Rebels on the Great Lakes

REBELS ON THE GREAT LAKES

Confederate Naval Commando Operations Launched from Canada
1863–1864

JOHN BELL

DUNDURN
TORONTO

Editor: Allison Hirst
Design: Courtney Horner
Printer: Webcom

Library and Archives Canada Cataloguing in Publication

Bell, John
        Rebels on the Great Lakes : confederate naval commando operations launched from Canada, 1863-1864 / by John Bell.

Includes bibliographical references and index.
Also issued in electronic formats.
ISBN 978-1-55488-986-0

        1. United States--History--Civil War, 1861-1865--Naval operations, Confederate. 2. Confederate States of America--Foreign relations--Canada. 3. Canada--Foreign relations--Confederate States of America. 4. Confederate States of America--History, Naval. 5. Canada--History--1841-1867. I. Title.

E596.B44 2011   973.7'57   C2011-903776-9

1   2   3   4   5   15   14   13   12   11

We acknowledge the support of the **Canada Council for the Arts** and the **Ontario Arts Council** for our publishing program. We also acknowledge the financial support of the **Government of Canada** through the **Canada Book Fund** and **Livres Canada Books**, and the **Government of Ontario** through the **Ontario Book Publishing Tax Credit**, and the **Ontario Media Development Corporation**.

Care has been taken to trace the ownership of copyright material used in this book. The author and the publisher welcome any information enabling them to rectify any references or credits in subsequent editions.

J. Kirk Howard, President

Printed and bound in Canada.
www.dundurn.com

Dundurn	Gazelle Book Services Limited	Dundurn
3 Church Street, Suite 500	White Cross Mills	2250 Military Road
Toronto, Ontario, Canada	High Town, Lancaster, England	Tonawanda, NY
M5E 1M2	LA1 4XS	U.S.A. 14150

For my two youngest grandsons,
Aidan William Bell in Gunning Cove, Nova Scotia
and Finnegan James Rowe, in Richmond, Virginia.

These men were not "burglars," or "pirates," enemies of mankind, unless hatred and hostility to the Yankees be taken as a sin against humanity, a crime against civilization.[1]

— John Yates Beall (1864)

Contents

Acknowledgements

The preparation of this book could not have been completed without the generous assistance of numerous people in Canada and the United States. I particularly want to thank the following individuals: Marcel Barriault, Peter DeLottinville, Colonel Bernd Horn, Élizabeth Mongrain, Pierre Ostiguy, Natasha Rowe, Kathleen Wall (McCord Museums), and Michel Wyczynski. I would also like to acknowledge the assistance that I received from various staff members of Library and Archives Canada in Ottawa and the Virginia Historical Society in Richmond.

Introduction

Despite its relatively small size and limited resources, the Confederate States Navy (CSN) made a very significant contribution to the overall Confederate war effort during the American Civil War.[2] Much of the success of the South's naval strategy can be attributed to the farsightedness of Stephen R. Mallory, the Confederate secretary of the navy, who recognized the importance of confronting the formidable Union Navy, which had imposed a blockade on Confederate ports, with "technical surprise."[3] Mallory's commitment to technological innovation encouraged the development of not only ironclads and commerce raiders, but also revolutionary forms of submarine warfare, including the extraordinary CSS *Hunley*, recently raised from Charleston's harbour.[4]

The Confederate Navy's willingness to innovate in its struggle against a vastly superior enemy was not restricted to technological developments. It also extended to other tactical and strategic initiatives. Starting in 1862, Mallory, who was, of course, aware of the success of Confederate cavalry raiders and partisans in various theatres of the war, became increasingly supportive of the idea of applying asymmetric guerilla tactics to naval warfare, creating amphibious commando forces that could seriously harass Union shipping and the blockading fleets — and perhaps even seize enemy warships.[5]

Not surprisingly, the commanders of these new forces were drawn from among the navy's younger officers, men who were eager to see action and win promotion through meritorious conduct in combat. John Taylor Wood, who went on to become probably the most prominent Confederate naval commando leader (he was sometimes referred to as the "Horse Marine"), spoke for this younger generation when he wrote, "promote for fighting; otherwise the Navy never can be kicked into vitality."[6]

While the Confederacy's overall naval effort had a strong international dimension, which involved blockade-running to and from various British ports (including colonial cities such as Halifax and Saint John), the procurement and construction of ships in the United Kingdom, and the cruising, throughout the world's oceans, of predatory commerce raiders such as the CSS *Alabama*, the South's naval commando operations were, by their very nature, mostly restricted to American waters. However, there were a few such incidents in British North American waters, the most notable — and ambitious — of which occurred on the Great Lakes in 1863–64.[7]

The lure of the Great Lakes for the planners of Confederate naval commando operations derived from two realities. First, as a result of the Rush-Bagot Agreement of 1817, North America's inland seas were, from a naval standpoint, largely demilitarized.[8] In fact, by the time of the Civil War there was only one real warship on the Great Lakes, the USS *Michigan*, launched in 1843. Second, in 1862 the Union established a prisoner-of-war depot for Confederate officers on Johnson's Island, located in Sandusky Bay, Ohio. Eventually protected by the *Michigan*, the Lake Erie camp would come to house several thousand prisoners and would thus become a tantalizing target for the South, which increasingly suffered from devastating manpower shortages.

In many respects, the template for the Confederate operations launched on the Great Lakes was what one of the key participants, Robert D. Minor of the Confederate States Navy, called the "old St. Nicholas game," a reference to one of the earliest naval commando actions of the Civil War.[9]

A Southern GORILLA, (Guerilla)

This unsigned caricature of a Confederate "Gorilla" was featured on a Union postal envelope intended to ridicule the Confederacy's reliance on guerillas and other irregular forces. Both sides used such envelopes, known as "patriotic covers," to give expression to popular support for their respective war efforts. Some covers were rather primitive, but others, such as this example, featured quite sophisticated iconography. [New-York Union Envelope Deport (sic), circa 1861, author's collection]

On June 28, 1861, a joint group of more than two dozen Confederate Army and Navy commandos seized the sidewheel steamer *St. Nicholas*, which plied the waters between Baltimore and Georgetown, DC. The commando force had boarded the vessel at various points disguised as passengers. In fact, one of the operation's leaders, Richard Thomas, had come aboard in drag, dressed as a "French lady." Once under the command of the Confederate Navy officer George N. Hollins, the *St. Nicholas* steamed to the Virginia shore, where the commandos rendezvoused with a party of CSN officers and a detachment of Tennessee infantry. The captured vessel then headed up the Potomac in search of the USS *Pawnee*. Failing to find the U.S. warship, the *St. Nicholas* made her way to Chesapeake Bay, where the Confederates quickly captured three American vessels — a brig and two schooners. (Robert D. Minor took charge of one of the schooners, the *Mary Pierce*.) The *St. Nicholas* then escorted her three prizes up the Rappahannock River into the Confederacy. This incident was celebrated in the South and would inspire even more daring operations, including the subsequent Confederate activities on the Great Lakes.[10]

Although the events of the Confederacy's three daring naval expeditions launched from Canada against Johnson's Island remain largely unknown in the two countries that border the largest group of freshwater lakes in the world, some of the players (both major and minor) in these forgotten historical dramas on the Great Lakes did make more indelible marks in history.

Among their number were a Scotsman who became the first prime minister of Canada, a famous American actor who assassinated a U.S. president, another Scotsman who emerged as one of the most celebrated British war correspondents of the Victorian era, a blockade-runner's captain's clerk who became a priest and one of America's most-beloved Catholic poets, the fighting son of the fiery abolitionist John Brown, a great Confederate naval hero who became a respected Halifax merchant, a noted Canadian artist who taught spy craft to Confederate operatives, and the scion of a prominent Toronto family who co-founded the nationalist Canada First movement and later emerged as one of Canada's greatest military theorists and who, after having supported the Southern rebellion, played a role in suppressing the Northwest Rebellion.

The improbable events that tie together all these disparate historical figures — and several hundred other committed Confederates, Americans, and British North Americans — is a story worth telling and remembering, but it is one that has frequently been marred by what one knowledgeable observer described as "much incoherence and more fiction."[11] Hopefully, the chapters that follow will bring both a new narrative coherence and a scholarly rigour to the little-known story of the Confederate commandos on North America's inland seas.

It is a story that reminds us, above all, perhaps, that the American Civil War was, in a sense, our war as well. Not only did British North Americans fight in the conflict in great numbers, but the war also spilled over at times (albeit in a limited fashion) into the Canadian colonies and ultimately shaped their destiny. The Confederates who sought to take the war to the Great Lakes in 1863–64 dreamed of creating their own nation. They failed. But their rebellion, of which these commando operations formed a small part, did contribute, in a very substantial way, to the creation of another new nation. It is called Canada.

1

William Murdaugh's Plan

As its uneven struggle against the industrial might of the North unexpectedly evolved into a protracted and extremely bloody conflict, the Confederate States of America was increasingly attracted to asymmetric forms of warfare that might provide it with an edge. Within the South's naval forces, this openness to tactical innovation in the area of irregular forces encouraged many volunteers, particularly among the Confederate States Navy's growing cadre of younger officers, to come forward with proposals for various commando operations.

There were, of course, aggressive young men chomping at the bit scattered throughout the various naval squadrons; however, one of the most renowned Southern commandos, John Taylor Wood, and many of the other early commando leaders, were drawn from the James River Squadron, which was charged with defending the Confederate capital of Richmond, or from the naval headquarters, which was located in the capital.[1] Following the North's Peninsula Campaign during the spring and early summer of 1862 (which saw the South turn back a much larger Union force under Major General George B. McClellan), service on the upper James became rather routine, prompting many officers in the "Capital Navy" to seek alternative duties.

Among the restless young officers in the James River Squadron during this period was Lieutenant William H. Murdaugh, then serving on the gunboat CSS *Beaufort*. A converted tugboat that had served earlier in the year as a tender to the ironclad CSS *Virginia* during her historic encounter with the USS *Monitor* in Hampton Roads, the *Beaufort* was not a particularly desirable assignment for an ambitious young naval officer hungry for action.[2] Rather than simply await a new assignment, Murdaugh took the initiative and tried to create an opportunity for more challenging service.

On February 7, 1863, following consultations with fellow CSN lieutenants Robert R. Carter and Robert D. Minor (a veteran of the Confederate operation that resulted in the seizure of the steamer *St. Nicholas* in 1861), Murdaugh wrote to the secretary of the navy, proposing a bold plan for a commando raid on the Great Lakes to be launched from British North America:

C.S.S. *Beaufort*,
Richmond, February 7, 1863

Sir: I have the honor to submit the following plan of operations proposed to be carried out on the Northern Lakes:

The party to leave the Confederacy at the earliest possible day, to be ready for commencing operations with the opening of navigation, which will be probably about the middle of April.

The commanding officer to be issued with a letter of credit for $100,000, although it is not presumed that more than half this amount will be expended.

After reaching Canada to purchase, through the agency of some reliable merchant, a small steamer, say one of 200 tons, that can pass through the Welland Canal. If practicable, to let the agent equip and victual the vessel and collect a crew of 50 men, ostensibly with a view to mining operations on Lake Superior. If this is not practicable the officers will separate and each collect a party and join the vessel at some point on Lake Erie. The object of the expedition not be made known to the men until the vessel is clear of the Canadian coast, when strong inducements in the way of pay, etc., must be held out to them for making the attempt and still stronger ones for its successful accomplishment. Those not willing to make the attempt to be returned to the Canadian shore; those who are willing to be shipped into the Confederate service. In collecting men much judgment must be exercised in the selections. The crew will be armed with cutlasses and revolvers. The vessel will be provided with a number of small buoys to be used as torpedoes and also the powder, fuses, etc., to charge and fire them. These are to be used in the destruction of canal locks. She must also have on board plenty of spirits of turpentine and incendiary composition for rapid work in starting fires.

The first point to be aimed at is Erie, Pa., the arrival there to be so timed as to make it about 1:00 a.m. The steamer to be laid alongside the USS *Michigan* and that vessel to be carried by boarding with as little noise as possible. If there is a reasonable hope that the vessel has been carried without its being known beyond the vessels engaged, both vessels will leave the harbor and proceed toward the Welland Canal, with a view to getting the small steamer through into Lake Ontario before the news of the capture should have reached the Canadians, who might interpose objections to her doing so should the objects of her voyage be apparent. But if the capture is not made secretly, then the work of burning every particle of Federal property afloat will be immediately commenced. Even in this latter contingency the attempt will still be made to get the small steamer into Lake Ontario, when she, under the command of the second officer of the expedition, would have a fine field, but the most important part of her work would be to destroy the aqueduct of the Erie Canal, which crosses the Genesee River at Rochester, 7 miles from the lake, and the locks of a branch of the canal at Oswego.

If a passage through the Welland Canal for the small steamer should be refused by the Canadians, both vessels would operate in Lakes Erie, Huron, and Michigan. In Lake Erie, after leaving the town of Erie, Buffalo would be the first point to be visited, the fleet of trading vessels in its harbor and the locks of the great Erie Canal to be destroyed. The next place would be Tonawanda, distant about 30 miles from Buffalo, where there is also an entrance to the Erie Canal, which would be destroyed. Then, coasting along the southern shore of the lake, destroy the locks of the canals leading to the Ohio River, four in number, and burn the vessels fallen in with. Then pass Detroit in the night, and if possible without notice; pass through Lake Huron and into Lake Michigan, and make for the great city of Chicago.

At Chicago burn the shipping and destroy the locks of the Illinois and Michigan Canal, connecting Lake Michigan and the Mississippi River. Then turn northward, and, touching at Milwaukee and other places, but working rapidly, pass again into Lake Huron, go to the Sault Ste. Marie, and destroy the lock of the canal of that name. Then the vessel would be run into Georgian Bay, at the bottom of which is a railway connecting with the main Canadian lines, and be run ashore and destroyed.

Four officers will be required for this expedition. I respectfully volunteer my services and ask that Lieutenants Minor, Robert Carter, and Wood may be selected.

Very respectfully, etc.,

Wm. H. Murdaugh,

Lieutenant, C.S. Navy[3]

Master Jeff—and his Navy.

This caricature of Confederate president Jefferson Davis, taken from a Union patriotic cover, reflects Northern attitudes toward the fledgling Confederate States Navy. Although it was seriously outnumbered and outgunned, the CSN ultimately played an important role in the Southern war effort. Furthermore, the Confederacy's commerce raiders did lasting damage to the American merchant marine. [D. Murphy's Son, Print., New York, circa 1861, author's collection]

Secretary Mallory, who by this time had already authorized successful naval commando operations in the fall of 1862 under the leadership of John Taylor Wood (whom Murdaugh hoped would be free to participate in the Great Lakes operation), was enthusiastic about Murdaugh's plan, strongly recommending it to president Jefferson Davis and the Confederate cabinet. With Mallory's backing, the operation was eventually approved (although Wood's participation was ruled out, as he was by this time serving as an aide to his uncle, President Davis), and $100,000 was earmarked for the expedition.[4]

However, as Murdaugh, Carter, Minor, and Lieutenant Walter R. Butt (Wood's replacement) prepared for their clandestine operation in Canada, Davis and his cabinet began to have second thoughts. According to Murdaugh, the Confederate leadership grew concerned about the expedition's potential impact on the Confederacy's crucial relations with Great Britain. "When everything was ready for a start," Murdaugh later recounted, "President Davis said that he thought the scheme practicable and almost sure of success, but that it would raise such a storm about the violation of the neutrality laws that England would be forced to stop the building of some ironclads which were on the stocks in England and take rigid action against us everywhere. So the thing fell through and with it my great chance."[5]

Robert D. Minor shared his friend's disappointment. Reflecting on the aftermath of the plan's collapse, Minor wrote, "With the expedition thus broken up, Murdaugh disheartened, sought other duty, and he, Carter, and Butt were ordered abroad, leaving me here on my regular ordnance duty, as the only representative of a scheme whose prospects were so inviting and so brilliant."[6]

However, as it turned out, Minor's involvement with the plan was not over. The summer of 1863 saw such momentous changes in the Confederacy's fortunes (most notably the defeat at Gettysburg and the fall of Vicksburg), that by the autumn of that year a Confederate raid on the Great Lakes took on not only a new viability, but perhaps even an urgency. Lieutenant Murdaugh's plan would be resurrected and revised to reflect new realities.

The chief reason for the survival of the plan was its basic soundness. Anyone contemplating a map of North America in 1863 from the point of view of naval defences could not help but be struck by the fact that the Great Lakes were a region of profound vulnerability for the Northern states. Under the provisions of the Rush-Bagot Agreement of 1817, America's inland seas were largely demilitarized, protected by a single warship of fourteen guns based in Lake Erie: USS *Michigan* (686 tons displacement), the U.S. Navy's first iron-hulled ship.[7] Seize this Union Navy vessel and the South could wreak havoc in some of the North's most important cities and industrial centres. Moreover, there was a very inviting target sitting three miles offshore in Sandusky Bay, Ohio: the prisoner-of-war camp on Johnson's Island (the southernmost of the Lake Erie Islands), which was now swelling with more than 1,500 prisoners (mostly officers), following the defeat at Gettysburg and the collapse of the Confederacy on the Mississippi.[8]

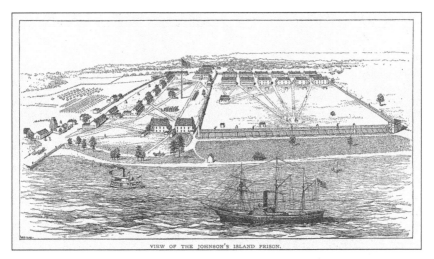

VIEW OF THE JOHNSON'S ISLAND PRISON.

A view of the Johnson's Island prison with the USS Michigan *in the foreground. As Confederate plans for an operation on the Great Lakes evolved, the prisoner-of-war camp for Southern officers became an increasingly central target.* [Engraved from a lithograph based on a wartime sketch made by a Union soldier, The Century Illustrated Monthly Magazine (March 1891)]

However, for the plan to work, the Confederates would confront serious logistical challenges launching their operations from British North America, where they ran the risk of precipitating a serious diplomatic incident and where they were obliged to rely on the assistance of sometimes untested Confederate expatriates and agents as well as local sympathizers, while at the same time confronting a new class of opponents, comprising detectives, secret agents, con artists, and opportunists. Naval personnel accustomed to service on blue water and brown water would now have to function in the even murkier waters of cross-border intrigue, counterintelligence, and dirty tricks.

2

John Wilkinson's Expedition

In August 1863, Robert D. Minor, the only member of the original group of officers designated for the proposed Great Lakes commando force still in Richmond, was summoned from the Naval Ordnance Works to a meeting with two members of the Confederate cabinet, Navy Secretary Mallory and secretary of war James R. Seddon. Minor listened as Seddon read to him from a letter proposing a raid on the Great Lakes. This new proposal centred on a goal that had not figured in Murdaugh's original plan, namely, the freeing of the prisoners at the Johnson's Island camp.

Although the letter's author was not identified by Minor, it is possible that it came from a senior Confederate imprisoned on Johnson's Island. One likely candidate would be Brigadier-General James Jay Archer, who had been captured on the first day of battle at Gettysburg. It is known that Seddon received the following unsigned message (by way of a paroled soldier) from Archer late in September:

We count here 1,600 prisoners, 1,200 officers. We can take the island, guarded by only one battalion, with small loss, but have no way to get off. A naval officer might procure in some way a steamer on the lake and with a few men attack the island and take us to Canada. C.C. Egerton of Baltimore, would, I think, furnish a fitting crew to one of our naval officers who carried your indorsement [sic] to him, and would give valuable advice regarding how to get the men armed, in steamer &c. There is no truer man in our service, and he has a large body of men sworn to obey him and help us. Lieut. George Bier or William Parker are suggested.[1]

In order to ensure that he succeeded in communicating with the War Department in Richmond, it is very probable that Archer used several different messengers over the course of the summer of 1863. Of course, it is also possible that other prisoners, perhaps even before Archer's arrival at the camp, were trying to contact Seddon to recommend a similar plan.[2]

Another possible candidate for the authorship of the letter was George Proctor Kane, the former Baltimore chief of police, who, after having been arrested on suspicion of sedition in June 1861, was subsequently confined in Fort Warren at Boston until November 1862.[3]

Following his release, Kane made his way to Montreal, where he made contact with various Southern sympathizers and began to hatch a plan to attack Northern lakeside cities. On July 17, 1863, Kane wrote to president Jefferson Davis from Montreal, outlining an ambitious proposal for simultaneous expeditions against Buffalo, Erie, Detroit, and other ports, with a view to "paralizing [sic] the lake commerce" and providing "a quickening impetus to the peace feeling." Kane also pointed to the importance of releasing the prisoners at Johnson's Island and stressed the need for experienced army and naval officers — and for proper funding.[4] (Robert D. Minor would later confirm that an expedition on the Great Lakes "had been vaguely talked of in Montreal.")[5]

Clearly, proposals for a major operation against American cities on the Great Lakes were coming from several different quarters, and it is likely that taken together they had an accumulative effect, culminating in the decision to proceed with an expedition.

In any event, Robert D. Minor, who had remained a firm believer in the potential of a Great Lakes raid, was asked for his opinion of a new proposed operation that would, in effect, combine Murdaugh's original plan with a proposal to free the prisoners on Johnson's Island. Minor did not hesitate to support the operation, remarking, "I need not inform you, gentlemen, how much pleasure it would give me to be engaged upon such duty."[6]

Following this consultation with Seddon and Mallory, Minor anxiously awaited word regarding the new raid's authorization. A month later he was summoned again to Mallory's office, where he received the welcome news that the operation was, indeed, a go, and was ordered to "organize the expedition, select the officers, [and] make all the necessary preparations." Mallory concluded his instructions by offering Minor command of the operation. Although Minor was keen on the expedition, he declined the offer to lead it, deferring, he later reported, "in favor of my friend, John Wilkinson (who was in a manner somewhat committed to the plan by the letter which I have mentioned as being shown to me by Mr. Seddon, the Secretary of War), with this proviso, however, that on our arrival in Canada, in the event of adopting two lines of operations, I was to have one of them as my command."[7]

Although Minor's friend Lieutenant John Wilkinson was an experienced and well-respected officer, best known, at this point, as the commander of CSS *Robert E. Lee*, a government-owned blockade-runner operating out of Wilmington, North Carolina, he was not an obvious choice for a secret commando operation in British North America. Nonetheless, he accepted the assignment, noting that his orders were deliberately vague: "It was left to the officer in command how the details were to be arranged, his sole explicit instructions being not to violate the neutrality of British territory."

The latter requirement was a dubious formality, as Wilkinson well knew. "How this was to be avoided," he remarked, "has ever seemed impossible to me, but having been selected to command the expedition, I resolved to disregard all personal consequences, and leave the responsibility to be borne by the Confederate Government."[8]

Clearly, the latter now had a different attitude regarding an attack on the Great Lakes. According to Minor, President Davis, who had previously agonized over the international repercussions of such an operation, stated that it was "better to fail than not to make the attempt."[9]

The rakish USS Fort Donelson *(former CSS* Robert E. Lee*) off Norfolk, Virginia, December 1864.* [Francis Trevelyan Miller, ed., The Photographic History of The Civil War in Ten Volumes; Volume Six: The Navies (The Review of Reviews Co., 1911)]

One likely reason that Wilkinson was chosen to lead the expedition was the fact that, as an experienced blockade-runner, he could not only be counted on to deliver the Lake Erie commando contingent to Halifax, Nova Scotia, on the *Robert E. Lee,* but he could also take charge of a sizable cargo of cotton from the War Department and negotiate its sale in order to complement the $35,000 in gold that had been supplied by the Navy Department, thereby providing, in Minor's words, "the sinews of the expedition."[10] Some of the gold would be spent in Halifax in order to outfit the men for their trip across the Maritime provinces to Montreal and then on to the Great Lakes; however, the lion's share would be reserved for the outfitting of the liberated POWs of Johnson's Island.[11]

Twenty-two men, mostly officers, were selected for the operation.[12] Among their number were several who had already served — or would later serve — with the renowned commando leader Wood, including Lieutenant B.P. Loyall, Lieutenant G.W. Gift, Chief Engineer Charles Schroeder, and Assistant-Surgeon William G. Shepardson. (The latter, in addition to serving as a medical officer, was also an experienced journalist and was probably assigned to the expedition so that he could prepare a stirring account of the operation — should it prove successful — for the Confederate newspapers, as he had done for other naval commando operations.)[13] The party also included two gunners, Crawford H. Gormly and John Waters. Only Wilkinson, Minor, and Loyall knew that their destination was Halifax.[14]

On the night of October 7, 1863, the *Robert E. Lee*, under Wilkinson's command, left Smithville, North Carolina (now Southport), below Wilmington.[15] The night was clear, but Wilkinson was confident he could run the gauntlet of the Union blockade. "The fact is," he later explained, "a blockade-runner was almost as invisible at night as Harlequin in the pantomime. Nothing showed above the deck but the two short masts, and the smoke-stack; and the lead-colored hull could scarcely be seen at the distance of one hundred yards."[16]

Despite her commander's assurance, the *Lee* did not entirely escape the notice of the blockading fleet. After running at full speed for nearly an hour, she came under fire. Following a first shot that was a little long and a second that was just short, the vessel was struck by a shell that hit the starboard bulwarks, setting a cotton bale ablaze, destroying a small hoisting engine, and wounding three men with splinters and shell fragments.[17]

The Confederates promptly threw the burning bale overboard and tended to the men, whose wounds were relatively minor. Although several more shots were fired, the *Lee* soon reached safer waters. As she sailed up the coast, the blockade-runner showed American colours to all vessels that she encountered, including, in very dirty weather off New York, a Union man-of-war.[18]

On October 16 the *Lee* reached Halifax, where Wilkinson consigned his cargo of cotton (worth $76,000) to the wholesale merchant Benjamin Wier, the port's unofficial agent for the Confederacy.[19] Wier, later a Canadian senator, was one of the most prominent and influential members of the large group of Confederate sympathizers found among Halifax's business and social elite.[20] Wilkinson then passed on the command of the ship to John Knox. (Much to Wilkinson's dismay, the *Lee* would be captured on her return voyage, soon thereafter becoming the Union blockader USS *Fort Donelson*.)[21]

The arrival of such a splendid Confederate States Navy vessel did not go unnoticed by the press. The Halifax *Journal* called her "a beautiful specimen of naval architecture, low and long and rakish, with a beautiful moulded stern, and a bow as clean and sharp as a knife." The paper also noted the evidence of her encounter with the Union blockaders, remarking that the "marks of shot and shell are plainly visible in different parts of the ship." The press also reported on the *Lee*'s unusually large compliment of

Confederate States Navy officers. However, the Confederates were able to offer a plausible explanation, which the *Evening Globe* of Toronto conveyed to its readers: " *Lee* has a number of naval officers on board on their way to England to bring out vessels building there." [22]

Concerned that the "arrival of so large a party of Confederates in Halifax attracted attention," raising suspicions in the wrong quarters, Wilkinson began preparations for the next stage of the operation — namely, the trip to Montreal in Canada East, where the commando leaders would rendezvous with George P. Kane. Assuming that they were now under surveillance, presumably by agents of the vigilant American Consul in Halifax, Judge Mortimer M. Jackson, and/or British authorities, Wilkinson took several measures to safeguard the integrity of his operation.[23]

First of all, he dismissed a civilian named Leggett, whom he and other officers suspected of being "a traitor and a spy." [24] Second, he broke the commando group into small parties of three and four, which were to travel to Montreal by one of two different routes: "one via St. John, New Brunswick, and thence up through the province via Fredericton and Grand Falls to Rivière du Loup, on the St. Lawrence, to Quebec and Montreal, and the other via Pictou, through the Northumberland Strait to Bay of Chaleurs, via Gaspé, up the St. Lawrence to Quebec, and thence by railroad to Montreal." [25] Finally, Wilkinson sent ahead his own agent, a "canny Scotchman," who would travel to Montreal via Portland, Maine, and prepare for the commandos' arrival.[26] By this time, Montreal was a hotbed of Confederate activity, much of it centred in one of the city's leading hotels, St. Lawrence Hall.[27]

As they made their way along "their long and devious route through the British Provinces," the Confederates were struck by the brazen activities of "recruiting agents for the United States army … scarcely affecting to disguise their occupation." [28] (These efforts at foreign enlistment were extremely fruitful for the North, as many Maritimers would serve in New England regiments or the Union Navy.)[29]

The various Confederate parties began arriving in Montreal on October 21. According to Minor (who apparently adopted two *noms de guerre*, Brest and Kelly), all members of the contingent were ordered to take precautions to avoid detection by Union and Canadian agents:

George Proctor Kane, the former police marshal — and future mayor — of Baltimore, who lived in exile in Montreal from 1862 to 1864. Kane, together with his associate Patrick C. Martin, played an instrumental role in the planning of the first Lake Erie expedition. It has been suggested that Kane had been involved in an 1861 plot to kill President-elect Lincoln in Baltimore. [Franklin Engraving & Printing, New York, author's collection]

As it was of vital importance that the utmost secrecy should be observed, the officers were directed to take lodgings in quiet boarding houses, to avoid the hotels, not to recognize each other on the street, and not to be absent from their rooms for more than half an hour at a time. Finding Marshal Kane and some of our friends in Montreal, we set to work to prepare and perfect our arrangements, the first object of the plan being to communicate with the prisoners on Johnson's Island.[30]

Accordingly, with the assistance of a cross-border network of Confederate sympathizers, Wilkinson utilized the personal columns of the *New York Herald* to contact Brigadier-General Archer and confirm that an attempt would be made to free the Confederate prisoners. Wilkinson's message stated that "a few nights after the 4th of November a carriage would be at the door, when all seeming obstacles would be removed, and to be ready."

"The obstacles alluded to," Minor later clarified, "were the USS *Michigan* and the prison guard."[31] (In response to rumours regarding Confederate attempts to free the prisoners on Johnson's Island, the *Michigan* was ordered to take up station in Sandusky Bay in late October.)[32]

Once he had established contact with the Confederate prisoners, Wilkinson was determined to act quickly, in the hope that he and his men could avoid detection. Over the course of the last week of October and the first week of November, he finalized the key elements of his operation, adjusting for changing circumstances and contingencies, including regular intelligence reports received from Ohio; all the while he was trying to weigh the reliability of the various sympathizers and agents who offered assistance and advice.[33]

Wilkinson soon realized that preparations would take longer than expected, which prompted the insertion of a new classified notice in the *Herald*:

> TO A.J.L.W. — CANNOT COMPLY WITH YOUR wishes till after Wednesday, the 4th of November. Your solicitude is fully appreciated, and a few nights after that date the carriage will call for you, and the present seeming obstacle will be overcome. Be ready.[34]

With logistical support from George P. Kane, Wilkinson focused on three key issues: ordnance, the composition of his commando force, and the final details of his assault plan. Assisting Kane and Wilkinson in this crucial role were Kane's close associate, the former Baltimore distiller, Patrick C. Martin, who was operating both a wine-importing business and a blockade-running operation out of Montreal, and Charles H. Haile, a former Bank of Tennessee cashier from Memphis.[35] (There is also evidence that two other prominent Southern exiles in Montreal participated to at least some degree in planning and logistical support for Wilkinson's expedition: James Brown Clay and Dr. Montrose A. Pallen. Clay, a former U.S. congressman and diplomat and the son of the famous statesman Henry Clay, had attended the Peace Convention of 1861 in Washington, where a concerted but doomed effort had been made to avert war between the North and South. Pallen, who had served for a time in the Confederate Army and held a commission as an acting surgeon in the Confederate Navy, was in Canada on secret service. He would eventually be authorized to inspect the main Union prison camps, including Johnson's Island, in order to report on conditions to the Confederate government.)[36]

Robert Minor described the creative approach that the Confederates adopted for weaponry:

> Two small 9-pounders were quietly purchased; Colt furnished us with 100 navy revolvers, with an ample supply of pistol ammunition, of course through several indirect channels. Dumb-bells were substituted for cannon-balls, as it would have excited suspicion to have asked for such an article in Montreal; powder, bullets, slugs, butcher knives in lieu of cutlasses, and grapnels were obtained, and all preparations made to arm the escaped Confederate officers and soldiers ...[37]

As for the final assault force, Wilkinson initially resisted the temptation to recruit a large number of men from among either the members of Montreal's sizable Confederate colony or several British North America volunteers; although, he did make an exception for a few former prisoners who had escaped from Johnson's Island.

Lieutenant John Wilkinson, CSN, commanding officer of the first Lake Erie expedition, who had achieved renown as the commander of the blockade-runner CSS Robert E. Lee. *He would later command the warships CSS* Chickamauga *and CSS* Chameleon *(formerly* Tallahassee *and* Olustee*). Following the war, Wilkinson lived in exile for several years in Halifax, Nova Scotia.* [J. Thomas Scharf, History of the Confederate States Navy *(Rogers and Sherwood, 1887)]*

Because they knew the lay of the land, these men might be able to provide crucial information. During the actual attack, Wilkinson's commando force would also be assisted by a number of prisoners who had volunteered to rise against their captors.[38]

However, as the Confederate's plans progressed, the enormity of the task of seizing the *Michigan* prompted a reconsideration of the size of the assault force. As one of the participants later recalled, the expedition leaders came to the realization that "more men were necessary, and some Confederates, who had recently escaped from camps Chase and Douglas, were taken as volunteers."[39] With this augmentation, the final commando party numbered fifty-four.[40]

Although no British North Americans figured among the members of the assault team, two did play important roles in the operation. The first, an unidentified retired British army officer, travelled to Sandusky, where under the pretext of duck-hunting, he observed the movements of the USS *Michigan* and relayed information about the vessel and other activities in the vicinity of the Johnson's Island camp to Wilkinson on a daily basis, using a "pre-arranged vocabulary," presumably in cables or newspaper advertisements.[41]

The second Canadian, Charles H. Haile's brother-in-law, James Simeon McCuaig, the manager of the Bay of Quinte and St. Lawrence Steamboat Company and later a federal member of Parliament, ultimately had an even more critical impact on the operation; however, his initial role was to convince Wilkinson to alter his assault plan.[42]

Wilkinson's original plan, probably developed in consultation with Minor and Loyall, was to travel to Windsor and take passage on a steamer to Detroit. Once out on Lake Erie, Wilkinson's commandos would seize the vessel and then make their way to Johnson's Island, where they would find a way to board the *Michigan*. However, based on information received from McCuaig, who had been introduced to the commando leaders by Kane, the plan was revised, with the Welland Canal chosen as the departure point.[43] Minor summarized the new plan as follows:

> From Ogdensburg, in New York, there is a line of screw steamers plying to Chicago in the grain and provision trade, and as they return nearly empty to Chicago, and sometimes carry the Adams Express Company's safe, we decided to take deck-passage on board one of them as mechanics and laborers bound to Chicago to work on the city waterworks there, and with this view one of our clever privates, named Connelly, was sent over to Ogdensburg, who paid the passage money for 25 of us in advance, to be taken on board at some point on the Welland Canal, and while doing so he made an agreement to take as many more laborers as he could obtain, their passage being fixed at the same price, to

which the New Yorker consented, and gave him the ticket to show to the captain of the boat.

We were then to assemble at St. Catharines, on the canal, go on board the steamer (one of our men, apparently entirely unconnected with us, having charge of the guns, powder, pistols, etc., boxed up in casks, boxes, etc., and marked "Machinery, Chicago," going on board the same steamer with us), and when fairly out in Lake Erie, and well clear of British jurisdiction, we were to rise on the officers and crew, overpower them, seize the steamer, mount our two 9-pounders, arm the men, secure the prisoners, and push on for Sandusky, timing our arrival so as to reach the *Michigan* about daylight, collide with her as if by accident, board and carry her by the cutlass and pistol, and then with her guns, loaded with grape and canister, trained on the prison headquarters, send a boat on shore to demand an unconditional surrender of the island, with its prisoners, garrison, material of war, etc., upon penalty of being fired into and the prisoners being released without restraint upon their actions.[44]

Once the *Michigan* and the POW camp were captured, the Confederates would seize several small steamers known to be at the wharf at Sandusky and then transport the bulk of the prisoners to Canada West. Then the *Michigan*, with a crew drawn from Wilkinson's commando force and about fifty freed POWs (some of whom would likely serve as marines), would set out to attack Northern shipping. As Minor observed, the Confederates would have "the lake shore from Sandusky to Buffalo at our mercy, with all the vast commerce of Lake Erie as our just and lawful prey."[45]

On October 31, Wilkinson ordered Minor to dispatch two officers to Toronto and two to Windsor in order to begin collecting the men who would comprise the commando force, indicating that the necessary funds would be supplied by the expedition's paymaster, William Finney. Wilkinson also noted that two Confederate army veterans in Canada West, Murray and Bishop, would help to assemble the men. As well, Wilkinson urged the officers to use "extreme caution" as they prepared and dispatched the various Confederate commando parties, due to the presence of "federal detectives in that portion of Canada."[46]

Having completed all his preparations, Wilkinson then placed a final notice in the *Herald*, notifying Archer that "the carriage will be at the door on or about the tenth."[47] The commandos then embarked — presumably once again in small parties — for St. Catharines, where they would meet and await the arrival of the steamer on which they had booked passage. About a month after the *Robert E. Lee*'s departure from Wilmington, Murdaugh's plan was about to be realized — or so it seemed.[48]

On or about November 12, with his commando force assembled on the canal at St. Catharines, awaiting the imminent arrival of the steamer that would carry them to Lake Erie, Wilkinson's party received devastating news, which, in his words, "fell among us like a thunderbolt."[49] The news came in the form of a proclamation, issued by the governor general, Lord Monck, warning of Confederate plans to launch a naval attack from British North America and threatening serious repercussions for anyone violating British neutrality. In addition, there were further reports indicating that Monck had ordered that the Welland Canal be carefully watched and that any suspicious parties travelling through its waters be arrested. As well, the governor general notified the U.S. authorities of Confederate designs, prompting the American secretary of war, Edwin M. Stanton, to send warning telegrams, on the evening of November 11, to the governors, mayors, and military commanders of the Great Lakes region and to order the defences at Sandusky to be significantly bolstered.[50]

Although Wilkinson was loath to abandon his operation, he promptly withdrew his force from the canal and endeavoured to obtain more intelligence. Meanwhile, his Canadian contact at Sandusky wisely ended his duck-hunting excursion and quickly returned to Canada, where he reported on the increased garrison at Johnson's Island and, in Wilkinson's words, "such other measures adopted as to render our success impossible."[51]

Following a council of war with his senior officers, Wilkinson concluded that the operation had been seriously compromised. "There was a possibility of a successful issue to this enterprise," he later wrote, "but not a probability."[52] Robert Minor summarized the final decision of the commando leaders:

With our plan thus foiled, and with the lake cities in a fever of fear and excitement, and with the rapid advance of reenforcements [sic], both naval and military, to reenforce the garrison at Johnson's Island against our compact little band of 52 Confederates, we had, as a matter of course, to abandon the design, and leave Canada as soon as possible, but to do so in a dignified and proper manner.[53]

As they prepared for the journey back to the South, the Confederates received intelligence indicating that they had been betrayed at the last moment by the Canadian McCuaig, who apparently had come to regret his connection with the operation and had revealed the details of the plot to Luther Holton, a noted steamship and railroad entrepreneur and the Canadian finance minister.[54] (Holton also apparently served as the unofficial liaison between Monck and U.S. Consul General Joshua Giddings.)[55] On November 24, a bitterly disappointed George P. Kane wrote to President Davis, confirming that "McCuaig, as we learn, turned traitor."[56]

John Wilkinson, on the other hand, was not entirely certain that McCuaig was solely to blame for the operation's failure. In fact, he later speculated that the expedition had been doomed from the start: "It is quite probable, indeed, that we were closely watched through the whole route ..."[57]

Whatever the case, the disappointed Confederates recognized that Monck was under enormous pressure to curry favour with the increasingly belligerent and hostile North by publicly thwarting the Confederate plan. Fortunately for the Confederates, the Canadian authorities were prepared, in the interests of maintaining neutrality, to let the commando force return to the South unmolested.[58]

For their trip back through British North America, the Confederates broke up into at least two groups.[59] As winter began to set in, the disconsolate commandos returned to Nova Scotia, travelling by various means and routes.

Robert Minor travelled by steamer down the Saint John River from Tobique to Saint John, where he and his party boarded the steamer *Emperor*, crossing the Bay of Fundy to Windsor and then taking the railroad to Halifax. Here, Wilkinson and Minor learned of the seizure on the morning of December 8, in New England waters, of the U.S.

steamship *Chesapeake* by a motley crew of Confederate sympathizers, including several British North Americans. The vessel, which was now in Nova Scotia waters and being pursued by Union warships, had been rechristened CSS *Retribution II.*[60]

Minor promptly volunteered to take command of the potential commerce raider. John Wilkinson approved the request, and tentative arrangements were made, probably through Benjamin Wier, to convey Minor to the captured vessel by means of what he described as a "dull, heavy-sailing collier," possibly the coastal schooner *Investigator*. However, after a brief flurry of enthusiasm for the venture, it soon became apparent that the prospects for success were far from encouraging, which prompted reconsideration and a decision to withdraw Confederate Navy participation. Minor later recalled his disappointment: "The attempt was abandoned, and thus I lost my chance of a command afloat, when I had invitingly open before me the prospect of much damage to the enemy's coasting trade."[61]

After visiting briefly with Halifax's Confederate sympathizers, Wilkinson, Minor, and their men took passage for Bermuda on the Royal Mail steamer *Alpha*, arriving on December 17. At St. George's, the commando force began to disperse. Wilkinson was soon offered command of a small blockade-runner, *Whisper*, which, after a rather harrowing voyage, arrived in Wilmington on January 7. Among his passengers were Minor and about one-third of the original commando force.[62]

While Wilkinson remained in Wilmington for a time, Robert Minor returned to Richmond, where he resumed command of the Naval Ordnance Works. Over the course of the next few weeks, as time permitted, he drafted a lengthy — and admittedly "prosy" — report on the Lake Erie expedition for CSN Admiral Franklin Buchanan. Completed on February 2, 1864, about a year after he and Murdaugh had first planned an attack on the USS *Michigan*, the report reflected its author's bitter disappointment. "So, but for treachery," Minor wrote, "which no one can guard against, our enterprise would have been the feature of the war, and our little Navy another laurel wreath of glorious renown."[63]

Although Robert Minor would have no further involvement in efforts to capture the *Michigan*, the Confederate States Navy would soon have another opportunity to win renown on Lake Erie.

3

The Propaganda War

Although the first Lake Erie expedition had the potential to seriously damage relations between the United States and British North America, decisive action by Governor General Monck and other British and Canadian officials resulted, instead, in something of a diplomatic coup, one that allayed, at least to some degree, Washington's fears that the British were turning a blind eye to Confederate efforts to launch hostile actions from Canada. However, not everyone in the North was convinced that British North America was acting in good faith. There were many in the United States who regarded Canada's claims of neutrality as spurious. For them, the province had, in fact, become a safe haven for Southern raiders.

Such distrust seemed to be justified by the publication, on November 19, 1863, of a *New York Times* article on the raid. Signed by "Canada," who was based in Toronto, the lengthy report offered a surprisingly accurate account of the Confederate operation and its participants, clearly drawing upon much behind-the-scenes information, presumably supplied by Secret Service sources. Although "Canada's" narrative was fraught with sarcastic wit, it provided a realistic appraisal of the threat to the North that Wilkinson's commando expedition had represented: "had it been successful, the deeds of the Alabama and Florida would have paled before the lights of the Michigan; for had not the plans miscarried, Uncle Sam's vessel of war would have been the rebel privateer upon the lakes; and Wilkinson, with such desperadoes as were associated with him, would have made terrible havoc upon the lakes after releasing more than twenty-five hundred officers and men on Johnson's Island." Pointing to the evidence of collusion on the part of Confederate sympathizers in the North, "Canada" also offered an ominous warning to *Times* readers: "We have traitors at home whom we have to fear more than our enemies abroad."[1]

Alarm about Confederate activities in Canada was further stoked nearly a month later, with the publication, on December 15, 1863, in another New York paper, the *Sun*, of what purported to be Confederate secretary of the navy Stephen Mallory's annual report for 1863. This document, which was widely reprinted, included a rather boastful section on the aborted Lake Erie expedition:

> During the months of July and August I sent twenty-seven commissioned officers and forty trustworthy petty officers to the British provinces, with orders to organize an expedition and to co-operate with army officers in an attempt to release the confederate prisoners confined on Johnson's island in Lake Erie. From time to time I learned that the arrangements made were such as to insure the most complete success. A large amount of money had been expended, and just as our gallant naval officers were about to set sail on this expedition, the English authorities gave information to the enemy, and thus prevented the execution of one of the best-planned enterprises of the present war.[2]

Although the report was short on corroborating details, it appeared to underscore the ease with which a Confederate military force was able to operate on British soil.

Trinidad-born Stephen Russell Mallory, the Confederate secretary of the navy. A former member of the United States Senate Committee on Naval Affairs, Mallory realized that the Confederate States Navy would have to embrace technological innovation and irregular forms of warfare in order to confront the much larger Union Navy and its blockade of Southern ports. [J. Thomas Scharf, History of the Confederate States Navy *(Rogers and Sherwood, 1887)*]

In any event, the impact of the publication of the Mallory report was soon felt in diplomatic circles. On December 20, the American secretary of state, William H. Seward, wrote to Charles F. Adams, the American ambassador in London about the document and its revelations:

> I send herewith a copy, which has accidentally attracted my notice, of what purports to be an extract from an annual report of S.R. Mallory, who is pretending to act as Secretary of the Navy for the insurgents at Richmond. So soon as I can lay my hand upon a full copy of that paper

I shall transmit it. In the mean time, it is proper to say that I have not the least doubt that the extract now sent is authentic.

It boldly avows the authority and activity of the insurgents at Richmond in the building of the rams in Great Britain and France on their account, and for their use in making war from British and French ports against the United States.

Secondly, it avows with equal boldness and directness the sending of twenty-seven so-called commissioned officers, and forty reliable petty officers from Richmond to the British North American provinces, to organize an expedition from thence to co-operate with the so-called army officers, in making war against the United States on our northern border lakes. And it confesses that this expedition has only been defeated through the watchfulness of the British provincial authorities.

For Seward, the implications of the Confederate naval report were such that he instructed Adams to issue a stern warning to the British:

Indications of popular favor towards this design of the insurgents are not wanting in British communities. If we correctly understand occurrences of the hour, there are not only in the British provinces, but also in the British realm, and in its very Parliament, many persons who are engaged in advancing that design, or who at least are pursuing practices which they must well know necessarily tend to exhaust the patience of the United States, and to provoke our citizens, in self-defence, either to seek their avowed enemies within British jurisdiction, or to adopt some other form of retaliation.[3]

Before broaching such a provocative matter with the Foreign Office, Ambassador Adams decided that he should review the full text of Mallory's report. On January 8, he wrote to Seward, complaining that he was still without a copy of the document, as it had been ignored by the British press: "It is much to be regretted that I cannot find a complete copy of the report of Mr. Mallory, referred to in No. 789, in any of the newspapers. I think, however, there is no doubt of a growing conviction here of the necessity of some decisive action to check the outrageous plots of the rebels and their British sympathizers."[4]

Less than a week later, Adams finally received the full text of the Mallory report. What he read gave him pause and prompted the following message to Seward:

London, January 14, 1864.

Sir: I have prepared a note to Lord Russell, based on the instructions contained in your despatch, No. 789, and the copy of the whole report of Mr. Mallory, which has been received here as printed in the *New York Times* of the 30th December. But on a close examination of this paper so much of it seemed to justify a suspicion of its entire genuineness that I have concluded to defer sending it at least until after the receipt of further intelligence from America. It is not unlikely that some further notice of the report, after it shall have reached you in its full extent, may accompany the copy you expressed an intention to transmit when obtained.

I have the honor to be, sir, your obedient servant,
Charles Frances Adams[5]

Despite his own skepticism about the Mallory report, on January 19 Adams wrote, as instructed, to Lord Russell of the British Foreign Office expressing American concern regarding the activities covered in the document:

My Lord: I have the honor to submit to your consideration a copy of what purports to be the annual report of Mr. S.R. Mallory, the person who is known to be officiating at Richmond as director of the naval operations of the insurgents in the United States. Although this paper has been received only in the form here presented, I entertain little doubt that, in substance, it may be relied on as authentic.

If this be once assumed, I am sure I need not point out to your lordship the great importance of the admissions therein made of the systematic violation of the neutrality of her Majesty's kingdom, which it has for a length of time been my chief labor to make apparent.[6]

Adams's lingering doubts about the authenticity of the Mallory report published in the *Sun* were soon reinforced by a letter that appeared in the London *Herald* on January 29. Written by Matthew Fontaine Maury, a world-renowned oceanographer and a respected senior Confederate naval officer then serving in the United Kingdom, it denounced the document as a total forgery, a "Yankee trick."[7]

Maury's letter was, in fact, the first Southern shot in what was becoming, particularly for the Confederate States Navy, a crucial propaganda war. Increasingly concerned that the report would damage the South's relations with Britain, where several Confederate warships were then on the stocks, the Southern authorities scrambled not only to cast doubt on the authenticity of the document that had appeared in the *Sun*, but also to offer their own account of the Lake Erie expedition, emphasizing the measures that had been taken to avoid any violations of British neutrality. To this end, an unsigned report on the expedition was published on February 18 in the *Index*, a semi-official Confederate organ published in Britain. Expressly designed "to correct some misstatements which have obtained currency through the federal press," the article, written by an unidentified participant, contradicted any suggestion of British collusion or assistance:

The assent of the confederate government was asked, but long refused, from a doubt whether it could be effected [*sic*] without violating the neutrality of British territory. This objection was at last so far overcome that a certain number of officers received leave to attempt the hazardous experiment, but under strict orders to do or permit no act directly or indirectly liable to be construed into such violation, to buy no materials of war and enlist no assistance on British soil, but only to exercise the right of passage as individuals. Accordingly, upon arriving in Canada, arms and cannon were purchased in New York, and were sent by parties there up to the lake, where we could get them. Not an article was obtained in Canada. Even medicines and surgical instruments were furnished from New York, and all correspondence with the prisoners was carried on through the personal column of the New York *Herald*. Several British officers wished to join, but they, as also the assistance of many Canadian gentlemen, were refused. The basis of our operations was to be on Yankee territory, the means for carrying out our object, viz: to release the prisoners, were to be obtained there alone. This principle was adhered to in perfect good faith, in spirit as well as in letter, though not without some difficulty.[8]

Although this account left much to be desired when it came to accuracy, it was a rather deftly crafted piece of propaganda intended to exonerate the British authorities.

Although the Confederates had succeeded in sowing serious doubts about the reliability of the *Sun*'s Mallory report, Secretary of State Seward remained convinced of its authenticity and the document continued to be cited in the British Parliament and elsewhere, much to the chagrin of Confederate authorities, who were increasingly worried about the report's deleterious impact on foreign relations. Writing from London on March 12, the Confederacy's chief propagandist in Europe, Henry Hotze, expressed considerable frustration with the widespread acceptance of what he perceived as a clumsy forgery:

The cautious language in which Mr. Adams ... forwards the alleged report of Mr. Mallory forms a strong contrast to the confident tone in which her Majesty's ministers speak of it as a public document of undoubted authenticity. This paper has done us an infinite amount of mischief; it has been publicly denounced as a forgery by Captain Maury, and Captain Bulloch, being equally convinced it is not genuine, has written to Mr. Mallory earnestly requesting that it might be contradicted. But meanwhile it is used in Parliament and in the press as the Government's best weapon of defense, and it may probably turn the scales in many judicial and political issues now pending.[9]

Unbeknownst to Hotze, Secretary Mallory had finally exposed the report as a fabrication on March 11, in a letter to the Richmond *Sentinel*. Mallory's forceful denunciation challenged even William Seward's willfully persistent belief in the document's validity and prompted an investigation into the New York *Sun*'s original publication of the report.[10] It was soon revealed that the so-called "Mallory Report" had actually been fabricated by the newspaper's co-editor, Moses Sperry Beach, who was engaged in a heated penny-press rivalry with James Gordon Bennett of the New York *Herald*. This news was conveyed by Seward to Charles F. Adams, who was then, in turn, obliged to send a formal notification to Lord Russell:

LEGATION OF THE UNITED STATES
London, April 4, 1864.

My Lord: In connexion with the subject of the report of Mr. Mallory, the insurgent secretary of the navy, about which I had some conversation with your lordship on Saturday, I have the honor to apprise you that I have just received a despatch from Mr. Seward, informing me that after most diligent inquiries it has been ascertained that the supposed report is admitted by the editor of the New York *Sun* to have been prepared for the columns of that newspaper, in which it first appeared.

The reason assigned for this extraordinary proceeding is the desire of creating the impression that he had means of communicating with the insurgent capital superior to those of his professional brethren. The fact is that the same newspaper already had earned that reputation, so that there seems to have been scarcely an adequate cause for resorting to so discreditable a step. I therefore still incline to believe in the correctness of the conjecture made by me to your lordship, that the information contained in the paper had been surreptitiously obtained from sources which the editor, being now forced to act, is unwilling to expose. This, however, can make no difference in regard to the manner in which the paper must now be viewed. I hasten to give this information to your lordship, in order that no further reliance may be placed upon it.

I pray your lordship to accept the assurances of the highest consideration with which I have the honor to be, my lord, your most obedient servant,

Charles Frances Adams[11]

Although Adams's admission was a vindication for the Confederates, they actually took little comfort from the belated exposure of the Mallory forgery. Beach's text had already achieved its ostensible goal, applying pressure on the British when it came to involvement in Confederate naval construction and tolerance for military operations launched from Britain's colonies. John Slidell, the South's representative in France, and one of the two Confederate commissioners who had been removed from the British vessel the *Trent* in 1862 (a provocation known as the Trent Affair and one that had almost culminated in war between Britain and the United States) gave vent to Southern anger about the Mallory report (as well as a second alleged forgery that was then making the rounds in Britain and the U.S.) and a perceived bias on the part of the British, particularly Britain's Ambassador in Washington, Lord Lyons:

The paper is, on its face, so palpably a fabrication that one could scarcely have supposed it could dupe even the most credulous. Lord Lyons, by not publicly and indignantly denouncing the tricks by which he has been twice made the instrument of palming upon his Government forged papers intended to influence its action in important matters in a sense favorable to the Lincoln Government, has, in my opinion, rendered himself fairly obnoxious to the charge of complicity at least after if not before the fact. His course, however, does not surprise me, as I had abundant evidence of his servile submission to the dictates of Seward in the manner in which Messrs. Mason and I, with our secretaries, were transferred from Fort Warren to the *Rinaldo*.[12]

Although the South had eventually recaptured some ground in this particular skirmish in the larger, never-ending propaganda war with the North, Moses Sperry Beach's forgery had clearly done some damage and would serve to complicate any future attempts to launch a naval operation on the Great Lakes. Nonetheless, it would not forestall such attempts.

4

The Order of the Brotherhood of the Southern Cross

As American, Confederate, British, and Canadian authorities contended with the diplomatic fallout from Wilkinson and Minor's failed expedition against the Johnson's Island POW camp, the camp's prisoners, whose ranks were continuing to swell, were determined to ensure that the next attempt against the camp would succeed. Rather than passively await rescue, they sought, as much as possible given their circumstances, to take the initiative.

Over the course of three days, December 17–19, 1863, senior Confederate officers on Johnson's Island, including the two generals who had communicated with John Wilkinson during the first commando expedition, Major-General Isaac Trimble and Brigadier-General James Jay Archer, met to secretly formulate a camp command structure that could facilitate future escape operations. These meetings resulted in the following document:

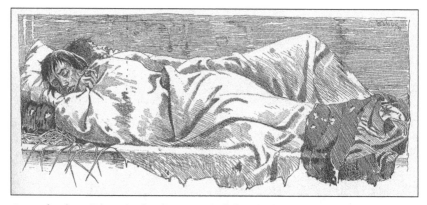

Prison bunks at Johnson's Island were stacked three high, with each bunk sleeping two men. The Southern prisoners found the Ohio winters particularly harsh. [Art by Walton Taber, The Century Illustrated Monthly Magazine *(March 1891)]*

Plan of Organization

Whereas the present posture of affairs in regard to the exchange of prisoners between the United States and the Confederate States governments leaves us but little hope of a speedy exchange, and whereas it is the privilege and duty of the Confederate prisoners of war confined on this Island to make their escape from imprisonment, and to adopt any plan by which so desirable an object promises to be successful; and whereas for the more effectual accomplishment of the proposed plan, we hereby agree to the following plan of organization of the Confederate officers here confined:

1. The plan to be adopted shall embrace the whole or such part of the prisoners as it may be deemed necessary for harmony, efficiency and success.

2. The whole organization shall be under the command of Major-General Isaac R. Trimble, of Maryland, as commander-in-chief of all the forces thus organized.

3. Corps commanders shall be appointed to the command of the twelve blocks respectfully, viz.:

General J.J. Archer, Maryland, to the command of blocks one' three and five; W.N.R. Beall, Arkansas, to the command of blocks seven, nine and eleven; Colonel R.S. Clarke, Eighth Kentucky Cavalry, to the command of blocks ten, twelve and thirteen. Colonel J. Miles, Thirty-ninth Mississippi, corps commander.

4. Each block shall be under the command of an officer, who shall organize companies or squads in each room or mess. Each company or squad to be under the command of a captain, who shall keep his men ready at any moment to carry out the orders and commands of their superiors in rank and position of their organization.

5. Block one shall be under the command of General J.R. Jones, Virginia; two, of Colonel D. Howard Smith, Kentucky; three, of Colonel B.D. Fry, Alabama; four, of Colonel L.M. Lewis, Missouri; five, of Colonel D.M. Shannon, Texas; seven, of A.G. Godwin, North Carolina; eight, of Captain L.W. Allen, Virginia; ninth, of General J.W. Frayser, Tennessee; ten, of Colonel R.M. Powell, Texas; eleven, of Colonel J.R. Herbert, Maryland; twelve, of Captain Johnson, Kentucky, and thirteen, General M. Jefferson Thompson, Missouri.

6. The commander-in-chief, the corps commanders, and of each block respectively, shall constitute a board of officers, who shall direct, arrange and superintend the formation of all plans and arrangements otherwise, concerning the escape of prisoners from this prison and of their return to the Confederate States, leaving all details of executing said plans to the direction of the commander-in-chief.

7. Commanders of corps shall be authorized to administer to subordinate commanders the following oaths [the

form of oath is not given], and they in turn shall administer them to each recruit.[1]

Apparently a major impetus for the adoption of the "Plan of Organization" was a document entitled "Plan of Escape" that had been presented to senior Confederate officers in the camp a few days before by Captain L.W. Allen, a Virginian cavalry officer. Allen, who was designated as a prison-block commander in the "Plan of Organization," had endeavoured to provide a comprehensive assessment of the prospects for escape:

Plan of Escape

Any plan of escape involves the necessity of organizing the prisoners is such a manner as will make them the most formidable and reliable, and may be regarded as embracing the following considerations:

I. Get out of the Enclosure.

II. Capture the Garrison.

III. Escape from the Island.

IV. Return to the South.

I. Get out of the Enclosure.
This is to be done in one of two ways, or by both combined.

1. By storming. This may be done by tearing down the plank enclosure, or by steps or ladders to climb over it, or by ripping off plank.

2. By bribing. This, I think, is practicable to some extent, by which the gates may be opened, or planks or posts loosened or removed, etc.

This being effected —

II. Capture the Garrison.

This will involve great danger and much loss of life, for the problem must be considered. How can fifteen hundred or two thousand unarmed men capture eight hundred or one thousand armed men and disarm them.

Allowing this to be accomplished.

III. How Can We Escape from the Island?

This is to be done in one of three ways.

1. By crossing on the ice to the main land.

2. By securing the steamer here and going to Sandusky, and there procure other transportation.

3. By being furnished transportation from friends on the outside.

The first two of these plans have serious, if not insurmountable objections and difficulty.

1. For the ice to be strong enough to cross on it will require such cold weather as utterly to unfit most of the prisoners to travel when they get to the main land.

2. It may be possible to capture the little steamer, but she can only take a small portion of the men and no plan must be entertained which does not provide for the absolute safety of all of our wounded and disabled comrades.

   No surprise of the garrison can be effected without the firing of guns, and this will give the Sanduskians notice. They having an armory and arms, one thousand men can be got under arms to receive us before we could steam from here or cross over on the ice.

3. The most hopeful plan of escape from the island is to secure outside aid.

IV. How Shall We Return South?

In one of three ways.

1. By reaching the main land, procuring horses and marching through Ohio to Pittsburg or Wheeling, or through Kentucky to Virginia, or Tennessee, or Georgia.

2. By reaching the main land and moving up towards Toledo, or the Straits, to Canada.

3. By crossing the lake to Canada.

When it is remembered that in the late gubernatorial election in Ohio the aggregate vote was upwards of four hundred and fifty-five thousand men; three-fourths of whom we may safely conclude are capable of bearing arms, to say nothing of the many garrisons and camps in the State, together with the great distance to be travelled in this inclement season, the very poor equipments of the prisoners, the whole trip to be performed among a most hostile population, all being taken together, make these plans most difficult and dangerous, if not utterly impracticable.

The third, to wit: Outside aid is the only one which may be considered practicable.

The conclusions at which I arrive from the above views are:

1. At least twelve hundred or fifteen hundred should be organized of the very best, truest and most trusty of the prisoners; each block to have at least one hundred men sworn to attempt any plan which may be sanctioned by the board of officers, that they will succeed or die in the attempt.

This one hundred men to be divided into two, or three, or four equal companies, under the command of brave, discreet and competent officers to be appointed by the commander of blocks, sanctioned by their respective corps commanders.

2. The most liberal use should be made of money, etc., in attempts to bribe; the full amount in no case to be paid in advance, and that this delicate and important duty should be entrusted specifically to one or two discreet men. This and all other matters should be conducted with the greatest caution, prudence and secrecy.

3. The details of the plan when adopted shall be entrusted for arrangement and execution to the commander in-chief.

4. Some one should be sent to Richmond, and secure the aid of our government to send us outside help.

5. In case we shall be successful in effecting our escape the organization hereby effected and acknowledged shall continue in force, and all who escape shall be under the control of the board of officers till we shall land on southern soil, or shall find it necessary to dissolve the organization.

6. In the mean time, if the weakening of the forces here, or any other circumstances shall arise by which the providence of God opens a way for our escape, we should not wait for the aid of our government, but rely upon ourselves.

Signatures of three Confederate officers (Captain Leonard E. Locke, Lieutenant William C. McGimsey, and Lieutenant J. Cabell Breckinridge), taken from an autograph book that circulated among the prisoners of war on Johnson's Island, 1862–64. Locke, who was a doctor from Alabama, provided medical assistance to his fellow prisoners. McGimsey, from Louisiana, had been captured after being severely wounded during the Battle of Gettysburg. Breckinridge, from Kentucky, was the son of the Confederate general (later secretary of war) and former U.S. vice-president, John C. Breckinridge. Following the war, young Breckinridge and his family lived in exile for several years in England and Canada. [Author's collection]

> I respectfully submit these hasty thoughts to the sound
> and better judgment of the board of officers, etc.
>
> L.W. Allen, Captain[2]

Early in February, the Confederates took further steps to increase unity and enhance morale in the camp by creating a new organization, the Order of the Brotherhood of the Southern Cross, with the object of reinforcing "union amongst the officers and men of our army."

According to L.W. Allen's diary, the following officers were to lead the new group: "Major General I.R. Trimble, of Maryland, was elected General; Colonel John Critcher, of Virginia, Lieutenant-General; Colonel Miles, of Louisiana; Colonel Cantwell, of North Carolina; Colonel

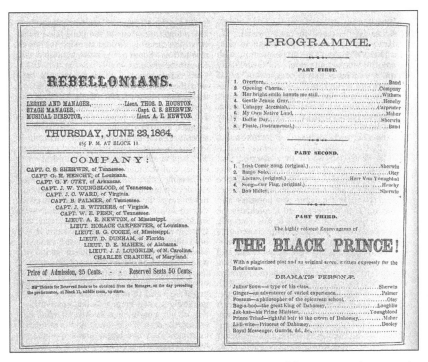

Playbill for an afternoon of music and theatre, presented by a prisoners' troupe, the Rebellonians. There was at least one other group of Confederate musicians and actors active in the camp — the Rebel Thespians. [The Century Illustrated Monthly Magazine *(March 1891)*]

Maxwell, of Florida; Colonel Shannon, of Texas; Colonel George, of Alabama; Colonel George, of Tennessee; Colonel D.H. Smith, of Kentucky; Colonel L.M. Davis, of Missouri; General Beall, of Arkansas; General Archer, of Maryland; Colonel Provence, of South Carolina; [rank or official position not stated] Major Hall, company secretary; Captain L.W. Allen, of Virginia, recording secretary; Captain W.F. Dunnaway, of Virginia, assistant secretary; Colonel Wood, of Alabama, Treasurer; Captain T.E. Betts, of Virginia, assistant treasurer."[3]

With the adoption of a command structure and an escape plan in December 1863 and the formation of a unifying patriotic organization in February 1864, the prisoners of Johnson's Island were now ready to challenge their Northern captors. They were prepared not only to participate in any escape efforts that might be organized externally by Confederate authorities, but also to take advantage of any opportunities that might arise within the camp. Clearly, their focus was not so much on escape by individuals or small groups, but rather a far more tantalizing goal: a mass breakout.

They would not have to wait very long for another concerted effort to bring about a major escape. Shortly after the organization of the prisoners' Order of the Brotherhood of the Southern Cross, the Confederate government would dispatch a senior official to Canada who was determined to strike numerous blows against the North. Among his priorities would be the capture of the USS *Michigan* and the freeing of the Southern prisoners on Johnson's Island. The Confederate dream of freedom on Lake Erie was not dead.

5

Privateers at Rondeau Harbour

As the Confederates prepared for a second attempt to free the prisoners on Johnson's Island, Union authorities continued to be deluged by rumours of menacing Rebel conspiracies taking shape across the northern border. Most of these proved to be groundless; however, even dubious threats had to be investigated and, where necessary, pressure brought to bear on Canadian officials to disrupt such activities.

One of the key figures responsible for the analysis of the plethora of intelligence received from Canada was Colonel Lafayette C. Baker, the head of the United States War Department's Secret Service, a powerful detective arm that maintained numerous undercover operatives in British North America. Early in 1864, Baker contacted Edwin M. Stanton, the secretary of war, to convey alarming — and apparently reliable — information concerning Confederate naval activity at two different locations on Lake Erie:

Washington, D.C., March 8, 1864

Sir — Herewith I have the honor to forward a statement furnished by one of my agents who has been in Upper Canada for some two months. The statement can be relied upon as being true in every particular. There is now lying in Rondeau Harbor, about 17 miles from Chatham, C.W., a fore and aft schooner, named the *Montreal*, commanded by one Captain Whitby, formerly a Lieutenant in the Confederate Navy. She has on board two 24 pounders, a quantity of ammunition, arms, chests, cutlasses, boarding pikes, &c.; she also has a crew of fourteen men, nearly all escaped Rebel prisoners.

There is also lying in New Creek, Long Point Marsh, and about 15 miles from Port Stanley, C.W., a schooner named *Saratoga*; she also has four eighteen pounders on board and is manned with a crew of 16 men.

Both of these vessels referred to, are not dismantled, as is usual during the winter months in that climate, but are kept in sailing condition at the shortest notice.

My informant has mingled and talked freely with the crews of these vessels, and they do not hesitate to avow their piratical intentions as soon as navigation is resumed in the Spring.

I am, &c.,
(Signed) L.C. Baker
Col., and Agent War Dept

Hon. E.M. Stanton,
Secretary of War[1]

The threat of two Confederate privateers operating on Lake Erie was not to be taken lightly. Upon receipt of this Secret Service report, Secretary Stanton promptly forwarded a copy to the secretary of state, William H. Seward, who, in turn, on March 11, wrote to the British ambassador in

Lord Charles Stanley Monck, fourth Viscount Monck, governor of the Province of Canada and the governor general of British North America during the American Civil War. Monck was charged with the difficult task of maintaining British neutrality while contending with the belligerent activities of the Confederate community based in Canada. Following the war, he played an instrumental role in the confederation of the British North American provinces, serving as the Dominion of Canada's first governor general until his resignation in 1868. [Photo by R. Carswell, Toronto, author's collection]

Washington, Lord Lyons, asking him to convey Baker's information to Governor General Monck, so that the latter could conduct an expedient investigation into "the piratical designs of insurgents against the United States, who have sought refuge in Her Majesty's Provinces."[2]

On March 13, Lyons sent Seward's letter and its enclosures to Monck. Five days later, Monck wrote to Lyons, assuring him that he would "take immediate measures to ascertain the accuracy of this information, and to prevent any violation of the neutrality of Her Majesty's Canadian dominions, should it prove well founded."[3] Monck then dispatched as a "confidential agent," Lieutenant-Colonel Thomas Wily, Canada's Keeper of Stores and Military Properties, to investigate the alleged Confederate vessels.

Although the British authorities were prompt in offering assurances and were moving with some dispatch to investigate Baker's allegations, Major-General S.P. Heintzelman, commander of the headquarters of the U.S. Army's Northern Department in Columbus, Ohio, was not content to leave the investigation of such a serious threat to the North solely to British and Canadian officials. Accordingly, on March 12, he ordered Brigadier-General Henry T. Terry, the commander of the U.S. forces at Sandusky and Johnson's Island, to leave for Canada in order to personally examine the schooner *Montreal* at Rondeau Harbour.

On March 22, at the village of Raglan, Terry met with Monck's agent, Wily, who had just completed his investigation of the suspect schooner. Wily informed Terry that the so-called *Montreal* was, in fact, a Kingston vessel, the *Catarauqui*, and that she had no connection with the Confederacy and offered no threat whatsoever to the Union. Despite such assurances, Terry insisted on making his own inspection, which he subsequently described in a report to Captain Carroll H. Potter, Assistant Adjutant-General:

> In obedience to instructions received from headquarters Northern Department, under date of March 12, 1864, to procure all the information in my power as to the truth of a report that a vessel loaded with small-arms and two 12-pounders was lying at Rondeau, Canada, and to report thereon to your headquarters, I have the honor to report that on Tuesday, March 22, 1864, I left Chatham, Upper Canada, with John Mercer, esq., sheriff of Kent County,

and proceeded to Rondeau. At the hotel at Raglan, a small village near the head of the bay (Rondeau), I met Colonel Wiley, of the staff of the Governor-General of the Canadas, who had been ordered by the Provincial military authorities from Quebec to investigate as to the character of the vessel in question. He had just returned from on board the suspected vessel, lying about a half mile out, and stated to me that there was not the slightest cause of suspicion.

I went on board the vessel with Sheriff Mercer and Capt. Nettleton B. Whitby, the master and owner, and found no arms on board except two fowling-pieces and an old gun of 21/2-inch bore, for signal purposes, weighing about 75 pounds. This piece had been on board, I found by inquiry, a long time.

Upon investigation and inquiry I learned that the vessel came to Rondeau in stress of weather, December 18, 1863, and was compelled to stay. Her name, *Catarauqui*, is on her stern, and she hails from Kingston. The crew, a mate, 4 hands, and a cook were discharged December 18, 1863, except 1 man, who is retained as a servant.

The captain, his wife, and this man stay on board the vessel. The captain is a man of more than ordinary ability, and has been engaged in the English merchant service. I examined the vessel thoroughly in every part and found nothing worthy of note. Saw her papers, and found they were in accordance with the captain's statements as to the character and business of the vessel. The collector of customs, with whom I conversed, confirmed all the statements of Captain Whitby. I feel assured that the *Catarauqui* is a harmless vessel, engaged in the transportation of staves.[4]

Having established first-hand that the mysterious schooner in Rondeau Harbour did not represent a threat to the Union and that Monck's agent was indeed a reliable and thorough investigator, Terry returned to Sandusky, leaving the pursuit of the second privateer vessel, the *Saratoga*, to Wily.

As Monck's agent later reported, the search for the second alleged Confederate schooner proved to be an extremely frustrating — and ultimately fruitless — exercise:

> From Chatham I next proceeded to Port Stanley, within fifteen miles of which place, at New creek, another vessel, called the *Saratoga*, of a similar character and designs, was stated to be lying.
>
> A diligent search on either side of that port, and for greater distances than that above specified as the place of her concealment, failed in revealing to me either such a place or vessel, and shipping masters born in that locality, who have sailed the lakes all their lives, informed me that they had no knowledge of any creek bearing that name on Lake Erie. The creeks from the Rondeau eastwards until you reach Port Stanley, a distance of about forty-five miles, are in the following order: Big creek, Clear creek, Sixteen-Mile creek, Number-Nine creek, Colonel Talbot's creek, and Kettle creek, otherwise Port Stanley. From the latter place, still following the coast line eastward to Port Burwell, a distance of twenty-five miles, are Silver creek, Catfish creek, or Port Bruce, and Otter creek, or Port Burwell.
>
> By the before-mentioned authorities I was further informed that it was not possible to winter a vessel at any of the creeks I have enumerated, except at the ports named, and there I saw and examined some fifteen or more vessels, but amongst them no *Saratoga*, the vessel I was in search of, nor could I find in the shipping list of Canadian vessels navigating the upper lakes any vessel bearing that name, although I searched it diligently for this purpose, nor had the master mariners whom I consulted knowledge of any such.[5]

Although Lieutenant-Colonel Wily and Brigadier-General Terry had succeeded in debunking Lafayette Baker's claims about Confederate privateering on Lake Erie, Terry's Canadian visit did leave him with a sense of foreboding about rebel activities in British North America:

> But I beg leave to add that there are many rebel refugees in Upper Canada, and that their headquarters are at Windsor, opposite Detroit; that they have some organization there is no doubt, nor that one of their leaders is a Colonel Snyder, of the Second Missouri (rebel) Cavalry. Mrs. Louisa Phillips now makes her headquarters at Windsor. I saw and conversed with her there.
>
> It is quite clear that they contemplate a raid of some kind, and that in its execution they have nothing to fear except the British authorities.[6]

As for the British authorities, they too remained concerned about the possibility of Confederate raids on the Great Lakes. Governor General Monck in particular was worried that, if left unchecked, increasing American anxiety about the possibility of Southern naval attacks might evolve "into a sentiment of hostility towards Canadians, from whose harbors they imagine an attack on their commerce might issue." Writing to the Duke of Newcastle on March 31, Monck urged London to give serious consideration to his proposal to station small Royal Navy vessels in each of the Great Lakes as a deterrent to Confederate operatives. Monck concluded his message to Newcastle with a blunt warning: "I trust that you will not think that I am pressing this request unduly, but I cannot conceal from myself the disastrous consequences which might result from any attempt at piratical aggression issuing from Canadian ports on the Lakes, and recent occurrences have shown that such events are at least not impossible, and ought, in my opinion, to be provided for."[7]

On the day after Monck conveyed his concerns to London, Major-General S.P. Heintzelman forwarded Brigadier-General Terry's report on Rondeau Harbour to Washington. In his covering letter, Heintzelman expressed some skepticism about Baker's intelligence-gathering in Canada: "I have at last been able to settle the question as to the existence of an armed vessel lying in Canadian waters, which has been such a bug-bear in some quarters. The inclosed report of General Terry, dated Sandusky, Ohio, March 29, 1864, will fully explain."[8]

LITTLE JOHNNY KANUCK. "Look here, Papa, you said if I'd abuse UNCLE SAM, you'd take my part when he came over to whip me."

PAPA JOHN BULL. "Ah! but that was before the rascal got his *Monitors* and *Parrott Guns*. You must take care of yourself, young man."

LITTLE JOHNNY KANUCK (*crying*). "Oh! oh! oh!

This unsigned cartoon, depicting an exchange between Papa John Bull and Little Johnny Kanuck, satirizes Canadian anxieties regarding the growing military might of the Union. As the war progressed, Canadian authorities were obliged to become increasingly sensitive to American perceptions of British North America and its role in the Civil War. [Harper's Weekly, *July 5, 1862*]

However, like Terry and Monck, Heintzelman was convinced that something was definitely afoot among the Confederate exiles in British North America. "I am satisfied, however," he wrote, "that there is an organized band in Canada watching for an opportunity to do us some damage should a favourable occasion offer. It will probably be turned into burning steamboats and warehouses of stores."[9]

Heintzelman's apprehensions were justified. A second Great Lakes operation was taking shape. Moreover, the South's "organized band in Canada" was about to be bolstered by new leadership and new financial resources.

Interestingly, subsequent events would also suggest that Lafayette Baker's suspicions concerning Nettleton B. Whitby and the *Catarauqui* were not completely unfounded after all. On September 30, the schooner sank off Presque Isle during a gale.[10] Several months later, Captain Whitby, who had survived the disaster, was engaged as master of a vessel that was unquestionably associated with Confederate plans for a privateering operation on Lake Erie.

6

Jacob Thompson's "Northwest Conspiracy"

As the South's military situation deteriorated throughout 1864 (one of the most devastating setbacks being General William Tecumseh Sherman's inexorable advance on Atlanta, starting in May), the Confederate leadership grew increasingly open to desperate measures that might serve to undermine Northern support for the war and perhaps even contribute to the electoral defeat of President Abraham Lincoln in the fall. One of the key figures given responsibility for implementing this new strategy was Jacob Thompson, a former United States congressman and secretary of the interior, who was dispatched to British North America as a Confederate commissioner in May 1864. Based at the Queen's Hotel in Toronto, in Canada West, Thompson was provided with large amounts of money to finance various irregular operations against the North.

His mandate was broad and deliberately vague:

Richmond, Va., April 27, 1864

Hon. Jacob Thompson:
Sir: Confiding special trust in your zeal, discretion, and patriotism, I hereby direct you to proceed at once to Canada; there to carry out the instructions you have received from me verbally, in such manner as shall seem most likely to conduce to the furtherance of the interests of the Confederate States of America which have been entrusted to you.

Very respectfully and truly yours, Jeff'n Davis[1]

Although President Davis did not mention the fact in writing, Thompson had the authority to sanction a wide variety of actions against the North, including sabotage and some plots that were probably best characterized as terrorism.[2]

Thompson's biggest challenge was to conduct his covert operations (which together came to be known as the "Northwest Conspiracy") under constant scrutiny by American and Canadian authorities. "The bane and curse of carrying out anything in this country," he later complained, "is the surveillance under which we act. Detectives, or those ready to give information, stand at every street corner. Two or three cannot interchange ideas without a reporter."[3] In this Canadian netherworld of Civil War intrigue, populated by detectives, double agents, fraud artists, criminals, and a large but motley pool of Confederate exiles (including paroled soldiers and numerous escapees from Union POW camps) and sympathizers, Thompson was also confronted with the problem of distinguishing between realistic and authentic plans and proposals that were unrealizable and/or fraudulent.

One plan that seemed particularly promising to Commissioner Thompson was the seizure of the USS *Michigan*. As a result, he was keen to authorize another commando operation against the vessel. He did not have long to wait. In July, Thompson was approached by Charles H. Cole, who presented himself as an escaped army captain who had served with Nathan Bedford Forrest's celebrated cavalry force. Cole also indicated that he held the rank of lieutenant in the CSN.[4] (In reality, Captain Cole had no naval commission. He had been paroled in April 1864 and allowed to

The Honourable Jacob Thompson in 1864. A former U.S. secretary of the interior, Thompson was sent to Canada in order to assume command of what became known as the Northwest Conspiracy, a series of covert operations intended to damage Union morale, divert Northern military resources, and encourage anti-war sentiment in the North, with a view to influencing the 1864 federal election. [John W. Headley, Confederate Operations in Canada and New York *(Neale Publishing Co., 1906)]*

return to his family home in Pennsylvania, after taking an oath of allegiance to the Union. He was thus taking a considerable risk by resuming hostile activities against the North.)[5]

In any event, Cole seemed to have the right stuff and was promptly sent by Thompson on a reconnaissance mission: "I sent him around the Lakes with instructions to go as a lower-deck passenger, to familiarize himself with all the channels and different approaches to the several harbors, the strength of each place, the depositories of coal, and especially to learn all that he could about the war steamer *Michigan*, and devise some plan for her capture or destruction. This duty he performed very satisfactorily."[6]

Cole ended his journey in Sandusky, where, with generous financing from Thompson, he presented himself as a free-spending oil-company executive, registered at the West House with a woman companion, and began a deliberate campaign to win the confidence of the *Michigan*'s officers, especially the vessel's commander, Captain John C. "Jack" Carter.[7] He also recruited a few conspirators from among Ohio's numerous Confederate sympathizers (known as Copperheads).[8] Reporting back to Thompson, Cole observed that "Lake Erie furnishes a splendid field for operations."[9]

He also asked Thompson to formally authorize his activities:

> Hon. Jacob Thompson:
>
> Sir: I have the honor to ask to be placed in secret detached service, in undertaking the capture of the gun-boat *Michigan* at Johnson's Island. Combination can be made without infringing the neutrality laws of Canada. I send this by special messenger. An immediate answer requested.
>
> Charles H. Cole,
> Captain, C.S.A.[10]

While Cole was engaged in his tour of the Great Lakes, Thompson had begun to seek other personnel for the Lake Erie operation. Fortuitously, he was soon contacted by John Yates Beall (pronounced "Bell") and asked to authorize a privateering expedition on Lake Huron. Beall, a recently exchanged Acting Master in the Confederate States Navy who had been involved in several daring commando operations in Chesapeake Bay in the fall of 1863 and who had subsequently lived in Dundas in Canada West for a few months in the late fall and early winter of 1863–64, was the ideal person to serve as Cole's second-in-command and to lead the naval side of the operation.[11] Accordingly, Thompson persuaded Beall to abandon his Lake Huron plans and to join the second Lake Erie expedition. This was probably an easy decision for Beall, as his primary goal was to strike against the Yankees on the Great Lakes, something he had been pressing for before his meeting with Thompson.[12]

In fact, in late May or early June of 1864, Beall had apparently received consent for an operation against Johnson's Island from Secretary Seddon of the War Department. Beall's original plan was to assemble some of the commandos who had served with him on the Chesapeake for "special service" in British North America.[13] However, before he could finalize arrangements, he abruptly left the Confederacy. According to William Washington Baker, who had been chosen to serve with Beall, the latter "learned … of an easy way to get through the lines of the enemy to Canada, and left several of us in Richmond because we could not be assembled in time to leave with him."[14] Beall was clearly very eager for action.

A post-war photograph of the American Great Lakes warship USS Michigan *(renamed USS* Wolverine *in 1905), which the Confederates had sought to capture and transform into a Southern raider. Launched in 1843, she was commissioned the following year. Decommissioned in 1912, the vessel was scrapped in 1949, although her prow has been preserved as a monument.* [Author's collection]

With Beall on side, Thompson did not hesitate to send authorization to Cole, albeit with the usual pro forma admonition regarding British and Canadian neutrality:

Charles H. Cole, Captain C.S.A. and Lieutenant C.S. Navy:

Sir: By the authority in me vested, specially trusting in your knowledge and skill, you are assigned to the secret detached service for the purpose mentioned in your letter. To aid you in this undertaking, John Y. Beall, Master in the Confederate States Navy, has been directed to report to you for duty. In all you may do in the premises, you will carefully abstain from violating any laws or regulations of Canada or British authorities in relation to neutrality. The

combinations necessary to effect your purposes must be
made by Confederate soldiers, with such assistance as you
may draw from the enemy's country.

Your obedient servant,
Jacob Thompson[15]

Thompson then sent Beall to Sandusky to confer with Cole and finalize an
assault plan. In many respects, the resulting plan resembled that of Wilkinson
and Minor; however, it deliberately avoided the bottleneck of the Welland
Canal, where the first expedition had come to such a disappointing end.

Essentially the plan called for Cole to stay in Sandusky and continue to
cultivate his relationship with Carter and the other officers of the *Michigan*,
with a view to arranging for a party on board the vessel on the evening of
September 19, at which Cole would ply the ship's officers with drugged wine.
Meanwhile, Beall would return to Canada and recruit a commando force.
Beall's raiders would seize the small sidewheel steamer *Philo Parsons* (222
tons) on the morning of September 19, during its regular run from Detroit to
Sandusky.[16] At Kelleys Island they would rendezvous with a messenger from
Cole who would confirm that all was ready for an attack on the *Michigan*.[17]
Beall's commandos would then steam to Sandusky, about twelve miles away,
and await a final signal from Cole to commence their nighttime assault.
Ordnance would consist primarily of Navy Colts and small axes, which,
together with grappling hooks, would be taken on board the *Philo Parsons* in
a trunk. As was the case with the first Lake Erie expedition, contact was also
made with senior officers on Johnson's Island and an uprising was planned to
coincide with the attack on the *Michigan*.[18] According to Thompson, "Their
plan was well conceived and held out the promise of success."[19]

With the plan completed, John Yates Beall returned to Windsor to
assemble his commando force. Here again, fortune seemed to be smiling on
the Confederate operation, as Beall was soon joined by another CSN officer
who had served with him during his depredations against Union shipping
in Chesapeake Bay: fellow Acting Master Bennett G. Burley, a Scottish
soldier-of-fortune, who had previously fought with — and then against
— the charismatic Italian revolutionary Giuseppe Garibaldi.[20] Burley had
arrived in Toronto following a harrowing escape, through a 25-yard-long

drain, from Fort Delaware, a notorious Federal prison on Pea Patch Island in the Delaware River.[21]

Beall also recruited an additional seventeen raiders, including an army surgeon, J.S. Riley.[22] Beall was assisted in his efforts by Thompson, who, in order to supervise preparations and provide logistical support, had taken up temporary residence at the home of Colonel Steele, a Confederate exile living outside of Windsor.[23]

On September 14, as Beall's preparations were nearing completion, he wrote from Windsor to a fellow Confederate operative:

> Dear Sir,
>
> This will be handed to you by _____ Esq., who will explain what I want. Please render him every assistance in your power.
> We want 3 dozen hatchets, also 4 grappling hooks.
> Please see Mr. B. If has met with any success — *we need that*. If there are any letters for me, forward them by him.
>
> Truly your friend,
> J.Y. Beall[24]

Two days later, Beall wrote again, cryptically indicating, "Everything is fair, and I believe he will be successful in business."[25] All was now in place. Beall's commandos were ready to embark on their "business" on Lake Erie.

Inside the camp on Johnson's Island, the Confederate prisoners were also ready. They had received messages alerting them to the new expedition and were thus preparing for Beall's attack, but probably not without some trepidation, given their limited resources when it came to the crucial matter of arms. Captain Archibald S. McKennon, an organizer in Block 13 of the prison, later recalled the preparations: "We were organized into companies and regiments and had armed ourselves with clubs, which were made of stove wood and other material at hand, with which to make the fight…. I had several conferences with the Colonel as to my duties, and we were in constant expectation of orders …"[26]

If Beall was successful, the long-awaited orders would come.

7

John Yates Beall Attacks

On September 18, Beall's second-in-command, the intrepid Scotsman Bennett Burley, was sent to Detroit with orders to contact the part-owner and clerk of the *Philo Parsons*, Walter O. Ashley, and arrange for the vessel's captain, Sylvester F. Atwood, to make an unscheduled stop at Sandwich, Canada West, in order to pick up a few men who would be joining Burley for an excursion to Kelleys Island. Burley explained that the stop would be a favour to one of the men, who was extremely lame. The next morning, Burley took passage at Detroit. As requested, the vessel stopped briefly at Sandwich, where John Yates Beall and two other commandos came on board. The *Parsons* then put in at Malden (now Amherstburg) on the Canadian side of the Detroit River, where a large group of passengers came on board.[1] Among them were sixteen Confederate raiders, who brought with them a large trunk. Ashley mistakenly assumed that they were skedaddlers (Union draft-evaders), a relatively common sight in the border communities during the war.[2]

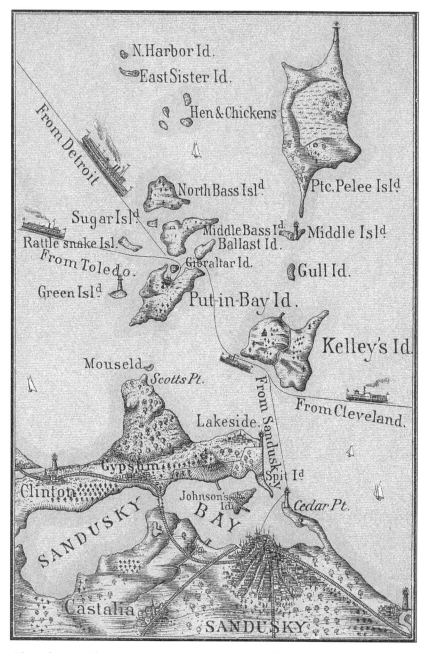

The Lake Erie Islands chain. Middle Island, the small island below Pelee Island, is the southernmost point in Canada. [Lake Erie Islands, Put-in-Bay, Gibraltar, Middle Bass, Kelley's, etc. *(Adolph Wittemann, 1886)]*

The *Parsons* then continued on to the Lake Erie Islands. At Middle Bass Island, the captain disembarked to spend the night with his family. The vessel, now under the command of the mate, De Witt C. Nichols, proceeded to Kelleys Island, the presumed destination for Burley and the men who had come on board at Sandwich. However, once at Kelleys Island, they informed the ship's clerk that they had decided to go on to Sandusky. Some new passengers got on at Kelleys Island, possibly including an associate of Cole's, but apparently not the promised messenger with news from Sandusky. Although Beall realized that this might point to a problem, it did not deter him from his mission.[3]

Shortly after the vessel left Kelleys Island for Sandusky, at about four o'clock, the commandos struck. Beall began the seizure of the vessel on the hurricane deck, where he confronted the mate. According to Nichols, Beall declared, "I am a Confederate officer. There are thirty of us, well armed. I seize this boat, and take you prisoner. You must pilot the boat as I direct you." Beall then pulled a revolver from his pocket and continued his instructions: "And here are the tools to make you. Run down and lie off the harbor."[4] An unarmed Nichols wisely complied.

Meanwhile, Burley and the other commandos promptly armed themselves and set out to take control of the vessel. About ten Confederates were assigned to the subduing of the clerk, the wheelman, the engineer, the fireman, and the deckhands. Two crew members tried to evade their captors, prompting the firing of several warning shots, which seemed to have the desired effect, as the outnumbered crewmen soon realized that resistance was ill-advised. The remaining commandos rounded up the passengers and made sure that they were unarmed before herding them into the fire hold. Much of the crew was also sent below. Any crew members not in the hold were accompanied by guards. Most commandos were armed with two Navy Colts. Some also brandished small axes.[5]

As the vessel steamed toward Sandusky, the Confederates brought the wheelman up from the hold, as well as several deckhands. The latter were ordered to clear the decks by throwing a cargo of pig iron overboard. Once the *Parsons* arrived outside of Sandusky harbour, at a point which offered an unobstructed view of the USS *Michigan*, Beall took stock of the situation. He also had one of the commandos press the mate, Nichols, for information about the warship and her current position in the harbour. Then Beall himself interrogated Nichols about the *Parsons'* fuel supply, determining that it was low. Following a brief council of war, Beall ordered the wheelman to turn back for the wooding station at Middle Bass Island.[6]

The *Parsons* arrived back at Middle Bass Island about dark and tied up at the wharf alongside the fueling station. Here, the Confederates were obliged to fire several warning shots at the owner of the wood supply and two other men on the wharf. They then released several deckhands from the hold to assist with the loading of the wood. They also apparently transferred the remaining prisoners from the hold to the cabin.[7]

As the loading continued, the commotion on the wharf soon came to the attention of the *Parsons'* captain, Atwood, who rushed from his home to the dock to find out "what in hell was up."[8] Within minutes, he found himself a prisoner on his own vessel. Dr. Riley, the surgeon assigned to the commando force, was then one of the guards in the steamer's cabin and tried to offer some comfort to Atwood. "He said," the *Parsons'* captain later recalled, "he thought I'd get my boat again."[9]

As Riley and Atwood conversed, the latter heard the familiar whistle of the *Island Queen*, a small steamer (173 tons) that also plied the waters of Lake Erie. As the *Queen* came alongside, Beall prepared to seize the boat, pulling guards from the cabin to assist in the assault.[10]

It was essential that Beall quickly gain control of the *Queen*. Although the crew and passengers (which included about twenty-five unarmed soldiers on their way to being mustered out at Toledo) were promptly subdued, this seizure met with some resistance. As a result, one person was cut in the head by a hatchet, several others were knocked down, and a number were struck with the butt ends of pistols or hatchets.[11] As well, the vessel's engineer, Henry Haines, suffered a minor gunshot wound. Perhaps because he could not hear very well above the noise of the engine, Haines had not responded to orders to stop it. He later recalled what happened next: "I heard some one exclaim, 'Shoot the son of a bitch,' and was immediately shot, the ball passing my nose and through my left cheek. The bell rang, and I stopped the engine, and came out on deck."[12]

Once the *Island Queen* was in Confederate hands, Beall had to address two urgent problems, namely, what to do with his surfeit of prisoners and what to do with the *Queen*.

The steamer Island Queen, *the second of two Lake Erie steamers seized by Confederate commandos on September 19, 1864.* [Theresa Thorndale, Sketches and Stories of the Lake Erie Islands (I.F. Mack & Brothers, 1898)]

His first step was to transfer the new prisoners from the *Queen* to the *Parsons'* cabin. Then, under the direction of Burley, most of the men were escorted, three at a time, to the hold. Beall then met with the *Parsons'* captain, Atwood, and asked him to give his word that he would not try to contact the mainland for twenty-four hours. Once Atwood agreed to these terms, Beall told him that he was releasing most of the prisoners into Atwood's care, starting with the women, children, and other prisoners held in the cabin. The released prisoners were also obliged to take an oath similar to Atwood's. Once Atwood was ashore and had begun to escort the prisoners to his house, Beall released most of the men from the hold. The only remaining prisoners were some crew members from the two steamers.[13]

One of the prisoners, a Cincinnati businessman named Frederick Hukill, later recalled the efforts to accommodate the numerous passengers stranded on Middle Bass Island: "Luckily for the ladies, room was found for them under roofs. The men had to bunk where they could. My companion and I slept in a haymow, and were fairly comfortable."[14]

With the bulk of the prisoners landed, the *Parsons* finally left Middle Bass Island and steamed toward Sandusky Bay with the *Island Queen* in tow. Before departure, one of the commandos had consulted with the *Queen's* engineer and verified the location of the boat's valves. The engineer later described what happened next: "I showed him the pony pipe in the hold, and he thereupon chopped it off. He then took a big sledge hammer and broke the big cock off the side of the boat and let the water in."[15]

After towing the smaller steamer for about five miles, the Confederates cut her loose and let her go adrift. They then imprisoned her crew members in the hold.[16] Beall's commandos next prepared for an attack on the *Michigan*. In addition to the equipment and ordnance that they had originally brought on board, they now had a supply of fireballs made from hemp, which they had ordered the *Parsons'* porter to fashion under their supervision.[17]

Beall was now finally ready to strike a blow against what he viewed as the United States' flagrant "war on Lake Erie against the Confederate States ... by transportation of men and supplies on its waters; by confining Confederate prisoners on its islands, and lastly, by the presence of a 14-gun steamer patrolling its waters."[18]

Unbeknownst to Beall, as the *Parsons* steamed toward Sandusky Bay, behind him on the lake, several Lake Erie Islanders were determined to thwart his plans. Among their number was a particularly formidable opponent: John Brown Jr., the son of the fiery abolitionist martyr. Brown was a fighter, a veteran of the violent, protracted war between pro- and anti-slavery forces that had torn apart "bleeding Kansas" in the 1850s.[19]

8

John Brown Jr. Fights Back

Despite their forced promises that they would refrain from contacting the mainland for twenty-four hours, some of the prisoners "paroled" by the Confederates on Middle Bass Island began to organize against the Southern commandos, whom they viewed as pirates, as soon as the *Philo Parsons* had left Middle Bass Island with the *Island Queen* in tow. These men quickly divided themselves into two parties of eight, one of which was apparently led by the *Island Queen*'s mate, George Magle. Determined to spread the alarm throughout the islands and to warn the military authorities at Sandusky and Johnson's Island, the two groups commandeered boats and set out to row across to Put-in-Bay on South Bass Island, the largest community in the Lake Erie Islands chain. The crossing proved to be a difficult one, as the lake waters were very rough that night.[1]

Magle's party was the first to arrive, and the news they brought with them quickly spread through the small island community, causing more than a little panic, as attested to by Francis C. Clark, whose father was then serving as a doctor on South Bass Island. According to Clark, her family was roused at ten o'clock on the evening of September 19, 1864, by the urgent pleas of a terrified young man whose mother had succumbed to an anxiety attack: "Oh, Doctor, come quick; my mother is in spasm. The rebs have captured the *Parsons* and the *Queen*, and there is no knowing how many are on the island."[2]

Although South Bass Island was soon in the grip of fear, most people managed to keep their heads, at least to some degree. The first priority for many islanders was to protect their valuables, lest the Confederate raiders attack. According to one observer, "Old stumps and hollow logs were utilized as banks of deposit for money, jewels and valuables of all sorts, while the numerous caves which perforate the island's sub-strata of limestone afforded refuge for the weak-kneed and faint of heart."[3]

Other islanders, however, focused on less selfish concerns, namely, the defence of the island and the best means, in the absence of a telegraph link, of reaching the mainland and notifying the Federal authorities. Those determined to resist the Confederate raiders turned to Captain John Brown Jr. for leadership. Brown, who had taken refuge on South Bass Island in 1862, not only had considerable experience fighting Southern partisans, but he also maintained a sizable personal arsenal, a legacy of his family's long and bloody war against slavery. His brother Owen, a survivor of John Brown's historic attack on Harpers Ferry (which had been partly planned at Chatham, Canada West), also lived on the island and quickly joined his older brother in the effort to counteract Beall's commandos.[4]

John Brown Jr.'s first concern was to organize a militia force. Hastily mustering the island's available men into companies, Brown distributed arms, arranged his forces in defensive positions at various landing points on the island, and devised signs and countersigns that would allow the defenders to identify one another in the darkness. He also had Admiral Perry's "Victory Cannon," Put-in-Bay's relic of a decisive American naval victory during the War of 1812, wheeled into a position commanding the community's wharves. The cannon was then charged with powder and loaded with the ordnance at hand: gravel and chains.[5] (Perhaps such improvisation would allow Brown to echo Perry's famous victory message: "We have met the enemy, and they are ours.")

As Brown took charge of the island's defences, the men who had crossed from Middle Bass Island proceeded to South Bass Island's west dock, where they arranged to sail with an islander named Stone across to Ottawa City, a small community on Catawba Island (actually a peninsula). From there they intended to make their way to Sandusky Bay. Unfortunately, the weather had deteriorated further and the lake's southern waters were simply too dangerous for Stone, who was forced to abandon his attempt to make the crossing.

Although the seas were extremely worrisome, the men remained determined to reach the mainland. Moving on to the east end of the island, they procured two skiffs and began rowing southeast for Kelleys Island. As was the case in the crossing from Middle Bass Island, one party soon took the lead, and eventually the two small boats separated on the dark, choppy waters of the Lake.[6]

Meanwhile, at the old South dock at Put-in-Bay, Brown's militia force was confronted with its first potential skirmish, as reported by Lydia J. Ryall, who later interviewed many of those who participated in the defence of South Bass Island:

> In the distribution of guards, two men had been picketed at that place. One was armed with a rifle, the other brandished an old musket. The men had been lying under a tree, when they perceived a squad of men approaching. One of the guards grew alarmed and wanted to run, but was rallied by his comrade. Together they faced the marauders, and in true military style demanded the countersign. The strangers couldn't give the countersign, but the spokesman of the party reported as captain of a small trading vessel anchored off shore, accompanied by his crew, and the newcomers were allowed to pass without molestation.[7]

Once he was convinced that the island's defences were in adequate order, John Brown, Jr. turned his attention to a far more dangerous task. Although two parties had already departed in small boats, heading toward Kelleys Island, Brown resolved to make his own attempt to apprise the military authorities at Johnson's Island of the Confederate raid and the seizure of the *Parsons*. He was also prepared to join in any fighting that might result from a Confederate attack on the prisoner-of-war camp. Accordingly, he decided to make the more direct and dangerous southern crossing to Ottawa City, despite the treacherous conditions that had earlier forced the experienced mariner Stone to turn back.

With the goal of reaching Colonel Charles W. Hill's headquarters at Johnson's Island, Brown and three volunteers, all heavily armed, set out in heavy seas and began rowing for Catawba Island, the northern tip of the Marblehead Peninsula. The trip across was harrowing and extremely difficult, but after many hours they finally made a landing. The four wet and tired men then hiked across the peninsula, until they reached the shores of Sandusky Bay, at a point opposite Johnson's Island. Here they scrambled to find a boat for the final stage of their journey: the short crossing to Johnson's Island. It was now about 6:30 a.m.[8]

Meanwhile, back on South Bass Island, as Lydia J. Ryall later recounted, Brown's militia force at Put-in-Bay was forced to confront a suspicious vessel:

> The second alarm occurred in the early dawn of morning, when a vessel entered the bay and cast anchor under the shadow of Gibraltar Island. Imagination had played wild pranks during the night, and become highly wrought. By its aid in the dim, uncertain light, the strange craft was readily resolved into a piratical cruiser upon evil intent. The shore battery was brought to bear upon her, and other preparations made for a gallant defense. The guards felt shaky, but anxious to ascertain the intruder's designs, a boat was manned and sent out to hail her. The first countenance that appeared over the "cruiser's" railing as they approached was that of a well-known sailor and fisherman — Meachem by name — a resident of the island. By this sign they knew that their fears were groundless, and that the vessel was an unoffending frequenter of the island waters.[9]

About the same time as the island defenders were contending with this second false alarm, out on the lake, one of the parties that had departed from the eastern side of South Bass Island was arriving on Kelleys Island.[10] Like

Captain John Brown Jr., the son of the fiery abolitionist whose attack on Harper's Ferry in 1859 hastened the coming of the Civil War. A veteran of his father's guerilla campaigns against slavery, John Brown Jr. had served in the Union Army at the start of the Civil War, but was living in quiet isolation when Confederate commandos captured the Philo Parsons *and the* Island Queen. *[Theresa Thorndale,* Sketches and Stories of the Lake Erie Islands *(I.F. Mack & Brothers, 1898)]*

Brown and his three men, they had risked their lives to make a dangerous, almost foolhardy crossing. Both groups were arriving at their destination with great trepidation. Uppermost in their minds were the obvious questions: Where were Beall's commandos, and had the Confederates succeeded in capturing the *Michigan*?

85

9

Rebel Mutineers

Of course, on the night of September 19, on board the captured steamer *Philo Parsons*, Confederate States Navy officers John Yates Beall and Bennett Burley and their fellow commandos were oblivious to the hornet's nest that they had stirred up on the Lake Erie islands they had left behind. Instead, their focus was very much on the challenge and danger that lay ahead, namely, Johnson's Island and the USS *Michigan*.

At about 10:00 p.m., the *Parsons* arrived opposite Marblehead Light, which marked the entrance to Sandusky Bay.[1] It was a clear night, and as they proceeded into the bay's entrance, the Southern commandos' target was visible in the bright moonlight. The Confederates now awaited Cole's signal to attack. It did not come, which was a serious problem. Two more would promptly follow.[2]

First of all, the *Parsons'* wheelman, Michael Campbell, told Beall that "it was too dangerous to run into Sandusky Bay by night ... the channel

Captain George W. Orr, master of the steamer Island Queen. *Following the capture and sinking of his vessel, Orr remained as a prisoner on the* Philo Parsons *until she was run aground and scuttled at Fighting Island in the Detroit River.* [Theresa Thorndale, Sketches and Stories of the Lake Erie Islands (I.F. Mack & Brothers, 1898)]

was too narrow."[3] This warning probably gave Beall pause, but apparently it did not deter him from his plans. However, the second problem proved to be fatal to the operation. "I then started back to attack the *Michigan*," Beall later recounted, "when seventeen of my twenty men mutinied and refused to go forward ... a most cowardly and dishonorable affair."[4] Beall's raiders had split along predictable lines. The experienced naval commandos, Beall and Burley, together with two other men, were determined to proceed. (Captain George W. Orr of the *Island Queen* later recounted that he had overheard a hurried council of war that ended with Beall stating: "I have a notion to make the attempt, anyhow.")[5] The other Confederates, consisting mostly, if not entirely, of ex-soldiers, viewed an attack on the gunboat under the current circumstances as suicidal and doomed to failure.

An angry Beall did not want his own record besmirched by what he viewed as a failure of courage on the part of his volunteers and thus insisted that they sign a declaration:

On Board the *Philo Parsons*
September 20, 1864

We, the undersigned, crew of the boat aforesaid, take pleasure in expressing our admiration of gentlemanly bearing, skill, and courage of Captain John Y. Beall as a commanding officer and gentleman, but believing and being well-convinced that the enemy is already apprised of our approach, and is so well prepared that we cannot by any possibility make it a success, and having already captured two boats, we respectfully decline to prosecute it any further.

J.S. Riley, M.D.	Wm. Byland
H.B. Barkley	Robert G. Harris
R.F. Smith	W.C. Colt
David H. Ross	Tom S. Major
R.B. Drake	N.S. Johnston
James Brotherton	John Bristol
M.H. Duncan	F. H. Thomas
W.B. King	J.G. Odoer
Joseph Y. Clark[6]	

As it turned out, the mutineers were right about the prospects for success — as Beall surely must have realized, despite his protests. Cole was not signalling the *Parsons* because he had been arrested that afternoon, before his party was scheduled to start. An attack on the vessel would thus have resulted in either certain capture or death.

Unfortunately for Beall and Cole, on September 17, the military commander of the District of Michigan, Bennett H. Hill, had received intelligence from a Confederate double agent indicating that an attack on the *Michigan* was imminent.[7] He had promptly conveyed this warning to John C. Carter. Two days later, on the day of the planned attack, Hill supplied Carter with far more explicit information:

Detroit, *September 19, 1864*
C.J.C. Carter, U.S. Navy

U.S. Steamer Michigan, *Sandusky, Ohio*:
It is said the parties will embark to-day at Malden on board the *Philo Parsons*, and will seize that steamer or another running from Kelly's Island. Since my last dispatch am again assured that officers and men have been bought by a man named Cole; a few men to be introduced on board under guise of friends of officers; an officer named Eddy to be drugged. Both Commodore Gardner and myself look upon the matter as serious.
B.H. Hill,
Lieut. Col., U.S. Army, Acting Assistant Provost-Marshal-General[8]

Later that day, Carter assured Hill that he had acted on the intelligence:

Sandusky, *September 19, 1864*

Col. B.H. Hill:
Your dispatch of 19th received. I have Cole and a fair prospect of bagging the party.
J.C. Carter,
Commander, U.S. Navy[9]

With Cole and several of his associates in custody, Carter prepared his vessel for an encounter with Beall's commandos. He was determined to capture the *Philo Parsons* and spent most of the night of September 19 awaiting her approach.

As the *Michigan* lay in wait, her quarry slipped away and made for the Canadian shore of the Detroit River. The ever-aggressive Beall intended to destroy all American shipping that he encountered on the way. As a prelude to such actions, he ordered the mate from the *Parsons*, Nichols, to assist with the raising of the Confederate flag, presumably the naval ensign.[10] However, according to Campbell, wheelman of the *Parsons*, Beall decided to forego his only possible capture: "We saw but one vessel near to us as we went up; they told me to go alongside of her, and then asked what waters she was in. When I told him she was in British waters, they said they would not touch her."[11]

Just above Malden, Beall sent two commandos ashore in one of the *Queen's* lifeboats with a cargo of seized property (and probably some Confederate materiel). Farther along, at Fighting Island, most of the prisoners were released. The *Parsons* then proceeded to Sandwich, where, shortly after 8:00 a.m., the vessel docked and the remaining prisoners and commandos disembarked. Before leaving the vessel, the Confederates removed a sizable amount of property, including such improbable plunder as a piano and an easy chair. They also forced the engineer to cut the ship's injection pipes. The Confederates then made their way to Windsor, accompanied much of the way by the wheelman, engineer, and mate of the *Parsons*. At Windsor, the commandos scattered.[12]

By this time, the federal authorities were finally responding to the seizure of the *Philo Parsons* and the *Island Queen*. The *Michigan* had left her station and was in pursuit of the Confederates. Furthermore, following John Brown Jr.'s arrival at Johnson's Island, the camp commander, Colonel Charles W. Hill, in an effort "to guard the commerce of the lake and the lake towns," promptly issued the following warning by telegraph:

Johnson's Island, September 20, 1864.

Major-General Heintzelman, Columbus, Ohio (and provost-marshals and military commanders at Detroit, Monroe, Toledo, Cleveland, Painesville, Ashtabula, Conneaut, Erie, Dunkirk, and Buffalo):

Rebels from Canada captured the steamers *Parsons* and *Island Queen* near the Bass Island yesterday afternoon and have gone down or across the lake; disappeared from the islands between 10 and 11 o'clock last night; probably gone for re-enforcements, guns, and ammunition.

A wartime view from the fort on Johnson's Island, looking toward Cedar Point. [Theresa Thorndale, Sketches and Stories of the Lake Erie Islands (I.F. Mack & Brothers, 1898)]

The capturing party were about thirty, with abundance of revolvers and bowie knives. No other weapons noticed. At Middle Bass Island captors took wood enough to last two days. Warn all vessels and steamers and send all important information here. We have one of the principal conspirators in arrest.

Hill, Colonel, Commanding[13]

As news of the Confederate's daring attack spread, the *Michigan* steamed to Kelleys Island, where she was unable to dock until the islanders were assured, by the familiar presence of the ship's pilot, William Hinton, that she was still in Union hands. Here, the warship's captain, Carter, met briefly with the group that had rowed from South Bass Island. Then, as she steamed northward, the *Michigan* encountered a second party, including the *Parsons'* clerk, Ashley, who were under sail and on their way to Sandusky. Information from this group prompted Carter to search for the *Parsons* in the vicinity of the Detroit River, but to no avail. The *Michigan* next changed course for Middle Bass Island, arriving just before 1:00 p.m. About forty-five minutes later, she spotted the *Island Queen* grounded on

Chicanolee Reef, in waters too shallow for Carter to safely manoeuvre. Having failed to find the *Parsons*, the *Michigan* then made for Sandusky Bay, still unaware of the fate of Beall and his commandos.[14]

As for Beall, upon his arrival at Windsor, he reported to Commissioner Thompson. The young naval officer was soon sent north into the Canadian woods on a hunting trip in the vicinity of Balsam Lake in the Kawartha Lakes region. Here, in hiding, he would be beyond the reach of American and Canadian authorities, thus ensuring that he would be available for another operation; for neither Thompson nor Beall were prepared to abandon their designs on the *Michigan* and Johnson's Island.[15] Beall's firm resolve was evident in a letter to a friend on October 11: "You know that I am not the giving up kind. We are going to try again on my plan."[16]

10

The Unlucky Cruise of the CSS Georgian

Although Jacob Thompson was eager to initiate another naval operation on Lake Erie, despite the increasingly formidable obstacles — logistical and otherwise — his first priority was to come to the defence of Charles Cole, who was now a prisoner on Johnson's Island and facing the prospect of a trial before a military tribunal. On September 22, Thompson, together with fellow commissioner Clement Clay Jr., wrote to Jefferson Davis asking for official support for Cole.[1] That same day, they also wrote to Colonel Charles W. Hill, the commandant at Johnson's Island, insisting that Cole be treated as an escaped prisoner, and not — as had been reported — as a spy. In addition to pleading Cole's case, the commissioners included a blunt warning: "If you proceed to extremities with Captain Cole we should feel it our duty to call on the authorities of the Confederate States to adopt proper measures of retaliation."[2] (Such admonitions usually had the desired effect.)

During the month of October, Thompson's colleague Clay was largely preoccupied with the final planning, execution, and aftermath of the St. Albans Raid of October 19, which saw a Confederate cavalry force of about twenty men launch an attack on a sleepy Vermont town located about fifteen miles from the Canadian border. The raid, which was led by a young cavalry officer, Lieutenant Bennett H. Young (who had briefly served as a courier for Thompson, delivering cash to Charles Cole in Sandusky), caused great panic and much outrage in the North and also became a major source of tension between British North America and the United States.[3]

In late October, undeterred by the diplomatic furor caused by the Vermont raid, Thompson, Beall, and Burley stepped up their preparations for a third Lake Erie expedition. The new plan differed from the previous commando operations in one key respect. Rather than seize a Great Lakes steamer, the Confederates would purchase a suitable vessel in Canada, outfit her for war, assemble a crew under Beall, and then commence attacks against Union shipping and cities on the eastern end of Lake Erie, beginning with Buffalo.

As the Confederate raids continued, three additional steamers would be captured and armed. Crews would be drawn from among Confederate volunteers at various lakeshore communities. Once assembled, the small Confederate fleet would be divided. Assuming that their attacks would lure the *Michigan* from Sandusky Bay, one group would continue diversionary raids in the eastern part of Lake Erie; the other, comprising two steamers under Beall's command, would steam west and take advantage of the *Michigan*'s absence, attacking Johnson's Island and freeing the prisoners. The four steamers would then rendezvous and confront the *Michigan*.[4]

In its broad outline, the plan was daring to the point of audaciousness. It was also extremely complicated and far-fetched, probably too much so. However, the crucial part of the operation, the acquisition and arming of a steamer, was potentially a feasible goal.[5] The key question was: Could the Confederates outmanoeuvre their most daunting enemies, namely, the informers in their own ranks and the American and Canadian agents who were determined to monitor their every move?

Confident that he could obtain a ship, Thompson's first step was to send Burley, probably at the end of September or early in October, to Guelph, where he stayed at the home of an apparent relative, the foundry-

Adam Robertson, the Guelph foundry owner, in 1864. Robertson worked with the commando Bennett Burley to fashion armaments for the Confederate-owned steamer Georgian. The photograph is found in an album that belonged to David McCrae, the father of the noted Canadian poet John McCrae. [Guelph Museums M991.9.2.46]

owner Adam Robertson. At Robertson's foundry, the Confederate naval officer, who was the son of a Glasgow master mechanic and handle-maker and who had previously designed and manufactured an "infernal machine" for the CSN, began work on the production of a gun carriage, torpedoes, solid shot, shells, grapeshot, and other ordnance.[6] (Burley's father achieved such renown for his experiments with submarine weaponry that he was actually mentioned in Jules Verne's 1869 science-fiction masterpiece *Twenty Thousand Leagues Under the Sea*.)[7]

Young Burley also arranged for the purchase of an old 14-pounder gun from a Guelph resident and paid for it to be rebored.[8] On October 17, he reported on his progress: "Everything is going on finely and I anticipate having the things finished early, perhaps this week, anyway in the fore part of next."[9]

Thompson then focused on the acquisition of a vessel, which he wanted to accomplish without alerting Union and Canadian authorities. In this effort he relied on a proxy, John Bates, a Kentucky expatriate and former steamboat captain then in Toronto. On October 29, after negotiating for about two weeks, Bates purchased the steamer *Georgian* (350 tons) from A.M. Smith and Co. and George H. Wyatt, for approximately $16,500.[10] Ostensibly acquired for use in the timber trade, the *Georgian* was an impressive ship. Launched in Georgian Bay early in 1863, she was powered by a screw propeller and would serve as an excellent Lakes raider.[11]

Now that they had a suitable ship, it was imperative that the Confederates move quickly and simultaneously on three operational fronts: preparing the vessel for warfare, completing the manufacture of the necessary naval ordnance, and assembling a crew and commando force. Probably in an effort to elude surveillance, Thompson undertook these activities under different leadership at several different locations.

Bates was given responsibility for overseeing the conversion of the ship, which was delivered to him at Port Colborne on Lake Erie, at the southern end of the Welland Canal, on or about November 1. Under the guise of strengthening her beams for the towing of lumber rafts, he sought to have her hull reinforced and a ram attached which could be used against the *Michigan*. Bates also hired a crew, including an experienced Great Lakes captain, Milne, who was known as a Confederate sympathizer.[12]

Meanwhile, as Burley continued his ordnance work at Guelph, Thompson established a second ordnance operation in Toronto at the home of a Confederate agent named William Lawrence "Larry" MacDonald. As ordnance was completed, the Confederates began shipping it (much of it in boxes and barrels labelled "potatoes") to various lakeshore towns, including Sarnia and Spanish River. This would allow the *Georgian* to acquire its armament and munitions in stages during its inaugural cruise as a warship. Among the weaponry being assembled was "Greek Fire," which was apparently being manufactured at Windsor for use in various Confederate operations.[13]

In Toronto, Thompson and MacDonald also worked on recruitment.[14] As was the case with the second Lake Erie expedition, naval veterans were in short supply, so the Confederates would have to rely mostly on army personnel to serve as naval commandos. However, they were able to recruit a number of experienced cavalry raiders, including Colonel Robert M. Martin, Lieutenant John W. Headley, and George S. Anderson, all of whom had served with the celebrated Kentucky cavalry commander General John Hunt Morgan. In an effort to avoid detection, it was decided that commandos would join the CSS *Georgian* in small groups at various points on the Great Lakes.[15]

Also recruited for the operation was a young soldier from Florida, Charles C. Hemming, who had made a daring escape in late September from the federal prison at Rock Island, Illinois. According to Hemming, he actually had little choice in his recruitment:

> I reported to Col. Jacob Thompson at the Queen's Hotel, and he turned me over to his principal assistant, who would listen to nothing but enlistment there in their Secret Service Company. I wanted to get back to the army but could not enforce preference under the conditions. Soon after this I was enlisted with Capt. J.Y. Beall, who was preparing an expedition to raid the lakes by armed steamers, which were then equipping at the shipyard at Collingwood.[16]

In addition to being assigned to the *Georgian* operation, Hemming was asked to undertake several dangerous reconnaissance missions across the border, apparently travelling at times with John Yates Beall. According to Hemming, "Beall from the first seemed to take a strong liking to me, and we soon became intimate, and every time he crossed the line I was with him, and the same blanket covered us both."[17]

Despite the seeming promise of the operation, the third Lake Erie expedition soon began to unravel. At Port Colborne, Bates discovered that the *Georgian's* propeller required repairs. Consequently, ensuring that the ship was seaworthy quickly took precedence over the installation of a ram.

Following repairs, the vessel began her westward cruise on November 6, heading for Sarnia on Lake Huron. It soon became clear, however, that the ship was being watched by both American and Canadian authorities. Not only was she boarded along her route, but she was carefully inspected by custom officials at every port where she stopped. Furthermore, the propeller malfunctioned again, and Bates had to go to Toronto and make arrangements for a new one to be shipped to Collingwood.[18]

To make matters worse, on November 19, J.J. Kingsmill, the county Crown attorney for Guelph, acting on instructions received from John A. Macdonald, the Attorney General of Canada West, arranged for the arrest of Bennett Burley at Guelph, where he was residing at Ferndell, the home of his relative, Adam Robertson.[19] Interestingly, it is evident from Kingsmill's initial report that the authorities first assumed they were arresting Beall: "The person was arrested here this morning as Captain Bell, who on the 20th September last on Lake Erie seized the steamer *Island Queen*."[20] In addition to arresting Burley, Canadian authorities intercepted several Confederate ordnance shipments.[21] Clearly, Monck, Macdonald, and other Canadian officials were no longer willing to tolerate Confederate acts of aggression against the North launched from British North America.

Difficulties also plagued the Confederates when it came to manning the vessel. For instance, the three veterans of Morgan's Raiders — Martin, Headley, and Anderson — were sent to Port Colborne by Thompson and told to await Beall's arrival. Headley later recounted what transpired: "We waited for him two days and nights. His failure to come (he being twenty-four hours overdue) became a mystery and we returned to Toronto."[22]

Upon his arrival in Toronto, Headley met with Commissioner Thompson, who informed him that the third Lake Erie expedition was being aborted. Thompson cited two main reasons:

> … Canadian authorities had instituted such surveillance of the vessel that it had been impossible to get arms or other supplies on board.… And besides the United States authorities … had alarmed all points on the lakes and tugs were being fitted up at Buffalo and other cities, with artillery for her destruction. The panic could not have been greater if we had captured a city.[23]

Lieutenant John W. Headley in 1865. The young Kentucky cavalry officer had served with Nathan Bedford Forrest and then John Hunt Morgan before being sent to Canada in 1864 on secret service. [*John W. Headley,* Confederate Operations in Canada and New York *(Neale Publishing Co., 1906)]*

Thompson could have added a third factor: winter would soon be setting in and the navigation season on Lake Erie would be coming to an end.

Once he had decided to terminate the operation, Thompson's first concern was to dispose of the *Georgian*. Probably with a view to taking heat off the vessel and thereby ensuring her availability for future use, he ordered Bates to transfer ownership to a young lawyer, George T. Denison III.[24] A noted militia officer and member of a prominent Toronto family with strong Loyalist connections, Denison was also one of the most rabid pro-Confederates in British North America and the author of several pamphlets arguing for the need to bolster Canada's defences in the face of Yankee belligerence.[25] In assuming ownership of the vessel, he, like Bates, was serving as a proxy. Although Denison insisted that he had personally purchased the vessel for $13,000 and intended to use her for commercial purposes, American and Canadian authorities were not convinced.

In fact, there were well-founded suspicions that Denison was actually acting in conjunction with his uncle, George Dewson, a Confederate Cavalry colonel, who had arrived in Canada on secret service in July. Based on intelligence received by David Thurston, the U.S. Consul in Toronto, the American authorities reported to the British that Denison "professes to have paid $13,000 for her; but Mr. Thurston states that no such sum has ever been in the Major's possession, and he understands that George [Dewson], a Canadian by birth, and a Colonel in the insurgent service, who spent some months in Toronto and who avowed that he was there as the agent of the insurgents and for a special object, left that city a few days before it was known that the vessel had passed into George T. Denison's hands; that Dawson [sic] had a family connection with Denison, and was very intimately associated with him during his residence in this city."[26]

Suspicions about the *Georgian* were probably exacerbated by the new owner's choices for the manning of the vessel. As captain, Denison engaged none other than Nettleton B. Whitby, who, as master of the schooner *Catarauqui*, had already been investigated by Canadian and American authorities as a possible Confederate privateersman. In addition, his crew included a well-known Confederate agent, William Lawrence "Larry" MacDonald, who was supposedly serving as ship's carpenter.[27]

In any event, the *Georgian*, now at Collingwood, remained under careful surveillance.[28] Of course, Denison, as he later recounted, was under no illusions about the attention he had invited from the detested Yankees as a result of his association with Thompson: "Any persons seen communicating with him about the hotel ... were shadowed by the United States secret service men ..."[29]

With no possibility for any further actions against Johnson's Island until the following spring, on December 13, Thompson sent Martin, Beall, Headley, Anderson, Hemming, and five other commandos on a dangerous raiding mission to Buffalo. Although it was to take place in New York State, the raid was actually designed to free officers who had been imprisoned on Johnson's Island. This action would prove to be the final raid for one of the Confederate States Navy's most daring commandos.

11

The Buffalo Raid

The Buffalo raid was prompted by intelligence that Jacob Thompson had received from Sandusky indicating that seven Confederate generals were about to be transferred by train on December 15 from Johnson's Island to Fort Lafayette in New York Harbor. Apparently among the group were Major-General I.R. Trimble and Brigadier-General J.J. Archer, both of whom had been involved in the first Lake Erie expedition. The other senior officers were Major-General Edward Johnson and Brigadier-Generals M. Jeff Thompson, J.R. Jones, W.N.R. Beall, and J.W. Frazier. Most of these men had participated in the escape plans that had been prepared at Johnson's Island during the winter of 1863–64. Moreover, several were leaders of the prisoners' secret organization, the Order of the Brotherhood of the Southern Cross.[1]

On December 13, Thompson summoned two of the veterans of Morgan's Raiders who had previously volunteered for service on the CSS

Georgian, Robert M. Martin and John W. Headley. After outlining the intelligence relating to the transfer of the generals, he asked the two cavalry raiders if they would be willing to serve with John Yates Beall in an effort to intercept the Yankee train and free Trimble, Archer, and their compatriots. Eager for action, Martin and Headley, in the latter's words, "promptly volunteered."[2]

Thompson then sent a message to Beall, who would share the command of the operation with Martin. Meanwhile, Thompson, Headley, and Martin finalized the selection of the remaining members of the raiding party, recruiting Lieutenant James T. Harrington, Captain Robert Cobb Kennedy (a recent escapee from Johnson's Island), Lieutenant John T. Ashbrook, Charles C. Hemming, George S. Anderson, W.P. Rutland (who had been at Rock Island Prison with Hemming), and Forney Holt.[3]

In addition to freeing the generals, the raiders were instructed to seize all the money in the train's express safe, which, according to Hemming, the Confederates assumed was "heavily laden with gold and currency for the army paymasters at Washington." This part of the operation would be the responsibility of a small group directly under Beall. The train's passengers were to be unmolested, unless, of course, they offered resistance. In such a case, Headley later recalled, "we would shoot them, just as we would shoot the Federal guards of the prisoners."[4]

In order to safeguard the operation, the raiders were ordered to restrict any discussion of the raid to fellow members of the commando party. As well, for the purposes of travelling, the party broke into pairs, some leaving on the night of December 13 and others the following day. Headley and Martin were among the first to leave, departing on the night of December 13 for Hamilton, where they were to rendezvous at a hotel with Beall in order to prepare an attack plan. Reaching the hotel late at night, they discovered that Beall had retired, so the meeting was postponed until the morning of December 14.[5]

Although the two cavalry raiders had by now been assigned by Thompson to two different operations with Beall, they had never actually met the elusive naval officer. Headley would later recall their first impressions, all of which spoke to Beall's leadership qualities:

Colonel Robert M. Martin in 1866. A veteran of Morgan's Cavalry, Martin arrived in Canada in 1864 and participated in several commando operations, including the aborted third Lake Erie expedition. He was the leader of the notorious attack on New York City in late November 1864 and co-leader (with John Yates Beall) of the ill-fated Buffalo raid a few weeks later. [John W. Headley, Confederate Operations in Canada and New York *(Neale Publishing Co., 1906)]*

We ... fell in love with him at once. He was a modest, unassuming gentleman. I soon observed that he did not talk to entertain but was a thinking man and was resourceful and self-possessed.[6]

Once they were acquainted, Beall, Martin, and Headley spent the morning of December 14 in Beall's room hammering out a plan for their operation. In the end, its basic contours were fairly straightforward. They would capture the train between Sandusky and Buffalo, overpowering the guards, freeing the generals, and securing the money in the train's safe. The passenger coaches would then be derailed and nearby telegraph wires would be cut. At the same time, appropriate clothing for the generals would be confiscated from the passengers, who would be reimbursed for any losses. If possible, the Confederates would then force the train crew to run the engine and express car to the outskirts of Buffalo, where they would both be derailed. The party of ten commandos and seven liberated prisoners would next walk into Buffalo, where they would break into pairs and board westbound and southbound trains, eventually making their way to Toronto and Jacob Thompson.[7]

With their plan finalized, the raiders then took the train to Buffalo, where they took rooms and rendezvoused with the other members of the commando party, briefing them on the next day's action. Expecting the generals to be travelling on the eastbound train from Cleveland, the commandos decided to take the train from Buffalo to Dunkirk early on the morning of December 15 in order to meet the generals' train. Everyone would disembark at Dunkirk, except Robert M. Martin, who would go on to Erie, Pennsylvania, in order to board the general's train early and probably do some reconnaissance. It was further agreed that Beall and Headley would make discreet inquiries at Dunkirk about the transfer of the generals. Martin would so the same at Erie.[8]

On the morning of December 15, as the commandos prepared to board the Lake Shore Railroad train for Dunkirk, they were greeted by a rather ominous proclamation in the Buffalo papers. Issued the day before in the form of General Orders No. 97 from the headquarters of the Union Army's Department of the East, under the command of Major-General John A. Dix, the document spoke to the North's determination, in the aftermath of the St. Albans Raid and other cross-border depredations, to act decisively and without mercy against "rebel marauders" attacking from British North America:

> All military commanders on the frontier are therefore instructed, in case further acts of depredation and murder are attempted, whether by marauders or persons acting under commissions from the rebel authorities at Richmond, to shoot down the perpetrators, if possible, while in the commission of their crimes; or, if it be necessary, with a view to their capture, to cross the boundary between the United States and Canada, said commanders are hereby directed to pursue them wherever they may take refuge, and if captured, they are under no circumstances to be surrendered, but are to be sent to these headquarters for trial and punishment by martial law. The major-general commanding the department will not hesitate to exercise to the fullest extent the authority he possesses under the rules of law recognized by all civilized states in regard to

persons organizing hostile expeditions within Montreal territory and fleeing to it for an asylum after committing acts of depredation within our lines, such an exercise of authority having become indispensable to protect our cities and towns from incendiarism and our people from robbery and murder.[9]

While this military order gave the raiders some pause, due to the fact that it obviously put them, in Headley's words, "in greater peril," it did not deter them from their mission. Accordingly, they made their way, as planned, to the Buffalo depot, and Martin, as agreed, took the train to Erie. The rest of the party awaited his return.[10]

Later that morning, Martin arrived on the second eastbound train to reach Dunkirk, signalling for the other commandos to join him on board. He then informed them that he had learned that the generals were not on any of the eastbound trains and that the party should return to Buffalo for the day. This turn of events called for an improvised plan, which was finalized by Martin and Beall. It was decided that on the following day, December 16, the Confederates would go to the Buffalo depot and spend the morning keeping a close watch on all incoming trains from Sandusky, with a view to boarding any train carrying the generals. However, if the prisoners did not arrive that morning, the Confederates would hire sleighs and find a place outside the city where the road crossed the railroad line, thus offering an opportunity to fake an accident and thereby stop the next eastbound train and permit the commandos to board it and rescue the generals. If the generals were not on board, the Confederates would still presumably proceed with the robbery of the express safe. And then, with or without the generals, the party would force the engineer to run back toward the west. Meanwhile, a small group of commandos would be assigned to stay behind and obstruct the railroad as the main body of commandos — and, hopefully, the generals — escaped in sleighs.[11]

As it turned out, the generals were not on any of the morning trains. Consequently, early that afternoon, Beall, Martin, Headley, and Anderson hired a double-seated sleigh and proceeded to reconnoiter the outlying countryside. About four miles outside of Buffalo, they found a deserted area where the road crossed the railroad tracks. They decided that this would be a suitable place to halt the evening eastbound train and carry through with their plan. Moreover, the location was close enough to Buffalo that they could rush back to the city in their sleighs and catch the night train for Canada. Returning to Buffalo, they contacted the other commandos and arranged for the full party to divide into two groups of five, each of which would hire a sleigh and meet at the junction of the road and tracks at 5:00 p.m.[12]

Martin, Beall, Headley, Anderson, and Hemming apparently travelled to the rendezvous point in one sleigh; Harrington, Ashbrook, Kennedy, Rutland, and Holt in the other. Hiding the sleighs and their teams upon their arrival, the Confederates assembled near the tracks. Martin, the experienced cavalry raider, proceeded to use a sledge hammer and cold chisel to remove a rail in order to lay it across the tracks. He intended to signal the train to stop with a lantern, but if that failed, the rail would force a stoppage. However, the Confederates had seriously mistimed their operation. Before Martin could position the rail properly or organize the commando force, the train was upon them, striking the loose rail and sending it flying about fifty yards. Aware that he had hit something, the train's engineer sounded his whistle and stopped about two hundred yards down the tracks. Then several men with lanterns got off the train and started back toward the point of the collision. Realizing that they had lost the element of surprise, the Confederates rushed back to Buffalo, where it was decided to abandon the operation and return to Canada.[13]

Now in considerable jeopardy, the commandos broke into several groups for their flight back to British North America. Six men managed to reach Canadian soil that night; four of them, Ashbrook, Kennedy, Holt, and Rutland, by taking the train from Buffalo; and two others, Martin and Headley, by taking a train to Suspension Bridge, New York, and then walking across the international bridge to Canada West. These men were followed by Harrington and Hemming, who apparently straggled back separately to Toronto within the next few days. Hemming, the last to arrive, claimed to have evaded capture through a series of hair-raising adventures.[14]

The remaining two commandos, George S. Anderson and the intrepid John Yates Beall, were not so lucky. Like Headley and Martin, they had made it to Suspension Bridge the night of December 16; however, probably due to the cold and their own exhaustion, they chose not to cross the bridge by foot, but rather, decided to await the train on the American

Charles C. Hemming in 1902. As a young man, Hemming had participated in the aborted third Lake Erie expedition, as well as Beall and Martin's Buffalo raid. Late in life, he sought to commemorate the Lost Cause in his home state of Florida. [John W. Headley, Confederate Operations in Canada and New York *(Neale Publishing Co., 1906)]*

side. This proved to be a terrible mistake, as their presence at the Central Railroad depot had attracted attention. At about 10:00 p.m., the two were approached by a Niagara City police officer, David H. Thomas, who was accompanied by a second policeman named Saule. Thomas confronted Beall, while Saule approached Anderson. Beall, who was armed with a Navy Colt, was completely taken by surprise. (It is likely that both commandos were asleep when they were first accosted by the police.) [15]

As he frisked the senior commando, Thomas asked him his name. The Confederate naval officer automatically blurted out "Beall." However, when, not long after, Thomas asked Beall a second time, with a view to getting his full name, Beall replied, "W.W. Baker" (the name of one of the young commandos who had served under him in Virginia). Assuming that he was dealing with escaped POWs, Thomas placed Beall and Anderson under arrest. [16]

Given the anger in the North over his earlier raiding activities on Lake Erie and General Dix's ominous new proclamation regarding the treatment of "rebel marauders," Beall realized that he was now in serious — perhaps mortal — danger. He thus insisted that his name actually was Baker. He also made the following admission to Thomas: "That I will acknowledge. I am an escaped prisoner from Point Lookout." It was far better to be dealt with as an escapee from a Maryland military prison than as the notorious rebel pirate John Yates Beall. Unfortunately for Beall, his ruse would not fool the federal authorities for very long.[17]

For Jacob Thompson, who had authorized the Buffalo raid on the basis of what was clearly faulty intelligence, the arrest of Beall and Anderson was a serious blow. As long as an experienced and aggressive naval commando leader such as Beall was available, there was always the promise of another operation on the Great Lakes. Without him, the possibility of such an action was seriously undermined.

As for Thompson's adversaries, with the arrest of John Yates Beall at Suspension Bridge on December 16, Union authorities in the Great Lakes region could take some satisfaction from the fact that all three leaders of the second Lake Erie expedition were in custody (Charles H. Cole had, of course, been arrested at Sandusky on September 19; Bennett G. Burley at Guelph on November 19). With some assistance from Thompson in Toronto and the Confederate authorities in Richmond, all three young men, then in their late twenties, would engage in legal battles in which their freedom — and perhaps even more — would be in the balance. A key issue in the various legal proceedings that followed would be the commandos' status. Were they spies, unlawful guerillas, or legitimate enemy combatants engaged in properly authorized actions?

12

Charles Cole's Imprisonment

Charles H. Cole had originally presented himself to Jacob Thompson as an escaped Confederate cavalry captain who also held the rank of lieutenant in the Confederate States Navy. Thus, when Thompson learned, shortly after Cole's arrest, that the officer might be tried as a spy, he was outraged. Accordingly, on September 22, Thompson and his fellow Confederate commissioner, Clement Clay Jr., dispatched a forceful defence of Cole to Charles W. Hill, the commandant at Johnson's Island. Their message also contained an explicit warning:

> We have just learned that Captain Charles H. Cole, an escaped prisoner, has been arrested by the military authorities of your post, and that he is to be tried on the charge of being a public spy. As agents and commissioners of the Confederate States we protest against his trial on

this charge. As a prisoner, he was brought into your lines against his will. Since his escape from prison he has never been able to return to his own country; therefore he was legitimately where he was found and taken. Whatever designs he may have conceived, he had done nothing whatever in violation of the law of nations, of any law of the United States, or regulations of the Army. It would be contrary to every principle of law, either public, common, civil, or statutory, to punish him for his designs or purposes, proved he had carried none of them into execution, on the hypothesis that you have reason to believe he contemplated an act of violence. If he fail [*sic*] to carry it out, or make any attempt looking to that end, he cannot surely be adjudged guilty of any offense. If you proceed to extremities with Captain Cole we would feel it our duty to call on the authorities of the Confederate States to adopt proper measures of retaliation. If you can justly condemn Captain Cole as a spy, every soldier and officer of the United States would be tried and condemned as spies.

That same day, Thompson and Clay wrote to President Jefferson Davis, requesting assistance for Cole, who, they insisted, "has been acting in the line of duty with a courage and discretion that deserves the highest commendation."[1]

However, Thompson's high opinion of Cole would not last. Both his Confederate defenders and Union captors soon discovered that Cole was a habitual liar and a conman, motivated far more by personal gain than any other factor. He was not an escaped prisoner. Nor did he have a commission in the Confederate States Navy. In fact, he was not even a southerner. A native of Pennsylvania, he had apparently been residing in the South at the outbreak of the war and had probably joined the Confederate Army seeking adventure. Moreover, despite his claims, he probably never did attain the rank of captain. Taken prisoner, he had been paroled at Memphis with the understanding that he would proceed to Harrisburg, Pennsylvania, where his parents lived, and report to the local provost-marshal. Furthermore, his "wife," who had carried Thompson and Clay's message to Colonel Hill, turned out to be a prostitute with a long list of aliases.[2]

Cole's lies discouraged any further Confederate efforts to mount a defence. However, he was such an incorrigible and breathtaking liar that his constant fabrications ultimately ended up undermining any Union efforts to prosecute him.

When he was arrested, Cole glibly named a number of co-conspirators, several of them respected members of the Sandusky community. All these men were promptly rounded up and placed under arrest. On September 21, with assistance from the district attorney and the U.S. marshal at Cleveland, Cole and his closest associate, John B. Robinson (both of whom were then being held, appropriately enough, in the brig of the USS *Michigan* before being transferred to Johnson's Island), were grilled by military authorities about the Johnson's Island conspiracy. The interrogations continued on the following day, this time in the presence of Major-Generals E.A. Hitchcock and S.P. Heintzelman. As a result of this testimony, four of the suspected conspirators were immediately released, leaving Cole and Robinson, together with two Sanduskians, the architect J.B. Merrick and the merchant Louis Rosenthal, as the main culprits in the conspiracy.[3]

Following the return of indictments in February by a federal grand jury, the hapless Merrick and Rosenthal were placed on trial at Cleveland on June 5, 1865. The main prosecution witness turned out to be none other than their erstwhile friend Charles H. Cole. However, the ever-dissembling Cole was not especially effective in his newfound role as state's evidence. Moreover, the defendants' attorney mounted an able defence that both emphasized their good characters and shed considerable doubt on Cole's motives and reliability. The defence even called a former Confederate prisoner from Johnson's Island, Major Richard J. Person, who testified to Cole's unsavoury reputation.[4]

After deliberating for about thirty minutes, the jury returned a verdict of not guilty. This outcome left the prosecutors in Ohio with a crumbling case involving only two conspirators: Cole and Robinson. And the only evidence against either man was the word of Cole, now exposed as an incorrigible liar.[5]

Clement Claiborne Clay, Jr. in 1867. A Confederate senator who had previously served in the U.S. Senate, Clay was sent to Canada in April 1864 to pursue the Confederacy's interests with his fellow commissioner Jacob Thompson. Clay was subsequently involved with many of the Confederate secret-service schemes launched from British North America, including the raid on St. Alban's, Vermont, in October 1864. Following the war, he was imprisoned at Fort Monroe for nearly a year. [John W. Headley, Confederate Operations in Canada and New York *(Neale Publishing Co., 1906)]*

Despite the absence of hard evidence, Union military authorities were loath to release Cole and Robinson, particularly the former. Realizing that prosecution in the civilian courts was problematic, if not impossible, on July 15 the commissary-general of prisoners, Brevet Brigadier-General W. Hoffman, wrote to the office of the Judge Advocate General seeking advice as to how best proceed against the two conspirators. Hoffman received a prompt reply indicating that Cole could be tried before a military commission for a variety of offences:

> For a treasonable conspiracy with Robinson, Thompson, Clay, Norris, and others.
>
> For a violation of the laws of war in engaging in an attempt to seize Government property and release prisoners of war.
>
> For a violation of his oath of allegiance.
>
> For a violation of his parole.
>
> Upon any and all of these charges he is believed to be triable by a military commission.

As to Robinson, although no doubt guilty of the first two offenses, yet in the absence of any other testimony against him than that of Cole, he could not well be convicted except upon the first; and it any therefore be deemed best, if it be determined to bring these parties to trial, to arraign and try them together upon the first charge, and not further prosecute Cole separately upon the other charges specified.

It would appear, however, that the criminality of Robinson is of a character much less grave than that of Cole, and also that he is not a person of influence or much intelligence. It is suggested, therefore, that the privilege be offered him of appearing as a witness against Cole, upon the usual terms of pardon, provided he fully and frankly discloses all the facts within his knowledge; and that should he so appear and disclose, the trial of Cole upon all the charges indicated be proceeded with.

That this man — at once a secret agent and hireling of the rebellion and a false and perjured traitor — should escape punishment would appear to involve a deplorable failure of justice.[6]

At least some Union authorities were still determined to punish Cole. On July 24, Cole apparently made an attempt to escape from Johnson's Island. A little more than a month later, he and Robinson were transferred to Fort Lafayette, a military prison located on an island in New York Harbor. In ordering the transfer, the commissary-general of prisoners urged caution: "Have them under a suitable guard and officer.... Give very particular written instructions to the guard to insure that there will be no escapes."[7]

For whatever reason, Northern military authorities did not, in the end, proceed with the prosecution of Cole and Robinson. Perhaps the latter refused to cooperate and thus precluded any proceedings against Cole, for there is evidence that while at Fort Lafayette, Cole had the opportunity to vigorously coach Robinson to lie about their respective roles in the Johnson's Island plot.[8] Whatever the case, on February 5, 1866, Brevet

Brigadier-General Burke, the commander at Fort Lafayette, reported that a writ of habeas corpus had been served on him, and that he was obliged to deliver Cole to the Brooklyn courthouse on the morning of February 10. The army could have resisted, but decided not to. Five days later, Burke reported on the outcome of Cole's court appearance:

> Headquarters Fort Lafayette,
> New York Harbor, February 10, 1866
>
> Bvt. Brigadier-General D.T. Van Buren, *Asst. Adjt. General, Headquarters Department of the East:*
> Sir: I have to state that Charles H. Cole, late prisoner at this post, has been discharged by Judge Gilbert at the Brooklyn court-house this day.
> Very respectfully, your obedient servant,
> Martin Burke,
> Brevet Brigadier-General, U. S. Army, Commanding Post

Although he had been incarcerated for nearly seventeen months, the slippery Cole had avoided prosecution and was now a free man.[9]

13

Bennett G. Burley's Fate

Unlike Cole and Beall, Bennett G. Burley had been arrested in British North America. As a result, any prosecution by American authorities would first depend on the outcome of an extradition request, which had promptly been made by W.H. Seward on November 29, under the terms of the Webster-Ashburton Treaty.[1] However, Burley's extradition would not be a straightforward matter, particularly since the Confederate naval officer was a British subject.

Not surprisingly, given the conflicted attitudes in Canada about the Civil War, Burley would also be tried in the court of public opinion, where Union and Confederate sympathizers in Canada West would fiercely contend with each other, mostly in lively skirmishes in the provincial press.

All in all, Burley's prosecution would be a rather tangled legal affair, starting, in fact, with unexpected complications relating to the warrant for his arrest. At the Toronto Police Court, it was determined that the document was flawed, and Burley was accordingly released, only to be promptly re-arrested on a second, revised warrant. However, this, too, was deemed to be deficient, and Burley was let go again. As he left the courtroom, he was apprehended a third time under yet another revised warrant, which proved to be acceptable to the court.[2]

Burley's extradition hearing, initially before George Duggan, Recorder of the City of Toronto, would see the dramatic interaction of many of Canada's leading legal figures of the day. The prisoner was defended by M.C. Cameron, Q.C., one of the attorneys who had successfully defended the fugitive slave John Anderson in 1860–61. The provincial government was represented by Robert A. Harrison, Q.C., who later became Chief Justice of the Queen's Bench. And acting on behalf of the United States was Stephen Richards, a member of one of Canada's most distinguished legal families. Assisting Richards was the assistant U.S. attorney at Detroit, Henry Billings Brown, later an associate justice of the U.S. Supreme Court.[3]

Although American authorities were tempted to charge Burley with a number of crimes, including piracy, they decided to simplify the case and base their extradition request on the commando's robbery, at gunpoint, on September 19, 1864, of $20.00 from the *Philo Parsons'* part-owner and purser, Walter O. Ashley. This strategy, supported by Major-General John A. Dix and partly devised by Henry Billings Brown, proved to be an astute one, as the defence could hardly dispute the claim. There were far too many witnesses to Burley's depredations.[4]

Instead, Burley's lawyer, Cameron, centred his defence on the argument that the robbery was merely an incidental part of a larger act of war that had been duly authorized by the Confederate States of America. As evidence, Cameron provided an affidavit signed by Burley and also pointed to corroborating evidence from a number of Confederates then in exile in Canada, including Larry MacDonald and Robert Cobb Kennedy (both of whom had been involved in Confederate commando operations), and William Cleary, Jacob Thompson's secretary. However, Cameron admitted that the real proof of Burley's status was found in the Confederate capital. He thus requested — and received — a month's adjournment in order to dispatch a messenger to Richmond in order to obtain the necessary documents.[5]

Portrait of the young Confederate naval commando Bennett Burley.
[Engraving by the noted Canadian illustrator John Henry Walker, probably from a contemporary photograph, Daniel B. Lucas, ed., Memoir of John Yates Beall: His Life; Trial; Correspondence; Diary; and Private Manuscript Found Among His Papers, Including His Own Account of the Raid on Lake Erie (John Lovell, 1865).]

The journey to the Confederacy would be extremely hazardous. In order to safeguard his courier and his message, Thompson apparently turned to a Canadian sympathizer, the civil engineer, artist, and photographer William Armstrong, who wrote out Thompson's message to President Jefferson Davis in large block letters, reduced the text by means of photography, and then cut the resulting negative into five small pieces that were hidden, with the assistance of a Toronto tailor, George Walker, behind the coverings on the buttons of the courier's coat. Thompson also sent a backup messenger, who carried the message in the lining of a carpet bag.[6]

By the time the second courier made it through enemy territory to Richmond, the first messenger had arrived, and President Davis had already dispatched the necessary documents northward to Canada with his own special courier. The man chosen for this dangerous mission was Lieutenant Samuel Boyer Davis, a nephew of one of the most senior prisoners at Johnson's Island, Major General Isaac R. Trimble, and a survivor of Pickett's glorious but futile charge at Gettysburg. Lieutenant Davis was carrying documents relating not only to Burley's case, but also to that of the

St. Albans raiders, who were also being threatened with extradition to the U.S. Davis arrived in Toronto on January 5, reporting, as ordered, to the Queen's Hotel, where he delivered the documents to Jacob Thompson.[7]

Thompson was alarmed to discover that Davis had foolishly registered at the hotel under his real name, even indicating his army rank. Realizing that Davis, who had been ordered to return to Richmond with dispatches from Canada, had made himself vulnerable to the ever-vigilant Union Secret Service, Thompson instructed the young officer to stay in his room so no one could identify him. Thompson then sent his secretary, Cleary, to confer with George T. Denison, who agreed to let Davis hide at his home, Heydon Villa, until the latter's departure for Richmond. That night, Cleary and Davis slipped out of the Queen's Hotel, taking measures to ensure they were not followed, and safely made their way to Denison's house. "Lieutenant Davis," Denison later recalled, "stayed with me for four or five days, until Colonel Thompson was ready to send him back. He kept in the house and only went out for exercise after dark."[8]

Davis's dispatches included two documents relating to Burley's case. The first was from the Confederate secretary of the navy, Stephen Mallory, and consisted of a single page. On one side was a copy of the warrant, dated September 11, 1863, appointing Burley as an Acting Master in the CSN; on the other, a letter from Mallory, dated December 22, 1864, certifying that the warrant was a true copy. The second document was a "manifesto" (or declaration) signed by the Confederate president Jefferson Davis on December 24, 1864, and certified by Judah P. Benjamin, the secretary of state, in which Davis stressed that the second Johnson's Island commando operation "was a belligerent expedition ordered and undertaken under the authority of the Confederate States of America, against the United States of America, and that the government of the Confederate States of America assumes the responsibility of answering for the acts and conduct of any of its officers engaged in said expedition, and especially of the said Bennett G. Burley, an acting master in the navy of the Confederate States."

While they were determined to defend Burley, Davis and Benjamin were also cognizant of the diplomatic ramifications of the second Johnson's Island expedition and the extreme pressure then being brought to bear on Britain by Union authorities. Davis thus added a proviso to his manifesto, noting that the officers engaged in the expedition "were especially directed

George Taylor Denison III (top row, second from the left), with his brother Clarence (third from the left), the poet Charles Mair (seated in the front, on the left), and other officers of the Governor General's Body Guard, at Humboldt, 1885, during the Northwest Rebellion. [Lieutenant-Colonel George T. Denison, Soldiering in Canada: Recollections and Experiences *(Morang, 1900)*]

and enjoined to 'abstain from violating any of the laws and regulations of the Canadian or British authorities in relation to neutrality.'" [9]

Cameron's introduction of these documents, with the resumption of Burley's hearing late in January 1865, made for riveting courtroom drama. This was especially true of the manifesto from President Davis. In fact, according to one legal commentator, writing fifty years later, "A more remarkable 'production' is probably not to be found in the records of our Canadian courts ..." [10]

As it turned out, Davis's somewhat disingenuous declaration proved to be fatal to Burley's fight against extradition. Cameron's adversaries, Robert A. Harrison and Stephen Richards, seized on the document's contradictions, arguing that there was clear evidence that Burley had disobeyed his instructions and had, in fact, violated the neutrality of Canada, thereby negating any rights he might claim as a lawful belligerent. Accordingly, on January 20, 1865, Duggan ordered that Burley be incarcerated in the "common gaol" until he could be surrendered to American authorities. [11]

Duggan's decision prompted Jacob Thompson to write the next day to James M. Mason, the Confederate's representative in London, about the case. Thompson gave vent to considerable anger, stating that "not only is a great outrage about to be perpetrated on a citizen, but a great wrong is to be done and an insult offered to the Confederate States." He urged Mason to lobby British authorities to release Burley. If this failed, he insisted that Mason strenuously protest the extradition.[12]

This decision also prompted angry public demonstrations in support of Burley and heated protests in the pro-Confederate press against the Recorder. Meanwhile, Cameron promptly applied for a writ of habeas corpus, which meant the case would end up before a superior court at Osgoode Hall. Given the importance of the principles at issue, a particularly august panel was assembled, consisting of W.H. Draper, Chief Justice of the Queen's Bench (who had earlier presided over the famous Anderson case); W.B. Richards, Chief Justice of the Court of Common Pleas; J. Hagarty, Queen's Bench; and J. Wilson of the Court of Common Pleas.

After several days of complicated argument and careful deliberation, relating to both Canadian and international law, the court rendered a unanimous opinion that the writ of habeas corpus should be refused and that the extradition of Burley to the United States should proceed forthwith. According to Judge Wilson, who forcefully dismissed Burley's claims that the robbery of Ashley was undertaken as part of a sanctioned act of war, "We must not permit, with the sanction of law, our neutral rights to be invaded, our country made the base of warlike operations, or the refuge from flagrant crime."[13]

Given that Burley's legal battles in Canada were occurring at a time of considerable tension between British North America and the United States, it was probably with a distinct sense of relief that Lord Monck wrote to the Colonial Secretary, Edward Cardwell, on February 5, confirming "that Burley was this morning given up to officers appointed to receive by the United States Government."[14] (Burley's extradition would soon be followed by a contrary decision in the case of the St. Albans raiders in Canada East, where most of the Confederates would be released.)

American authorities shared Monck's satisfaction with the outcome of Burley's extradition hearing. This was particularly true of Henry Billings Brown, who had played an instrumental role in devising the U.S. strategy in the case. "I had a very lively time with him [Burley] in Toronto, which was filled with rebels," Brown later recalled, "and for a time it looked as though I should fail to get my man."[15] However, while Brown had succeeded in getting his man, his strategy of focusing on a rather minor transgression, the simple act of robbery, ultimately hampered the prosecution of Burley in the United States.

Fortunately for Burley, not long after his extradition his father began lobbying for him in Britain. The elder Burley wanted to ensure that his son was tried on the robbery charge cited during the extradition hearing and not for the more serious offence of piracy, which could result in much more severe punishment. The father's efforts were rewarded on March 15, when J. Hume Burnley, the British chargé d'affaires in Washington, wrote to American secretary of state Seward expressing British concerns over this matter and strongly asserting that Her Majesty's Government would "protest against any attempt to change the grounds of accusation upon which Burley was surrendered in pursuance of the treaty." Clearly, for the British, the Burley case involved an important legal principle.[16]

Seward replied on March 20, indicating that he was not prepared to recognize any legal constraint on America's scope of prosecutorial authority; however, he also noted that in the Burley case the point was irrelevant: "The question raised ... has become an abstraction, as it is at present the purpose of the Government to bring him to trial for the crimes against municipal law only." Nonetheless, while the American's were prepared to back off the federal charge of piracy, they did reserve the right to prosecute Burley not only for robbery, but also, Seward insisted, for "assault with intent to commit murder." As a result, the young commando was potentially still in a great deal of legal jeopardy.[17]

While the American authorities debated the best approach for his prosecution, Burley was held in the House of Correction at Detroit, then under the supervision of the zealous penologist Zebulon R. Brockway. Well aware that Burley was a particularly high risk for escape, the superintendent was determined to retain custody of the daring young Confederate naval officer. "I wakened," Brockway later recalled, "in the small hours of every night to inspect personally the corridor where he was confined and to note the vigilance of the patrolling guard."[18]

After several months awaiting trial, it was finally decided that Burley would be tried at Port Clinton, the capital of Ottawa County, Ohio, where his crimes had been committed. In June, a grand jury in Port Clinton indicted him for assault and robbery. Not long after, on July 10, 1865,

Burley found himself once more out on the waters of Lake Erie on board the *Philo Parsons*, as he was transported from Detroit to Sandusky Bay. Here he was met by Sheriff James Lattimore, who escorted him to the Ottawa County jail, located in the courthouse at Port Clinton.[19]

Burley's trial started the following week. The presiding judge was John Fitch of Toledo. The prosecution team consisted of William Annesley, Alfred Russell, and J.M. Root. Burley was defended by Sylvester Larned and Rufus P. Ranney. The prosecution's case focused on the basic facts of the armed robbery of Walter Ashley by Burley and Beall. The main witnesses were Ashley, Captain Orr of the *Island Queen*, and a passenger named William Rehberg, one of the Lake Erie Islands' leading businessmen. Also placed in evidence were the official Confederate documents that had been introduced in Burley's extradition hearing in Toronto.[20]

The crux of the prosecution's case was that Burley was a common criminal and had robbed Ashley strictly for personal gain. The defence, on the other hand, argued that Burley was a lawful combatant participating in an authorized military action, and, as such, had the right to seize not only the *Philo Parsons*, but all that belonged to the vessel, including her clerk Ashley's money.

In his charge to the jury, Judge Fitch made a major concession to the defence, stating that at the time the money was forcibly taken from Ashley, a state of war did obviously exist between the Union and the Confederate States. Consequently, the jury's choice was relatively simple. If Burley had committed the act as part of a military action authorized by his government, then at war with the United States, he had to be accorded the rights of a belligerent and could not be prosecuted in a civil court for what was actually an act of war. However, if Burley took the money for his personal use, then his commission from the Confederate government would not protect him from civil prosecution. After deliberating for several hours, the jury announced that it was deadlocked. Fitch then dismissed them and remanded Burley for retrial, setting his bail at $3,000. No bail was forthcoming, so the commando was returned to the Ottawa County jail.[21]

Reaction to the trial's outcome in the Lake Erie region was mixed. The most intemperate response probably came from the *Detroit Tribune*, which launched a vitriolic attack on the trial judge for failing to deliver the appropriate verdict: "Judge Fitch evidently needs looking after. If he is an ignoramus he ought to be removed. If he is a rebel sympathizer he ought to be impeached."[22]

Meanwhile, Burley resumed his prison life; however, the regime in Port Clinton under Sheriff James Lattimore was a far cry from the tight control and scrutiny that the commando had experienced in Detroit. This relative laxity derived from both Burley's winning personality and the inadequacies of the courthouse jail. Burley was a charmer, and soon became very friendly with Lattimore, who lived with his wife in the jail compound. Lattimore even took walks in Port Clinton with the likable Scots adventurer. As for the jail facility, it left much to be desired with regard to security. Burley's first-floor cell had a window that permitted him to talk to, and receive messages from, local visitors, of which there were many. Such unsupervised contact with friends and sympathizers was, of course, especially conducive to the preparation of escape plans. As the summer proceeded, it thus became increasingly unlikely that the Port Clinton jail would continue to hold the Confederate daredevil for very long.[23]

On September 17, 1865, Lattimore and his wife decided to spend the day at their property in the country. They took their two servants with them and gave Burley the run of the jail, including the hallway which led to Lattimore's residence. This proved to be a mistake, as Burley had somehow obtained a key which gave him access to Lattimore's quarters. Once inside, he exited the building through a window that had been propped up from the outside by a limb cut from a nearby tree by an accomplice. Before leaving the jail, Burley thoughtfully wrote a note, which he left on his bible for Lattimore to find: "Sunday — I have gone out for a walk — Perhaps (?) I will return shortly. B.G. Burley."[24]

But Burley never returned. Apparently, he first hid in Bay Township with a sympathizer named William Mulcahy. After a week or so, Mulcahy escorted Burley, who was in disguise, to Detroit and then across the river to Windsor. From there, Burley made his way to Toronto and the Queen's Hotel. Not long after, the audacious young Scotsman wrote to his friend Lattimore and asked that the many books he had left behind in his cell in the Port Clinton jail be shipped to him in Canada. After consulting with the county commissioners, who were actually glad to be rid of the expense of holding the Confederate prisoner, Lattimore advised Burley of the cost of express shipping. Burley sent the necessary money, and his prison library, as improbable as it might seem, was returned to him.[25]

Like Charles Cole, he had managed to avoid any serious punishment for his commando activities. The same could not be said for the main leader of the second Lake Erie expedition, John Yates Beall. In fact, the latter's fate underscored just how lucky Burley had been.

14

John Yates Beall's Trial

On December 18, two days after his arrest at Suspension Bridge, the commando leader John Yates Beall was transferred to the New York City police headquarters on Mulberry Street. Upon his arrival, Beall decided to keep a record of his incarceration in a small diary, in which he wrote the following description of his place of confinement:

> My *home* is a cell about 8 feet by 5, on the ground floor. The floor is stone; the walls brick; the door iron, the upper half grated, and opens into a passage running in front of three other cells; this passage is lighted by two large windows doubly grated, and has an iron door; at night it is lighted with gas. The landscape view from my door, through the window, is that of an area of some 30 feet square. By special arrangement I have a mattrass [*sic*]

and blanket. There is a supply of water in my room, and a sink. My meals are brought three times a day, about 9, 3 and 7. My library consists of two New Testaments. I am trying to get a Book of Common Prayer.[1]

At this point, Union authorities were still referring to Beall as "Baker," the name that he had given at the time of his arrest; however, there were strong suspicions that this was an alias. Furthermore, authorities in New York wondered whether their mysterious prisoner was somehow connected with the brazen attempt by Confederate operatives, on November 25, the day after Thanksgiving, to burn New York City using the incendiary Greek Fire. (In fact, several of Beall's associates in Canada had been involved in this ill-conceived terrorist attack, one of Jacob Thompson's most far-fetched and desperate schemes.)[2]

On New Year's Eve, at about 7:00 p.m., the then acting chief of detectives at police headquarters, Sergeant Kelso, approached the station's doorkeeper, Edward Hays, and asked him to initiate a conversation with "Baker," with a view to obtaining information, including, if possible, the Southern prisoner's true identity. Later that evening, during a lull in his work, Hays approached the Confederate naval officer. Beall quickly seized upon the opportunity to solicit Hays's assistance, asking the doorkeeper if he would be willing to help him send a letter to Canada (presumably a request for assistance addressed to Jacob Thompson). Hays, who had previously obtained a copy of the *Book of Common Prayer* for Beall, was non-committal, but did say that he would try to obtain some stationery.[3]

Reporting to the Detective's Office, Hays briefed Kelso, who encouraged him to return to the cell and continue pumping the prisoner for information. According to Hays, when he returned to Beall's cell, the prisoner changed tack and offered a substantial bribe if the doorkeeper would help him escape:

[He said] "Hays, I tell you what you can do for me," I said, "What?" he said, "You can let me go;" I said I could not; he said, "If you do I will give you $1,000 in gold." I asked him if he had that amount of money with him; he said no, but if I would take his word, his word was good for the money when he would get to Canada; that a man there had that amount of money and more belonging to him; that it would surely be given as soon as he would get there. I asked him if he had any hand in the fires here in New York; he said no, but that he knew the parties, and that they were then in Canada. I told him I did not think I could let him go for the money, as it would place me in a bad position; that I did not like to do it; that it would be too much risk for me to run.[4]

Not long after this exchange, Hays once more reported to the Detective's Office. He then returned to Beall's cell and resumed his discussions with the prisoner, endeavouring to learn more about the latter's escape plans, his previous activities, and his identity. While Beall avoided any mention of his predations on Lake Erie and refused to divulge his real name, he did try to assure Hays that, if given the chance to escape, he would be able to avoid recapture. (Beall could not be sure whether Hays was actually tempted by his bribe, so his intention here was probably to allay any possible concerns Hays might have about his role in Beall's escape being exposed.) Hays later described the encounter:

I again went back to him and told him that I thought it was pretty hard for me to do it, but if I did it what time in the night would he like to get away. He said he would like to get away in the fore part of the night; that he had two friends living up, he thought, in Thirtieth Street; that if he could get to their house, he wanted to get out in time so he could get there, so nobody would hear him make a noise around the place; he thought he could get arms there, and then it would take somebody to arrest him if he could get arms after he got out; for, said he, "I know well what would happen to me if I was to be caught and brought back again." I then asked him if those friends of his could not furnish him the money before he would leave New York. He said that very probably they could furnish a part of it, probably half of it in greenbacks, if not in gold, before he would leave New York; if not, that he would leave me an order that would positively get it in Canada. I asked him how did he think he could get clear from New York, and if he had any friends that he thought would get him clear on the way going. He said first he would go to this man's house in Thirtieth Street, and then he would start for a friend of his in Jersey, about five miles from Jersey City, who did business in New York, who came every morning and went back at night, and by getting there he knew he would be safe.[5]

Although Beall was obviously desperate and felt compelled to take a chance with Hays, he probably revealed more than was necessary — or advisable — to the doorkeeper. As detectives mulled over the information extracted that night by Hays, their suspicions regarding Beall could only have increased markedly, for the commando had revealed much, including confirmation that his name was not Baker, that he had indeed been involved in significant actions against the Union, that he was familiar with the operatives who had attempted to burn New York, and that he was intent on escape. Clearly, he was not just another POW escapee.

On the evening of January 1, police officials descended on Beall's cell. His description of what ensued comprises the bulk of the last entry in his prison diary:

> *Jan. 2d.* Last night was called out, and a search made of my room and my person. The captures consisted of two knives.... They gave me two newspapers, which do seem to bear out the statements of Southern loss, &c. Savannah, indeed, is fallen; but its garrison was saved, so that Hardee and Beauregard have an army. And Butler did not take Wilmington, though the fleet did storm long and heavy. Poor Bragg has some laurels at last. Oh that Gen. Lee had 50,000 good fresh veteran reinforcements! But what are these things to me here! I do most earnestly wish that I was in Richmond. Oh for the wings to fly to the uttermost part of the earth![6]

Landing state prisoners at Fort Lafayette, New York Harbor, 1861. Charles Cole, John Yates Beall, and Robert Cobb Kennedy were all imprisoned within its walls at various times. Kennedy was hung in the prison yard on March 25, 1865. [Frank Leslie, Frank Leslie's Illustrated Famous Leaders and Battle Scenes of the Civil War *(Mrs. Frank Leslie, 1896)]*

From this point on, Beall found himself in increasing jeopardy. On January 2 (or possibly the following day) his diary was confiscated. Worse still, sometime between January 1 and January 4, Walter Ashley, the clerk and part-owner of the *Philo Parsons*, and William Weston, the vessel's fireman, were escorted to the Mulberry Street jail by Colonel William H. Ludlow, one of the Union's prisoner-exchange agents. Ashley and Weston were taken to a room with twenty-five to thirty men and asked if they could identify Beall. Neither had any trouble confirming that the prisoner known as "Baker" was, in fact, the naval commando leader John Yates Beall, something that the Union authorities had clearly suspected, probably as a result of information received from George S. Anderson, the young man who had been arrested with Beall.[7]

In any event, on January 5, 1865, Beall was transferred to Fort Lafayette, which was then holding about sixty Rebel prisoners. His fate was now in the hands of Northern military authorities at a time when Union anger over Confederate cross-border actions was at a boil; when, in fact, many in the North viewed Beall and his compatriots as illegal combatants, if not terrorists or spies.[8]

On January 17, Major General John A. Dix ordered that Beall be brought to trial on January 20 at Fort Lafayette before a military commission consisting of seven officers. The commission president would be Brigadier-General Fitz Henry Warren; the judge advocate, Major John A. Bolles. The charges against Beall were serious indeed, namely, violation of the laws of war and acting as a spy.[9] As Beall scrambled to prepare his defence, he asked that a cellmate, the distinguished Virginia jurist — and rabid secessionist — Roger A. Pryor (who, in 1861, had declined the "honour" of firing the first shot at Fort Sumter and thereby starting the war), be permitted to serve as his counsel. Major-General Dix saw no reason to object to such an arrangement, but he wrote to Secretary of War Stanton on January 17 for authorization.[10] Two days later the assistant secretary of war, Charles A. Dana, replied, refusing to accede to Beall's request: "Under no circumstances can prisoners of war be allowed to act as counsel for a person accused of being a spy."[11]

Dana's refusal meant that when Beall appeared before the military commission on January 20 and was asked whether he was ready to proceed to trial, he had to state that he was not, making an eloquent plea for time to procure counsel and to prepare his defence:

> I am a stranger in a strange land; alone and among my enemies; no counsel has been assigned me, nor has any opportunity been allowed me either to obtain counsel, or procure evidence necessary for my defence. I would request that such counsel as I may select in the South be assigned me, and that permission be granted him to appear, and bring forward the documentary evidence necessary for my defence. If this can not be granted, I ask further time for preparation.

Beall was also asked whether he objected to any members of the military commission. According to Bolles, the CSN officer "answered that he did not, but that he desired to protest against being tried by any Military Commission." The commission disregarded Beall's objection, but did agree to postpone his trial until January 25, in order to give him additional time to find counsel; however, there was no sympathy on the part of Union authorities for Beall's request to be represented by Southern counsel.[12]

John Yates Beall's defence counsel, the New York criminal lawyer James T. Brady, who was probably best known for his defence, in 1859, of the Tammany Hall politician Daniel Sickles (later a Union major-general), who had murdered his wife's lover in a jealous rage. Sickles's case marked the first time that a temporary-insanity plea was successfully used in an American court. Sickles would later play a controversial role in the Battle of Gettysburg, during which he lost a leg. [Engraving from a photograph by Rockwood of New York, Harper's Weekly, February 27, 1869]

Barred from engaging a lawyer from the South, Beall drafted a letter later that day to the eminent New York jurist James T. Brady, requesting his services as counsel before the commission. This letter was conveyed by the commander of Fort Lafayette, Colonel Martin Burke, to the Judge Advocate, Bolles, who, in turn, delivered it by hand to Brady's office. Brady was out, but his partner, William C. Traphagen, indicated that if Brady was unable to take the case, their firm would endeavour to procure "competent counsel" for Beall, prompting Bolles to issue a pass that would permit Brady — or any other member of the bar — to visit Beall as often as required for his defence.[13]

As he awaited a reply from Brady, Beall focused on his defence case. He was particularly determined to acquire copies of the official papers that would prove he was not an unlawful combatant (a "guerrillero") or spy, but rather an officer in the Confederate Navy acting on official orders. Accordingly, on January 22, he drafted separate letters, to be delivered under a flag of truce, to two Richmond friends, Daniel B. Lucas, a lawyer, and Alexander R. Boteler, a congressman. He also wrote to Commissioner Jacob Thompson in Toronto. In all three letters, Beall succinctly explained his situation and asked for exculpatory evidence to be used in his forthcoming trial. In his letter to Thompson, Beall expressed a surprising degree of optimism: "The Commission so far have evidenced a disposition to treat me fairly and equitably. With the evidence you can send, together with that I have a right to expect from Richd. and elsewhere, I am confident of an acquittal."[14]

On January 25, Beall was once more brought before the commission and asked if he was ready to proceed to trial. He replied that he had written to James T. Brady, but had not yet received a reply, which meant that he was still without counsel. At this point, the Judge Advocate produced a letter that had been received from Brady that very morning. In the letter, Brady indicated that he was currently busy with another case; however, he also stated he was unable to procure alternative counsel for Beall that he could "in all respects commend" and thus asked that the commission postpone the trial for a week; at which time he would be available to defend the Confederate prisoner.[15]

Following the discussion prompted by Brady's letter, the Judge Advocate then exhibited more correspondence, namely, the three letters requesting assistance that Beall had written several days before. These had not been sent to their intended recipients. Instead, Union military authorities had held the letters and had decided to make the following offer to Beall:

> The Judge Advocate ... informed the accused that, if
> he would reduce to writing in the form of an affidavit a
> statement of the facts he expected to prove by the persons

or documents named in those letters, he should probably admit that the witnesses or documents, if presented in Court, would so say, and thus save the Government the delay, and the accused the trouble and expense of getting them here.[16]

Beall agreed to this arrangement, asking that his trial be delayed until February 1, in order to give him the time necessary to prepare his statement and to ensure that Brady could serve as his counsel. The commission granted this postponement; however, the haste with which the Northern authorities were otherwise proceeding with their case against Beall suggested that his belief in their fairness toward him might be unwarranted and that he might be in far more peril than he had hitherto realized. In fact, the magnitude of the danger confronting Beall was confirmed by the fate of another Confederate prisoner connected to Jacob Thompson's raiders.

On January 14, Lieutenant Samuel Boyer Davis, who had served as a courier, transporting documents from Richmond to Toronto to be used in the trials of Bennett Burley and the St. Albans raiders, was arrested at Newark, Ohio, on his return journey to the Confederacy. Davis was once again carrying dispatches, this time written in pencil on five pieces of silk carefully hidden in the lining of his coat — a rather ingenious stratagem devised by the Confederate sympathizer George T. Denison, whose wife, Caroline, was responsible for making the necessary alterations to Davis's clothing. At the time of his arrest, Davis had dyed his fair hair black and was travelling under an assumed name, that of Denison's friend Willoughby Cummings, a Toronto lawyer who had obtained a passport in his own name specifically for Davis's use. Within four days of his arrest, Davis appeared before a court martial convened in Cincinnati, where he was promptly tried and convicted as a spy and sentenced to hang.[17]

Davis, who had managed to remove and burn his dispatches under the noses of his captors, protested his innocence, but faced his sentence with great courage and defiance, stating: "Young as I am, scarcely verged into manhood, I would like to live; but gentlemen I am no coward, and I deem one who would stand here before his fellow men, before soldiers who have faced the foe and felt bullets and ask pity does not deserve the name of man."[18]

On January 26, Major-General Hooker approved and confirmed the court martial proceedings, findings, and sentence, and ordered that Davis be delivered into the custody of the commanding officer at Johnson's Island, where the prisoner was to be held until he was "duly executed at that place between the hours of 10 o'clock a.m. and 3 o'clock p.m. of Friday, the 17th day of February, A.D. 1865 …"

Clearly, at a time when the North was increasingly apprehensive and angry about Jacob Thompson's cross-border attacks, particularly the attempt to burn New York City, conviction as a spy would more than likely lead to the gallows.

On the day Davis's conviction was confirmed, efforts were underway within Toronto's Confederate colony to come to Beall's assistance. Beall's close friend Daniel B. Lucas (who, unbeknownst to Beall, had left Richmond and travelled to Canada in response to the earliest newspaper reports of Bennett Burley's arrest, in which it had been assumed that Burley was, in fact, Beall) wrote that same day to Major-General Dix, respectfully requesting "permission … to come on to New York and appear for Captain Beall, and to bring with me such papers as I may deem pertinent to his case." Much to Lucas's frustration and bitter disappointment, Dix ignored his letter.[19]

At about the same time as Lucas attempted to intervene on his friend's behalf, Jacob Thompson wrote to Major-General Dix and to James T. Brady, sending an affidavit signed by Colonel Robert Martin, indicating that the real object of the Buffalo raid had been to free Confederate officers being transferred from Johnson's Island. Martin also stated that the true purpose of the raid was only known to him and Beall, leaving the other participants "to their own conjectures upon the subject."[20] (This latter declaration was probably intended to counter any speculation by Beall's fellow prisoner, the boy Anderson, as to the goal of the Buffalo raid.) As was the case with Lucas's appeal, the commission disregarded Martin's evidence.

On February 1, Beall's trial finally began at Fort Lafayette. The commission proceedings commenced with the formal reading of the charges and specifications against Beall, to which the Confederate officer pleaded not guilty. The prosecution then presented its case, which was largely based on the testimony of five individuals: Walter Ashley, the clerk and part-owner of the *Philo Parsons*; William Weston, the *Parsons*' fireman;

David H. Thomas, the police officer who had arrested Beall; Edward Hays, the doorkeeper at police headquarters on Mulberry Street; and George S. Anderson, the seventeen-year-old boy who had been arrested with Beall. Ashley, Weston, and Thomas testified on February 1, Hays and Anderson on the following day. All five were cross-examined by Beall's counsel, Brady.

Taken together, the testimony of the five witnesses established several key facts, including Beall's leadership role in the seizures of the *Philo Parsons* and the *Island Queen* and the attempted attack on the USS *Michigan*; his participation in the Buffalo raid; his presence at Suspension Bridge; his use of weapons, civilian dress, and an alias; and his attempt to escape custody. Hays's testimony also suggested a possible connection between Beall and the raiders who had recently attacked New York City with incendiaries.[21]

Following the completion of the witnesses' testimony on February 2, Judge Advocate Bolles then read into evidence the three letters that Beall had written on January 22. These became Exhibits A, B, and C. Bolles next read Beall's pocket-diary entries, which comprised Exhibit D. The prosecution then rested its case, prompting the commission to ask Beall whether he was prepared to proceed with his defence. He replied that he was not, requesting an adjournment until the following week. It was agreed that the trial would be postponed until February 7.

When the trial resumed on that date, James T. Brady began his defence with the introduction of two documents: a certified copy of the warrant signed by the Confederate secretary of the navy, Stephen R. Mallory, appointing Beall as an Acting Master in the CSN and a copy of the manifesto signed by Jefferson Davis that had recently been introduced in Bennett Burley's extradition trial in Toronto. This latter document confirmed that the second Lake Erie expedition was "ordered and undertaken under the authority of the Confederate States of America, against the United States of America." These documents became Exhibits E and F. Brady did not call any witnesses; instead he based his defence on an impassioned and eloquent address (Exhibit G) to the members of the commission.[22]

Very much aware that Beall's trial was taking place in the shadow of the recent Confederate attack on New York City, Brady began his address with assurances to the court that, despite highly prejudicial speculation in the city's newspapers, Beall was not in any way connected with the "incendiary attempt." Such actions, Brady implied, would be beneath his client, a man "of highly respectable origin" and a "gentleman of education," who was fighting against the North for misguided, but nonetheless "most laudable motives."[23]

Brady then proceeded to present the key points of his defence, focusing initially on the issue of the court's jurisdiction, arguing that Beall should be tried before a general court martial, not a military commission. However, as he began to cite the relevant case law and legislation, Brady was interrupted by the Judge Advocate, who drew his attention to a relatively recent act of Congress that rendered the defence's arguments moot. Brady thus promptly shifted to "another proposition" relating, once again, to jurisdiction. His argument here was that Beall was being improperly prosecuted in two different capacities: "one as a mere individual, engaged in the perpetration of an offence against society at large; and the other in the character of a military man, offending against the laws of war." If Beall's offences were, in fact, against society, he should, Brady insisted, be tried before a judge and jury, for the prisoner remained a citizen of the United States, despite his allegiance to the Southern "revolting States."[24]

Next, Brady conveyed his client's objections to the first charge against him, namely, "violating the laws of war." According to the Confederate naval officer, this charge was far too general and vague to warrant trial by a military commission. Brady presented Beall's argument with great reluctance, even pointing out to the accused and the court that "usually the objection to anything on account of its generality is not of practical value, because if it be erroneous, it is only informing your adversary to make it more specific. It is of no advantage to the accused ..."[25]

Having dealt with the issues of jurisdiction and having met his obligation to bring forward Beall's objections to the "generality" of the charges, Brady moved on to the two most serious charges against Beall: "in the first place, that he was a spy; and, in the second place, a guerrilla."[26] Brady's response to these charges would comprise the crux of his defence. For his client, these were matters of life and death.

With regard to the charge that Beall was a spy, Brady offered a lengthy argument, addressing the precise definition of "spy" and challenging the accusations that his client was in "disguise" and captured within "the lines of the United States Army." He concluded this part of his presentation with a forceful assertion of Beall's innocence, insisting that his client was a misled Virginian engaged, not in espionage, but rather "honourable warfare":

Under those circumstances he was not a spy — he was anything and everything but a spy. He was acting under a commission; he was in the service of the rebel Government; he was engaged in carrying on warfare; he was not endeavouring to perpetrate any offence against society. And if he were not acting under a commission or with authority, but was acting upon his own responsibility and from the wicked intent of his own heart for motives of personal malice or gain, he is not amenable to this tribunal, but must answer to the ordinary courts of the State within which the crime was committed.[27]

Brady then turned his attention to the accusation that Beall was not a lawful combatant, but rather a guerilla. Again, he began with an explication of "the real meaning of the term," eventually pointing to the blurred line between "legalized" war and so-called unlawful warfare:

It is death, desolation, mutilation, and massacre that you are permitted to accomplish in war. And you look at it not through the medium of philanthropy, not through the Divine precept that tells you to love your neighbours as yourself, but through the melancholy necessity that characterizes the awful nature of war.... Where do you draw the line of distinction between the act of one you call a guerrilla and the act of one you call a raider, like Grierson? Where do you make the distinction between the march of Major-General Sherman through the enemy's country, carrying ravage and desolation everywhere, destroying the most peaceable and lawful industry, mills and machinery, and everything of that nature — where do you draw the line between his march through Georgia and an expedition of twenty men acting under commission who get into any of the States we claim to be in the Union, and commit depredations there? And what difference does it make if they act under commission, if they kill the innocent or the guilty? There are no distinctions of that kind in war.[28]

Brady next focused on the issue of legal authorization, underscoring the fact that Beall was acting as an officer of the Confederate military and was thus engaged in lawful "depredations for the purposes of war." As a result, he argued, the attempt to capture the USS *Michigan* must be viewed as a proper military expedition. As for the planned attack on the railroad outside Buffalo, Brady stressed that the only witness to testify against Beall in this regard was an accomplice, the young man Anderson. Otherwise, there was no proof regarding the nature or purpose of the attack. Anderson's testimony alone should not be sufficient to convict, Brady insisted, for such questionable, self-serving evidence "is tolerated rather than approved." [29]

Having dealt with the two main charges against Beall, Brady briefly addressed the issues relating to Beall's refusal to identify himself and his efforts to escape. Here the lawyer scoffed at any suggestion that Beall's behaviour was improper or suspicious, noting that "in warfare if a man is taken prisoner and afterwards escapes, his escape is sometimes the most poetical transaction in his life; and his daring in getting away entitles him to as much glory as courage on the battle-field." [30]

Brady then brought his remarks to a conclusion, urging the court to base its final judgment on logic and reminding its members that they were able to "look at war with its grim visage, with the eye of educated intelligence" and not be swayed by the "natural detestation of violence and bloodshed" that would prevail in civilian courts. Following this appeal to reason, Brady made a somewhat abrupt turn, with a shameless attempt to tug on the commission members' heartstrings by evoking the pathetic image of Beall's mother and sister, "who would not care if he should be shot down in one hour in open battle, contending for the principles which they, like him, have approved; if he were borne back to that mother like the Spartan son upon a shield, she would look at his corpse and feel that it was honoured by the death he received. But she would be humiliated to the last degree if she supposed that he had departed from the legitimate sphere of battle, and turned his eyes away from the teachings of civilization, and become a lawless depredator, and deserving and suffering ignominious death." [31]

Brady's eloquent address was followed by that of the Judge Advocate, Major John A. Bolles, who set out to methodically dismantle the key elements of Beall's defence. Bolles began by addressing a few minor points raised by Brady. First of all, he dismissed any suggestion that there had been an attempt to link Beall with the Confederate attack on New York City. Second, he urged the court to disregard any references to Beall's "wealth, family ancestry, and university education," as they "have nothing to do with the real inquiry before this tribunal." Third, he questioned Beall's character by insisting that the Confederate had lied about being a prisoner at Point Lookout. Next, utilizing Beall's diary against him, Bolles implied that the Southerner lacked a true Christian conscience and that his relation to the "rebel service" was involuntary, not one motivated by an idealistic devotion to a "just cause."[32]

Bolles next dealt with the issue of legal authorization. While conceding that Beall did have an appointment in the "rebel navy" and that his activities were apparently authorized by the Confederate government, Bolles argued that a naval commission and authorization by President Davis himself could not be utilized to justify acts that were violations of the law of war: "If, then, such unlawful command be given and obeyed, its only effect is to prove that both he who gave and he who obeyed the command are criminals, and deserve to be gibbeted together."[33] Bolles then set out to prove that Beall had, in fact, engaged in unlawful warfare, acting as both a spy and a guerilla.

Bolles began his argument by quoting at length from Chief Justice Wilson's decision in Bennett Burley's earlier trial in Toronto. In particular, the Judge Advocate pointed to Wilson's dismissive comments regarding President Davis's manifesto, which had been intended to provide legal cover for Beall's activities. For the Chief Justice, the document actually served to indict the commandos, as they had, in his view, disregarded the president's explicit instructions to avoid the violation of neutral rights and to engage only in a "proper and legitimate belligerent operation." Among the remarks quoted by Bolles was Wilson's assertion that he saw "no authority for the doing of the act, and as an assumption of what was done, therefore the whole justification fails."[34]

Having thus challenged Beall's case with regard to legal authorization, Bolles moved on to briefly discuss the testimony of Anderson, arguing that the members of the commission had to decide for themselves whether Beall's accomplice was telling the truth. If they found the young man believable, then they could "with or without corroboration … convict the accused." Bolles next dealt with the disputed phrase "within our lines," which he insisted was a comprehensive term: "There is no shore or border so remote that it is not now within our lines, and lines that bristle everywhere with bayonets, and frown everywhere with forts and cannon." [35]

Bolles then addressed the issue of jurisdiction, arguing that not only was "the offender ... a rebel officer in disguise," but it was obvious: "The acts charged and specified being military offences are triable by a military court, and the accused has no constitutional right to a jury trial." [36]

Having dispensed with many of Brady's objections, the Judge Advocate was now ready to focus on the key issue: Beall's alleged role as a spy and guerilla. What followed was an extremely learned and methodical explication of the law, in which Bolles quoted from a wide range of authorities, first on the issue of spying and then on that of unlawful guerilla warfare, while at the same time carefully examining Beall's actions within both these contexts. Bolles bolstered his argument by quoting at length from a letter that he had recently solicited from the eminent jurist Dr. Francis Lieber, who had advised the Union government on the proper conduct of war, including the treatment of guerilla parties. Lieber clearly had no sympathy whatsoever for Beall and his fellow commandos: "The insolence — I use the term now in a scientific meaning — the absurdity and reckless disregard of honour, which characterize this proceeding, fairly stagger a jurist or a student of history ..." [37]

As he concluded his remarks, Bolles sarcastically dismissed Beall's claim that the real object of his Lake Erie expedition was the seizure of the USS *Michigan*, portraying the Confederate naval officer and his fellow commandos as cowards, criminals, and cross-border terrorists:

> An act of lawful war! Seizing two passenger steamers, robbing the clerk, throwing overboard the freight, committing the crimes of pirates and of thieves, and not moving one barleycorn of distance toward what is pretended to be the object and end of their warlike enterprise? Such a case does not admit of argument.
>
> And so in regard to the defence of that scandalous attempt upon the train — that it was a simple attempt at robbery, and a mere civil offence, on the part of this "humane and conscientious" prisoner and his worthy

associates, who with a force of five men, armed with five revolvers, a sledge-hammer, and a cold chisel, expected to capture a train of fifteen cars and fifteen hundred passengers, and to plunder the express-man's iron safe! It is a glaring absurdity. Why, sir, the moment the train halted and they saw the approach of three or four lanterns, this squad of express robbers jumped into their sleigh and fled for the Canada border!

All the evidence in this case, may it please the Court, tends to show that the accused was part and parcel of a wide-spread scheme of unlawful and irregular warfare along our whole Canadian line; whose purpose was, in any way and in every way, except by open and honourable hostility, to endanger the lives, destroy the property, and weaken the strength of those Yankee citizens whom these brigands of the border so bitterly hate.

The piracy of the lake, and the outrage on the railroad, were parts of that system of irregular warfare, under the fear of which no man, woman or child can sleep with any feeling of security in our midst.[38]

While Beall's lawyer, James T. Brady, had, under very challenging circumstances, conducted an able defence, Major Bolles's prosecutorial address was a bravura performance. Given that it was delivered in a city that was still reeling from a recent Confederate terrorist attack and before men who represented a military leadership that was under extreme pressure to thwart cross-border attacks by participants in Jacob Thompson's Northwest Conspiracy, it did not augur well for the prisoner, as proved to be the case when the commission reconvened for deliberations on February 8 and found Beall guilty on all charges, except the third specification under the second charge; namely, that Beall had been acting as a spy in the state of New York on or about September 16, 1864.

On February 14, the verdict was endorsed by Major General John A. Dix, who found that Brady's client was obviously guilty as charged: "In all the transactions with which he was implicated — in one as a chief, and in the others as a subordinate agent — he was not only acting the part of a spy, in procuring information to be used for hostile purposes, but he was also committing acts condemned by the common judgment and the common conscience of all civilized States, except when done in open warfare by avowed enemies. Throughout these transactions, he was not only in disguise, but personating a false character." [39]

The sentence for such a conviction would not have come as a surprise: "It is hereby ordered that the accused, John Y. Beall, be hanged by the neck till he is dead, on Governor's Island, on Saturday, the 18th day of February, inst., between the hours 12 and 2 in the afternoon." [40]

For Jacob Thompson, the loss of first Burley and then Beall was a serious blow, precluding any possibility that the Confederates would ever resume their efforts to capture Johnson's Island and cause havoc on the Great Lakes. However, far worse calamities would soon follow — and in quick succession.

15

Commandos on the Gallows

On February 17, 1865, the day before Beall's scheduled execution, Jacob Thompson's courier, Lieutenant Samuel B. Davis, who had been captured in Ohio in January, was slated to hang at Johnson's Island. At the same time, a second Confederate connected with Thompson's clandestine operations, the raider Robert Cobb Kennedy, who had participated in the Buffalo raid and the subsequent incendiary attack on New York City, was now in custody — and in great jeopardy. Incarcerated at Fort Lafayette following his arrest in Detroit on December 29, he awaited trial before a military commission for activities as a spy and for violations of the laws of war, charges that would likely lead him to the gallows.

Given his involvement with the egregious attack on New York City, Kennedy' s fate was probably sealed, but there remained hope among the Confederates in Canada and Richmond that both Davis and Beall could be saved from the hangman's noose.

The efforts to save Davis began as soon as the Confederate authorities learned of his conviction. On February 2, Jacob Thompson wrote a beseeching letter to President Lincoln:

Toronto, Canada, February 2, 1865

To His Excellency, A. Lincoln, President of the United States

Sir: The telegraph announces that Lieut. S.B. Davis, identified at Newark, Ohio, confessed, on his arrest, to being the bearer of important despatches from Richmond to Canada, has been sentenced to be hung at Johnson's Island on the 17th of February. Another paper states that Lieutenant Davis has been condemned as a spy. This young man's life is in your hands, and I hope you will allow me to discharge a duty I owe to you, to myself, to Lieutenant Davis, to justice, and to humanity, to demonstrate fully the facts in the case, so far as they are known to me, on honor.

Lieutenant Davis is a citizen of the State of Delaware, and has been for some time an officer in the Confederate service. No braver or truer soldier can be found in either army. He is a gentleman of education, true in all his transactions, and beloved and respected by all who know him. In the trial of Acting Master Bennett G. Burley, a case for extradition, the Recorder at Toronto has postponed the investigation for thirty days to enable the accused to obtain certain documentary evidence deemed important to his defense, from Richmond. The Government at Richmond was duly informed of this. Mr. Burley's counsel deemed these documents essential, and Lieutenant Davis volunteered to bring them to Canada. As he was pressed for time, he came direct through the United States and reached here in six days, which was regarded a most expeditious trip. It was impossible for him on this trip to have acted the spy in any sense of that term. He remained here but three days in all. Lieutenant Davis was directed to return by the most certain route to Richmond, with all possible despatch, in order that the authorities might furnish the documents asked for by the counsel of the accused. The whole object and aim of his coming here was to obtain the proofs deemed necessary to secure the administering of justice to his former companion in arms.

As I received the despatches he brought and wrote those he carried, I know every word in them, and as every word related to the case then undergoing judicial investigation, there could have been no objection to your reading them; hence I know that, however much you may desire to crush out the Confederate States Government, it must be repugnant to your sense of right and justice and humanity to pursue individuals with unnecessary harshness. When Lieutenant Davis was arrested he was on the very route he had advised me he would take in order to avoid all contact with the military authorities. He was expecting to gain no information with respect to the movements of your armies, nor do I believe he sought to do so. As a private citizen speaking to one clothed with authority, I ask you to spare this young man's life, not from any favor to me, but for the sake of justice, humanity, and all the conditions which control intercourse between hostile people. You have a right to retain him as a prisoner of war, but I declare on honor he is not a spy.

Very respectfully yours,

[Signed] Jacob Thompson

At the same time that he sent this letter to the American president, Thompson dispatched a similar letter, but with some personal content, to his former cabinet colleague, Edwin M. Stanton, the Union secretary of war.[1]

Two days after Thompson had drafted his missives to Washington, Robert Ould, Confederate Agent for the Exchange of Prisoners, wrote from Richmond to the Union's assistant agent of exchange, Lieutenant-Colonel John E. Mulford, insisting that Davis was not a spy, but rather was simply "acting in obedience of orders." He also indicated "that proof will be furnished to that effect."[2]

When Ould finally received a reply, it was good news — and from General Ulysses S. Grant himself:

> City Point, VA., February 13, 1865.
>
> Col. R. Ould, *Agent of Exchange*:
> Your communication in relation to Lieutenant Davis, condemned to death as a spy, was received and forwarded to the Secretary of War with the recommendation that his execution be suspended until you could have time to forward evidence in his behalf. I send you now the action taken in his case, which you will perceive was taken prior to the receipt of your letter.
> U.S. Grant,
> *Lieutenant-General*

Enclosed with Grant's letter was a copy of a letter dated February 7, from Major-General Joseph Hooker to President Lincoln, indicating that Davis's sentence had been commuted to "confinement and hard labor" for the duration of the war.[3]

Timely appeals had clearly worked in the case of Davis, who would spend the remainder of the war in a penitentiary at Albany, New York. It was now hoped that similar interventions would result in Beall's life being spared, and, in fact, there was an early sign of encouragement. On February 17, Major-General Dix ordered that Beall's sentence be suspended.

However, this decision proved to be prompted by a legal technicality, not by any consideration of commutation. Dix, concerned with loose ends, had ordered the commission to reconvene and review its finding with regard to "the 3d. Specification under Charge 2d." As it turned out, Beall had been found not guilty on this specification of spying in New York state due to the fact that a mistake had been made in the written charge: the month cited should have been December, not September. The probable result of any review would actually be a strengthening of Beall's conviction. Nonetheless, the resulting delay did serve to buy the commando and his defenders some time.[4]

MAJ·GEN·JOHN·A·DIX

Major-General John A. Dix, who was determined to end Confederate raids launched from British North America. As a young man, Dix had been sent to the Sulpician-run Collège de Montréal, in order to obtain a classical education and strengthen his command of Latin and French. He remained there from early 1811 until the summer of 1812, when the outbreak of hostilities between the United States and Britain necessitated his return to America. Not long after, as a young ensign, he fought in several engagements, including the bloody Battle of Lundy's Lane. Dix remained very fond of his time in Montreal, and took great delight in visiting the college in 1865. [Engraving by J.C. Buttre from a Matthew Brady photo, Lillian Buttre, The American Portrait Gallery (J.C. Buttre, 1877)]

Although Confederate authorities did attempt to assist Beall, the most concerted efforts to save his life were undertaken by a group of devoted friends. Chief among them were Daniel B. Lucas, then in Canada, and two Baltimore residents, James A.L. McClure and Albert Ritchie, all of whom had attended the University of Virginia with Beall. On Wednesday, February 15, McClure hired the Baltimore lawyer Andrew Sterrett Ridgely, the son-in-law of the distinguished Maryland jurist and statesman Reverdy Johnson, to prepare an appeal to be presented to President Lincoln. The following day, Ridgely travelled to Washington, where he met with Lincoln. The president offered no encouragement, explaining that he had already received numerous appeals on behalf of Beall, but had decided to leave the matter in the hands of General Dix, who, as one commentator noted, "was none of the yielding kind."[5]

Aware of Dix's reputation for sternness, Beall's friends decided that their best strategy was to persist in their efforts to sway Lincoln, in the hope that he would ultimately intervene on Beall's behalf. With a view to furthering their cause, late on Thursday night they appealed for help from another prominent Baltimorean, Francis L. Wheatly. Roused from his bed, Wheatly promptly agreed to join in the attempt to save Beall from the hangman's noose. The next morning, on February 17, Wheatly and Ritchie travelled to Washington, where they met a delegation of Beall's supporters from New York. The two parties quickly decided to act in concert, retaining the services of Orville H. Browning, a former Illinois senator and close friend of the president.[6]

While Browning prepared a presentation for the president, Beall's supporters made their way to Congress, where, with the assistance of the noted Baltimore Presbyterian minister Reverend Dr. John J. Bullock, they circulated a petition calling for the commutation of Beall's death sentence. As they moved about the capital, Beall's friends were heartened to learn of numerous efforts on the parts of various people — mostly strangers to them and to Beall — who had tried, or were trying, to intervene on the Confederate commando's behalf.[7]

Late that afternoon, Browning met with Lincoln for more than an hour. In addition to delivering a petition in support of Beall signed by ninety-one members of Congress, Browning included his own letter conveying the appeal of Beall's friends. Rather than pressing Lincoln on the issue of a commutation, Browning focused, instead, on a request for a respite that would allow Beall's defenders more time to prepare a proper defence:

Washington D.C., Feb 17, 1865

The President:

Capt. John Y. Beall has been tried by a court martial at New York, found guilty and sentenced to be hung as a spy and guerrilla.

The sentence was approved by major General Dix on the 14th of Feb'y, and directed to be carried into execution tomorrow the 18th.

This is brief time for preparation for so solemn and appalling an event. The friends of Capt. Beall desire to appeal to your clemency for a commutation of the sentence from death to imprisonment and that they may have the opportunity to prepare and present to your consideration the reasons which they hope may induce to a commutation.

They now beseech you to grant the unhappy man such respite as you may deem reasonable and just under the circumstances. As short respite is all that is asked for now and as that can in no event harm, I forbear at present to make any other suggestion.

Most respectfully your friend,

O.H. Browning[8]

Following his interview with the president, Browning met again with his clients, assuring them that it was unlikely that Beall would be executed, as originally scheduled, on the following day, Saturday, February 18. This delay, prompted not by a change of heart on Lincoln's part but rather by General Dix's request for a revision of the commission's findings relating to the charge of spying in the State of New York, provided some gratification and hope to Beall's supporters; however, they were less encouraged by their final interview with Browning on Saturday afternoon. According to Ritchie, Browning indicated that Beall's fate rested with Dix, not Lincoln: "He told us that he had little hope that we would be able to accomplish more than the respite; but added that if we could obtain the approval of Gen. Dix, he felt assured the President would commute the sentence."[9]

On Saturday, Wheatly and Ritchie returned to Baltimore in order to coordinate presentations for General Dix. On Monday, February 20, McClure went to Washington, where, with Ridgely and Browning, he would continue to push for a commutation. That same day, the military commission reconvened in New York City to review the specification in one of the two main charges against Beall. Not surprisingly, the result of this reopening of the case was conviction on the revised specification — and reaffirmation of the sentence against Beall, who had, by this time, been transferred from Fort Lafayette to Fort Columbus on Governor's Island. The next day, General Dix endorsed the findings and rescheduled Beall's execution for Friday, February 24. Meanwhile, the efforts to save the Confederate prisoner intensified in both Washington and New York.[10]

In the capital, Lincoln was besieged by an impressive and almost improbable parade of prominent Baltimoreans and other dignitaries, all calling for the commutation of Beall's sentence. Among the callers were the Librarian of Congress, Richard S. Spofford; the governor of Massachusetts, John Andrew; and Montgomery Blair, a former member of his own cabinet. Lincoln even met with Confederate Brigadier-General Roger Pryor, who had just been released from Fort Lafayette, where he had been imprisoned with Beall, forming a very high opinion of the young man. Pryor was accompanied by two influential newspaper editors, both of whom joined the Rebel general in urging Lincoln to issue a commutation. In response to their pleadings, Lincoln finally showed them a telegram from General Dix stating that Beall's execution was necessary "for the security of the community," a clear indication that Union authorities suspected that there was a link between Beall and the incendiary attack on New York City.[11]

At the same time that Beall's friends were futilely pressing his case in Washington, Ritchie, in Baltimore, was procuring letters of support to be presented to General Dix. Finally leaving for New York on the night of Wednesday, February 22, he was startled to learn upon his arrival, on Thursday morning that Beall would be executed the next day. Rushing to General Dix's headquarters, Ritchie was able to arrange for an immediate interview with the Union commander. Dix accepted the letters carried by Ritchie, but made it clear that "there was not ... a gleam of hope" that Beall would be spared.[12]

Although Dix was determined to proceed with Beall's execution, he was prepared to indulge Beall's friends in at least one regard, as recounted by Ritchie:

> Gen. Dix tendered me a pass very promptly, adding at the same time, that while he had been strict, in order to prevent intrusion, any one whom Capt. Beall wished to see, would be permitted to go to the Island.
>
> I at once telegraphed to our friends in Washington the information I had received, and to Mr. McClure in Baltimore, telling him to send Mr. Ridgely and Mr. Wheatly to Washington, and himself to come on to New York, that we might both be prepared, when the last hope died, to carry out what had been our purpose from the beginning — which was, should it be impossible to arrest the coming of that hour, to at least share it with him if permitted.[13]

In fact, Dix was positively generous in his distribution of passes, as noted by Isaac Markens, then a young journalist working in New York: "In striking contrast with Dix's firm stand against Beall was his complaisance in the distribution of passes to witness the execution. These were given out without question, promiscuously and for the mere asking, the writer ... being one of the many thus favored."[14]

Even though appeals for clemency for Beall continued even into Friday in both Washington and New York, the fight to save the naval commando was really over. For his friends and family it was now time to provide comfort to the doomed young man. For General Dix, Beall's execution was obviously intended to serve as a message, one particularly addressed to the participants of Jacob Thompson's Northwest Conspiracy. The more people who witnessed Beall's fate, the more effectively Dix's message would be spread, not only in the North and South, but also in the border regions of Canada.

During the days preceding his execution, Beall was able to meet with his mother and several other supporters. He would spend much of the last twenty-four hours of his life with his two close friends, Ritchie and McClure, who were permitted to stay in Fort Columbus, most of the time in Beall's cell, where the three young men reminisced about their university days and where Beall recounted his Confederate service. Interestingly, when Ritchie had first arrived on Thursday, Beall revealed that he had a small saw, ingeniously cut from a steel watch spring, hidden between the double leathers of his shoe. Precluded from making use of it to cut his prison bars, due to the winter conditions in New York Harbor, Beall remarked, with some black humour, "I could have opened a vein at any moment, had I wished to do so — and I would like you to remind me of it in the morning."[15]

Sustained by his strong Christian faith, Beall accepted his fate with great dignity and composure. When marched to the gallows after one o'clock on Friday afternoon, February 24, he remarked to the accompanying Union chaplain, Reverend Dr. Weston, "As some author has said, we may be as near God on the scaffold as elsewhere." Once he reached the platform, Beall was then forced to listen to the full litany of the charges against him, which in the words of his friend Lucas, included "the whole prolix, and unmilitary, and unsoldierly pronunciamento of General Dix." This "hypocritical cant" became too much for Beall, who first shook his head in denial at the charges and then laughed outright at the overblown justification for his execution. This, in turn, prompted the executioner, an imprisoned Union deserter who had agreed to serve as the hangman in exchange for a pardon, to cry out: "Cut it short! Cut it short! The Captain wishes to be swung off quick!"[16]

In the moments before his death, Beall deliberately turned so that he was facing south. His friend Lucas described what then ensued:

> Thus he faces when the last duty save one of the executioner is performed; and while standing thus, the provost-marshal asks him whether he has anything to say. Turning upon the officer of the day, he speaks in a calm, firm voice: "I protest against the execution of this sentence. It is a murder! I die in the service and defence of my country! I have nothing more to say."

Acting Master John Yates Beall, the daring Confederate naval commando who led the second and third Lake Erie expeditions and who was subsequently captured following the ill-fated Buffalo raid. This photograph was taken on the morning of his execution on February 24, 1865. [Isaac Markens, President Lincoln and the Case of John Y. Beall *(Isaac Markens, 1911)]*

A moment afterwards a sword-flash is seen behind him, which is the signal to the executioner, and the soul of the hero springs upward with his body. Thus died in the thirty-first year of his age, on the scaffold, John Yates Beall.

Beall's lawyer, James T. Brady, was particularly impressed by his client's conduct, remarking, "I never before saw a human being whose composure in meeting his doom was equally perfect, while at the same time he displayed nothing of the bravo." It was the perfect death for a Confederate martyr.[17]

In Montreal, a bereaved Daniel B. Lucas began work on a volume commemorating Beall's short life and his sacrifice to the cause of Southern independence. Meanwhile, in New York, the publisher T.R. Dawley, the self-styled "Publisher for the Million," rushed to issue a dime novel about the Confederate commando's exploits and death. Appearing within a month or so of Beall's execution, the book, which was entitled *John Y. Beall, the Pirate Spy*, recognized Beall's courage on the gallows but was contemptuous of his misguided ideals and convictions: "He doubtless thought himself a martyr to the cause of liberty, whereas he was only aiding in the attempt to establish the most abominable despotism the world ever saw."[18]

In the Confederate capital, there was considerable outrage over the execution, once it was reported in the Richmond newspapers on February 27. The Confederate House of Representatives promptly demanded to know what President Davis and his government had done to assist Beall. On March 14, Davis forwarded to the House reports from Secretary of the Navy Mallory and the commissioner of exchange, Robert Ould, who had had some success in the case of Samuel Davis. While Mallory indicated that he had been able to furnish proof of Beall's appointment as acting master, Ould reported that he had been unable to act on Beall's behalf: "The cruelty of the enemy was so swift that no sufficient time intervened between a knowledge of the facts and the execution to enable any proceedings to be taken."[19]

Just as the Confederate leadership was coming to terms with Beall's execution, General Dix endorsed the trial and conviction of Beall's associate in the Buffalo raid, Robert C. Kennedy. Again, the sentence was death by hanging: "The major general commanding considers his duty as clear in this case as in that of Beall.... Crimes which outrage and shock the moral sense by their atrocity must not only be punished and the perpetrators be deprived of the power of repeating them, but the sternest condemnation of the law must be presented to others to deter them from the commission of similar enormities."[20]

Kennedy was hung at Fort Lafayette on March 25. Unlike Beall, he did not meet his death like a true Christian gentleman. A non-believer, Kennedy was more agitated than Beall — and more given to bravado, alternating between displays of humour, anger, and contempt. According to the *New York Times*, he departed life with a flourish as he interacted in his final moments with a marshal named Isaacs:

> Isaacs stepped forward, but Kennedy, placing his back against the upright plank, said: "Colonel, I wish to make a statement. Gentlemen, this is a judicial murder. Colonel, I am ready. This is a judicial, cowardly murder. There's no occasion for the United States to treat me in this way. I say, Colonel, can't you give me a drink before I go up?"
>
> At the signal, Isaacs again approached to adjust the knot and pull down the cap, when Kennedy startled every one present by suddenly shouting forth the stanza:
> "Trust to luck, trust to luck,
> Stare your fate in the face,
> Sure your heart will be aisy
> If it's in the right place."
> The final note of which rang in our ears when the whirl of Lieut. Black's blade brought down the fatal blow, and the broken-necked corpse of the incendiary swung before us.[21]

Kennedy, it seems, was too defiant by nature to play the role of a proper martyr. Like Beall, he had been executed by a deserter, in this instance a soldier from Maine.

John W. Headley, who had served with Kennedy in operations that formed part of Thompson's Northwest Conspiracy, later offered a brief eulogy for the young commando: "He possessed all the attributes of a gentleman, and was sincere, true, intelligent, and absolutely fearless."[22] In the North, Kennedy would soon be immortalized by a wax-figure likeness that was placed on display at the Barnum Museum in New York City, one of the targets of the Confederate terrorist attack.[23]

Although there was anger in the South over the executions of Beall and Kennedy, their deaths did not become Confederate *causes célèbres*, as the two hangings would very soon be obscured by events of far greater import. These events would not only have a huge impact on Confederate operations launched from Canada, but on the Confederacy as a whole. On April 2, Richmond fell and the Confederate government, in disarray, fled southward. On April 9, Robert E. Lee surrendered the Army of North Virginia at Appomattox. Other surrenders by key Confederate military commanders still in the field soon followed. On April 14, President Lincoln was assassinated in Washington by the renowned actor and rabid secessionist John Wilkes Booth. (Among the physicians who attended the dying president was Anderson Ruffin Abbott, the first Canadian-born black doctor, then serving as a surgeon in the Union Army.) Within weeks, the Confederacy collapsed and the war was over.[24]

As many senior Confederates escaped to Canada to avoid what they assumed would be certain prosecution for their role in the rebellion, Jacob Thompson resolved to flee from British North America to the even greater safety of Europe. Accordingly, on April 14, he left Montreal, making his way to Halifax, where he took passage for England. Uncertain of his possible legal jeopardy, he would live in exile for several years. Before leaving Canada, he had paid several visits to the Montreal branch of the Ontario Bank, the Confederacy's main bank in British North America, arranging for several hundred thousand dollars to be transferred to the Confederate government's bank in England — Fraser, Trenholm and Company of Liverpool. He had also withdrawn tens of thousands of dollars to finance his own escape. The disbursement of the Confederate funds had prompted a bitter dispute with his fellow commissioner, Brigadier-General Edwin Gray Lee (the cousin of Beall's good friend Daniel B. Lucas), who had arrived in Canada in February. Writing to Lee on April 9, Thompson had been emphatic in his determination to retain control of the funds and withdraw the amount necessary to secure his future: "In other words, when I leave here, I intend to be a free man."[25]

Confederate operations in British North America had come to an end. Although, it should be noted that George T. Denison, probably the most fanatical British North American supporter of the Confederate cause, would mount an unsuccessful legal fight for several months after the war to regain possession of the steamer *Georgian*, which had been seized by Canadian authorities on April 7 in preparation for her transfer to the American government.[26] Interestingly, one of Thompson's last acts as commissioner would be to accompany Denison on the evening of April 10 from Montreal to Quebec City, where the well-connected young Canadian would spend several days lobbying government officials about "the boat business." Thompson's involvement, at a time when he was very much preoccupied with winding up his financial affairs, tends to support the contention that the Confederates continued to have a stake in the vessel's disposition.[27]

In the wake of the fleeing Thompson, rumours and accusations would quickly emerge, tying him — and other participants in the Northwest Conspiracy — to the assassination of President Lincoln. It was even suggested that Booth had served with Beall on the Great Lakes and that the actor had killed Lincoln to avenge the death of his dear friend the naval commando leader.[28] Most of these stories proved to be apocryphal; however, there were very definite connections between Booth and at least one of the key participants in the Lake Erie expeditions.

16

John Wilkes Booth's Connection

Possibly inspired, in part, by an audacious but failed Union cavalry raid of March 2, 1864 (known as the Dahlgren Affair or the Kilpatrick-Dahlgren Raid), apparently aimed at the heart of the Confederate government in Richmond, John Wilkes Booth's original plan had been to kidnap Abraham Lincoln. He would then transport him to the Confederate capital, where, as a hostage, the U.S. president would serve as a crucial pawn in negotiations with the North for the release of Confederate prisoners and perhaps even a peace settlement and recognition of the Confederacy.[1]

However, with the fall of Richmond and the surrender of Robert E. Lee, Booth became intent on revenge, resolving to kill not only the Union president, but also the vice-president and the secretary of state. Booth later noted in his "diary" that "for six months we had worked to capture. But our cause being almost lost, something decisive and great must be done."[2]

After shooting Lincoln at Ford's Theatre in Washington on the night of April 14, Booth, together with fellow conspirator David Herold, fled the city and disappeared into the Confederate underground, through which they hoped to make their way southward across the Potomac and Rappahannock Rivers — and then beyond to the safety of the Confederacy. Their flight was complicated by the fact that Booth had broken a leg as he had leapt to the theatre's stage from the president's box, where he had fired point blank at the back of Lincoln's head.

As the Union authorities hunted the assassin and his accomplice, detectives were dispatched to Canada to ensure that Booth did not make his way north.[3] However, the main thrust of the Union pursuit logically focused on Maryland (Booth's home state) and Northern Virginia, where a well-established network of Confederate sympathizers and agents had been operating since the war began.

Chief among those chasing Booth at the end of the manhunt was a detachment of cavalry under the command of Lieutenant Edward Doherty, a Canadian from Ste-Hyacinthe, Quebec.[4] Doherty had been sent in pursuit of the assassin by the U.S. Secret Service chief, Lafayette C. Baker. In the early hours of April 26, Doherty and his men finally tracked the fugitives to a barn located on the farm of Richard Garrett, near Port Royal in Caroline County, Virginia. Booth had managed to cross the Potomac, but had received a cool reception on the Virginia side of the river. After failing to convince Booth to surrender, Doherty considered burning the barn, but decided to wait until daylight and then rush the fugitives; however, as he later recounted, events took an unexpected turn just as Booth's accomplice gave himself up:

> At this moment Herold reached the door. I asked him to hand out his arms; he replied that he had none. I told him I knew exactly what weapons he had. Booth replied, "I own all the arms, and may have to use them on you, gentlemen." I then said to Herold, "Let me see your hands." He put them through the partly opened door and I seized him by the wrists. I handed him over to a non-commissioned officer. Just at this moment I heard a shot, and thought Booth had shot himself. Throwing open the

door, I saw that the straw and hay behind Booth were on fire. He was half-turning toward it.

He had a crutch, and he held a carbine in his hand. I rushed into the burning barn, followed by my men, and as he was falling caught him under the arms and pulled him out of the barn. The burning building becoming too hot, I had him carried to the veranda of Garrett's house.

Booth received his death-shot in this manner. While I was taking Herold out of the barn one of the detectives went to the rear, and pulling out some protruding straw set fire to it. I had placed Sergeant Boston Corbett at a large crack in the side of the barn, and he, seeing by the igniting hay that Booth was leveling his carbine at either Herold or myself, fired, to disable him in the arm; but Booth making a sudden move, the aim erred, and the bullet struck Booth in the back of the head, about an inch below the spot where his shot had entered the head of Mr. Lincoln. Booth asked me by signs to raise his hands. I lifted them up and he gasped, "Useless, useless!" We gave him brandy and water, but he could not swallow it. I sent to Port Royal for a physician, who could do nothing when he came, and at seven o'clock Booth breathed his last. He had on his person a diary, a large bowie knife, two pistols, a compass and a draft on Canada for 60 pounds.[5]

The bank draft found among Booth's personal effects was actually for sixty-one pounds, twelve shillings, and ten pence. Dated October 27, 1864, it was signed by Henry Starnes, the manager of the Montreal branch of the Ontario Bank. Starnes, who lived in an apartment above the bank at Place d'Armes, was, of course, very well acquainted with Jacob Thompson and other leading Confederate operatives, as much of the funding for the Northwest Conspiracy had passed through his bank, including, eventually, the money stolen in Vermont by the St. Albans raiders. As Union authorities investigated the conspiracy to kill the president, a key question quickly arose: what was Booth doing in Montreal in October 1864?[6]

St. Lawrence Hall on St. James Street in Montreal, 1865–70. During the American Civil War, the fashionable hotel served as the headquarters of the Confederacy in Canada East. [Photo by James George Parks, McCord Museum MP-1975.36.5.1]

The complete answer will never be known; however, some intriguing details would emerge as Union authorities investigated the connection between the assassin and the Confederate community in Canada.

Booth was known to have been in Newburgh, New York, on October 16, until about noon. His whereabouts after that are unknown until 9:30 p.m. on October 18 (the evening before the St. Albans Raid), when he checked into St. Lawrence Hall in Montreal, one of the hubs of Confederate activity in British North America.[7] In fact, according to a Shakespeare-quoting *New York Times* correspondent writing about blockade-running from Montreal in 1863, the hotel was "as full of secesh as an egg is full of meat."[8]

Booth would remain in Montreal for the next ten days. Unfortunately, not all his contacts and encounters during his sojourn in the city have been documented and much of the information that subsequently did become public about his activities in Montreal came from sources that were tainted by perjury. However, there is reliable evidence of significant meetings with three people: the theatre impresario John Wellington Buckland and two prominent Confederate agents, George N. Sanders and Patrick C. Martin.

Booth's encounter with Buckland, the manager of the Theatre Royal and the husband of the well-known American actress Kate Horn, would be a perfectly natural contact for a noted stage actor to make. Their meeting, which apparently centred on a possible theatrical engagement, was probably beyond reproach.[9] However, the same cannot be said of Booth's connections with the other two men.

George N. Sanders was one of the most ruthless and fanatical supporters of the Confederate cause. A fervent admirer of the 1848 revolutions in Europe, he revelled in revolutionary chaos and nationalist violence. Sanders was also a firm believer in regicide and tyrannicide, and thus was someone who would not have hesitated to support Booth's original plot to kidnap Lincoln — or probably any other threat directed against the Union president. In fact, even his fellow Confederates were sometimes aghast at Sanders's recklessness and extremism. For instance, the Confederate commissioner Clement Clay, writing just a few days before Booth's arrival in Montreal, expressed his dismay at Sanders's constant, unrealistic scheming and his "pretentions of luck, liberty and independence."[10]

Patrick C. Martin, on the other hand, was, in many respects, a far more sophisticated and effective operative — and a shrewd businessman. Since arriving in Montreal in 1862, he had established a wine-and-spirits importing and distilling business with J.T. Carroll.[11] He had also secretly developed strong connections with the Confederate Navy. In 1863, he and his wife had played an important role, together with fellow Baltimorean George P. Kane, in the first Lake Erie expedition (in fact, there is some evidence suggesting that Martin might have been the first person to conceive of such an operation).

A few months later, in the spring of 1864, he served, under an assumed name, as his own supercargo, shipping provisions, clothing, and ordnance stores from Montreal to Bermuda on board the British schooner *Marie Victoria* (90 tons burden), under the command of Captain John B. Carron and manned by a French-Canadian crew. (Martin had also arranged for an escaped Confederate POW, J.W.A Wright, to ship with false papers provided by a British North American sympathizer, John N. Colclough of Le Bic, Quebec.) From St. George's, the cargo was trans-shipped to Wilmington, North Carolina, on board a blockade-runner (probably the *Lilian* or the *Clio*), eventually selling to the Navy Department in Richmond for the rather princely sum of $31,507.97 on August 27.[12] (Interestingly, Martin and Wright had taken passage from St. George's to Wilmington on board the *Lilian*, commanded by the noted Confederate Navy officer John Newland Maffitt. Among their fellow passengers were the famous war correspondent Frank Vizitelly and the young cavalryman Bennett Young, who would lead the St. Albans Raid later that year.)[13]

To understand the import of Booth's meeting with the merchant and blockade-runner Martin, it is necessary to consider the context of the actor's Montreal trip. As Booth later confirmed in his diary, by the time he arrived in the city, he had recently made a crucial decision about his future; namely, that he would spend the next few months organizing the kidnapping of President Lincoln, an action that would forever sever his ties with the North. This meant that he had to quickly wind down his theatrical career and wrap up his financial investments in the North — and also begin preparations for the kidnapping plan. Martin had a role to play in all three areas.

As Booth may have already known when he arrived in Montreal, Martin was then in the process of preparing for his second run of 1864 through the blockade, this time by way of Nassau in the Bahamas.[14] Once again, he had engaged the schooner *Marie Victoria*. On paper, she was British, owned by the Confederacy's main banker in Canada, Henry Starnes; however, this might have been a ruse to disguise her true ownership, as it is known that Starnes frequently allowed Jacob Thompson to transfer money using the names of employees of his branch of the Ontario Bank.[15]

Henry Starnes in 1866, the year he was re-elected as mayor of Montreal. During the Civil War, Starnes was the Confederacy's main banker in British North America and the owner, at least on paper, of the blockade-runner Marie Victoria. *[Photo by William Notman, McCord Museum I-20691.1]*

In any event, the imminent departure of the *Marie Victoria* provided Booth with an opportunity to ship his extensive theatrical wardrobe, in several trunks labelled "J.W.B., New Providence," to the Confederacy, where, presumably, he could later resume his illustrious career in the independent Southern States.[16] However, this might not have been the only portion of the schooner's cargo that was of interest to him, as the vessel's main cargo consisted of 540 barrels of coal oil (kerosene), worth nearly $10,000 in British North America — and certainly far more in the Confederacy.[17]

It is sometimes forgotten that Booth was not only an actor, but also one of America's early oilmen, having invested thousands of dollars in the Pennsylvania oil fields, where an oil boom was then underway. In fact, in September, before making his trip to Montreal, Booth had travelled to Venango County, Pennsylvania, to close out his petroleum holdings.[18] According to official records, the coal oil on the *Marie Victoria* belonged to Alexander Saunders, a Montreal jeweller; however, since Martin was once again serving as a supercargo on the impending voyage and because it was common for him to utilize Canadian associates and sympathizers to provide cover for his operations, it is very probable that the cargo was connected, in some way, with Martin, and possibly other Confederate investors — maybe even Booth (there were strong ties, after all, between many early petroleum producers and the then more-established coal-oil industry).[19]

In any event, on October 24, the *Marie Victoria* cleared port under the command of Captain Thomas Ellis, with a crew of six men that included Patrick C. Martin.[20] Before her departure, Martin had provided Booth with a letter of introduction to Dr. William Queen, a Confederate sympathizer in southern Maryland. As it turned out, this letter would contribute significantly to the conspiracy to kill the president.[21]

The day after the departure of the *Marie Victoria*, George N. Sanders checked into Booth's hotel, presumably to facilitate further contact with the actor.[22] However, at this juncture Booth was mostly concerned with last-minute financial matters. Sometime during his Montreal trip he had visited the exchange brokers Davis & Co., a small firm that reputedly had strong Southern connections and which had set up business on St. James Street, across from St. Lawrence Hall. Here Booth had obtained a cheque for $255 drawn on the Merchant's Bank. On October 27, Booth, accompanied by Davis, opened an account at Henry Starnes's Ontario Bank, depositing the cheque from Davis and $200 in cash (Montreal bills). He also used $300 in American gold to purchase the bill of exchange that was found in his pocket at the time of his death. According to Robert Anson Campbell, the teller who served Booth that day, the actor had been looking for a flexible and secure form of currency:

> When Booth came into the bank for this exchange, he bought a bill of exchange for £61 and some odd shillings; and at the time he bought the exchange, he said, "I am going to run the blockade; and, in case I should be captured, can my capturers make use of the exchange?" I told him no, not unless he indorsed the bill: the bill was made payable to his order.[23]

Booth apparently left Montreal the next day and made his way back to New York, where, on October 29, he signed off on the final disposition of his oil properties. (The fact that he had left behind a substantial amount of money in a Montreal bank suggests that he might have had a contingency escape plan, in case things went awry and he later found himself unable to flee southward from the United States.)

A few days later, Booth would travel to Charles County, Maryland, introducing himself, by way of Martin's letter, to Dr. William Queen. This initial contact would, in turn, quickly lead Booth to a network of Confederate agents and sympathizers in Maryland, people who would be able to identify potential escape routes from Washington and perhaps even join in his kidnapping plot. Among these new Maryland associates were Queen's neighbour, Dr. Samuel Mudd; the innkeeper Mary Surratt; and Surratt's son, John, all three of whom would play pivotal roles in Booth's assassination plot.[24] Meanwhile, unbeknownst to Booth, the blockade-runner Patrick Martin was meeting with disaster in the St. Lawrence River.

Very early on the morning of November 7, the veteran pilot Louis M. Lavoie, then at the lookout station at Pointe-au-Pére, Quebec, where he was scanning the river with a glass as he awaited the arrival of the mail steamer, spied a schooner in obvious distress and adrift in the river about fifteen miles away. The weather at the time was exceedingly rough, with heavy seas and strong gales from the south, which were driving the hapless vessel down the river toward the rocky north shore, where she was certain to be wrecked. Lavoie could not abandon his station; however, he quickly contacted other mariners from his village and alerted them to the disaster. Four men — Napoléon Lavoie, Captain Pierre Lavoie, James Banville, and Daniel Banville — agreed to try and reach the schooner in a large, open boat; a very dangerous undertaking over such a distance in the prevailing conditions. Only the most experienced seamen could have survived their ordeal as they rowed and sailed for more than six hours through rain, hail, sleet, and snow in violent and heavy seas, arriving at the stricken schooner at about one o'clock in the afternoon.[25]

As they reached the vessel, which was plunging violently in the heavy seas and full of water up to her deck, they rowed around her and hailed her, but received no response. As they inspected the seventy-three-foot schooner from a safe distance, the men realized that her bow was smashed, probably stove in when she had hit rocks farther up the river. They then resolved to board her, an extremely risky undertaking which they nonetheless managed to accomplish without incident. Once on the vessel, they confirmed that there was no one else on board. Presumably, Captain Ellis, Patrick Martin, and the crew had abandoned the drifting schooner soon after she had first hit the rocks, trying to make for safety in a small boat. Given the terrible conditions and the extreme difficulties encountered by the would-be rescuers from Pointe-au-Pére in what was probably a much larger and more seaworthy boat, it is unlikely that the captain and crew of the *Marie Victoria* ever reached shore. Whatever the case, they were never seen or heard from again.[26]

What had begun as a rescue operation now became a potential salvage operation, as the men from Pointe-au-Pére endeavoured to inspect the cargo and determine the damage to the vessel. They soon discovered that the hundreds of barrels of coal oil had dramatically shifted in the violent seas, making the vessel too deep forward, which might have contributed to her nearly fatal accident. In any event, through great effort they were able to shift the cargo enough to make the vessel sufficiently navigable that they could make sail on her and safely secure her to their boat. Then the wet, cold, hungry, and exhausted men rowed back through the rough seas, towing the lumbering *Marie Victoria* southwest toward Pointe-au-Pére, finally reaching a safe anchorage at Saint-Barnabé Island, about three miles west of the village, at about two o'clock on the morning of November 8, having accomplished something of a miracle.[27]

Under the direction of Louis Lavoie, who had initiated the rescue and salvage operation and who was then in Quebec City, the men arranged for the schooner to be pumped day and night to ensure she did not sink. Lavoie's intention was to have the derelict vessel brought to Quebec City before the close of the navigation season, which was fast approaching. Accordingly, on November 10, the *Marie Victoria* left Saint-Barnabé Island under sail for Quebec. It was a slow, laborious, and dangerous journey, as her pumps had to be manned constantly. In fact, after a week of such difficult progress, it became apparent that the schooner would not make it, as she was taking on too much water and her pumps were wearing out. Faced with the threat of the loss of the vessel and her valuable cargo — if not their own lives — the crew deliberately ran her ashore on November 17, near the mouth of the Rivière Oty, on the south shore of the St. Lawrence, near the village of Le Bic.[28]

Over the course of the next three weeks, Louis M. Lavoie oversaw the unloading and removal of the cargo (including Booth's wardrobe trunks), which was then transported to Quebec City for disposal and adjudication by the Vice Admiralty Court. Once the cargo was discharged, the vessel was hauled up to avoid ice damage. This complicated salvage operation would cost Lavoie and his partners nearly $500, then a considerable amount of money.[29] However, they hoped that the court would ultimately compensate them for their many risks and hard work. Little did they know, at this point early in December, that the abandoned schooner which they had just rescued in the St. Lawrence would soon be connected to one of the most infamous acts in American history.

Following Lincoln's assassination, as Union authorities investigated Booth's activities in Montreal, information — and misinformation — about the connections between the actor and Confederate operatives in Canada began to emerge. By this point, Jacob Thompson, had, of course, fled Montreal, leaving on the very day of Booth's attack on the president. His departure was so precipitous that R.A. Campbell of the Ontario Bank later noted, "I know, at the time, I thought it strange that he was going overland, when if he had waited two weeks longer, or about that time, he could have taken the steamer. That was the talk in the bank, at the time, among the clerks."[30] In Thompson's absence, it was left to other Confederates to disassociate their government from Booth's actions, something that soon became imperative.

On April 24, Edwin M. Stanton, the U.S. secretary of war, wrote to Major-General John A. Dix, informing him that "this Department has information that the President's murder was organized in Canada, and approved at Richmond." Stanton's provocative dispatch was released to the press, causing great consternation among the Confederates in Canada and prompting an indignant response from Edwin G. Lee. Writing from St. Lawrence Hall on April 25, Lee denied any involvement in the assassination plot on the part of the Confederate government; however, he was much less vehement with regard to Booth's Canadian connections: "Whether President Lincoln's murder were 'organized' in Canada, or not, is a matter of which I am equally ignorant and careless. I believe this statement to be false: I know it to be so, so far as it involves any imputation of instigation, complicity or remotest connection on the part of myself or any other Confederate, so far as my knowledge extends."[31]

Lee's rather equivocal denial did nothing to allay Union suspicions about the activities of his predecessor Thompson and others involved in the Northwest Conspiracy. In fact, the Confederate operatives in Canada were very soon confronted by far more serious accusations. On May 2, the new president, Andrew Johnson, issued what was for them a very alarming proclamation:

BY THE PRESIDENT OF THE UNITED STATES OF AMERICA
A PROCLAMATION

Whereas it appears from evidence in the Bureau of Military Justice that the atrocious murder of the late President, Abraham Lincoln, and the attempted assassination of the Hon. William H. Seward, Secretary of State, were incited, concerted, and procured by and between Jefferson Davis, late of Richmond, Va., and Jacob Thompson, Clement C. Clay, Beverley Tucker, George N. Sanders, William C. Cleary, and other rebels and traitors against the Government of the United States harbored in Canada:

Now, therefore, to the end that justice may be done, I, Andrew Johnson, President of the United States, do offer and promise for the arrest of said persons, or either of them, within the limits of the United States, so that they can be brought to trial, the following rewards:

One hundred thousand dollars for the arrest of Jefferson Davis.

Twenty-five thousand dollars for the arrest of Clement C. Clay.

Twenty-five thousand dollars for the arrest of Jacob Thompson, late of Mississippi.

Twenty-five thousand dollars for the arrest of George N. Sanders.

Twenty-five thousand dollars for the arrest of Beverley Tucker.

Ten thousand dollars for the arrest of William C. Cleary, late clerk of Clement C. Clay.

The Provost-Marshal-General of the United States is directed to cause a description of said persons, with notice of the above rewards, to be published.

In testimony whereof I have hereunto set my hand and caused the seal of the United States to be affixed.

Done at the city of Washington, this 2d day of May, A.D. 1865, and of the Independence of the United States of America the eighty-ninth.

ANDREW JOHNSON.
By the President:
W. HUNTER,
Acting Secretary of State[32]

Although Johnson's hasty accusations were later dropped by Union authorities, their initial appearance prompted a round of forceful denials from those identified as conspirators. In fact, several, presumably recognizing that a good offence was the best defence, even accused Johnson himself of complicity in the assassination. As Beverly Tucker asserted in a letter to the Montreal *Gazette*, the former vice-president was "the only solitary individual of the thirty-five millions of souls comprised in that land who could possibly realize any interest or benefit from the perpetration of this deed."[33]

Even though Edwin Lee and Beverly Tucker were quick to loudly profess their innocence, they did not hesitate to surreptitiously assist in the escape of John Surratt, one of Booth's associates in the original kidnapping plot. Surratt, who had also served as a courier for Lee, managed to evade Union detectives, arriving in Montreal three days after the assassination. With assistance from fellow Confederates and the Catholic Church, he was able to hide at St. Liboire, Quebec, until September, when Lee and Tucker helped him take passage on the steamer *Peruvian* from Quebec to Liverpool. He would remain as a fugitive in Europe for more than a year. (As Surratt hid in Canada, his mother, Mary; Dr. Samuel Mudd; David Herold, who had been captured with Booth; and five other defendants were tried before a military commission and convicted of conspiracy to kill President Lincoln. Mary Surratt, who was hung on July 7 with three other conspirators, became the first woman to be executed in the U.S. by the federal government.)[34]

As the controversy over the possible involvement of Canadian-based Confederates in the assassination simmered, Union authorities learned of Booth's connection with the *Marie Victoria* and of the vying claims then before the Vice-Admiralty Court of Lower Canada at Quebec, on the part of Louis M. Lavoie and his associates on the one hand, and Henry Starnes and Alexander Saunders on the other. Secretary Seward thus instructed the newly appointed consul in Quebec City, William H.F. Gurley, to inspect the trunks belonging to Booth that had been salvaged from the schooner. Gurley examined Booth's belongings but was unable to find anything of an incriminating nature or of apparent relevance to the assassination investigation.[35] This meant that arrangements could finally be made to dispose of the trunks at a public auction.

Accordingly, on July 10, the Quebec City auctioneer Thomas Casey, acting on behalf of the Vice-Admiralty Court, announced a forthcoming auction slated for July 18, at Champlain Auction Hall in Quebec, of the "effects saved from the schooner *Marie Victoria*, consisting of a small quantity of Dry Goods, Theatrical Costumes, Swords, and various other articles; half-barrel Salmon, half do Mackerel, 1 case Smoked Salmon, Tea, 2 cases Wine, &c."[36]

As a result of the Booth connection, there was, according to the Quebec *Morning Chronicle*, considerable interest in the salvaged items:

> Amongst the wardrobe, which unfortunately had been injured by salt water, there was a splendid collection of theatrical clothes, in fine silk velvets, silks, satin, ermine, crimson clothing, hats, caps, plumes, boots and buskins, shoes, &c. In swords and pistols, there was a case or trunk packed with a large variety of some very beautifully mounted ones among them. The competition on the whole was very spirited, and several articles were sold at exceedingly high prices.[37]

In total, Booth's theatrical wardrobe sold for about $500. Among the main bidders were the New York antiquarian and collector W.W. Snaith, who happened to be in Quebec City, and George Rankin, who was representing his brother, McKee Rankin, the famous Canadian actor.[38] (The auctioneer Casey later noted that he personally retained some of the more severely damaged items from among Booth's possessions.)[39]

On September 5, 1865, the Vice-Admiralty Court finally rendered its verdict in the salvage suit involving the *Marie Victoria*. The court had appraised the schooner at $2,280 and her cargo of coal oil at $9,656. When combined with the $560 realized at the Casey & Co. auction of July 19, this made for a total salvage value of $12,496. The judge, the Honourable Henry Black, acknowledged the salvagers' "great gallantry and humanity" and further recognized that "actions of this kind should be properly appreciated and liberally compensated." He thus expressed his inclination to provide Louis M. Lavoie and his associates with the lion's share of the value of the schooner and her cargo; however, Black finally concluded, with some obvious regret, that he was bound by precedent, ruling that the salvagers would receive one half the total value plus their legal costs — still a very handsome sum in 1865.[40]

President Lincoln's assassin, the strikingly handsome actor John Wilkes Booth. Following the assassination, cartes-de-visite *depicting the killer were in high demand, prompting many enterprising local photographers to print images from copy negatives. This particular example was issued by the Halifax photographer Isaac Parish, who was active in the city during the Civil War period and was closely associated with Halifax's military community. Today, Parish's most sought-after photograph is an 1864 view of* CSS Tallahassee *in Halifax Harbour, the only known photograph of the Confederate warship.* [Author's collection]

With the deaths of Patrick Martin and John Wilkes Booth and the disposition of the *Marie Victoria* and her cargo, the tangled story of the American actor's involvement with the Montreal-based Confederate operative and blockade-runner who had helped plan the first Lake Erie expedition receded into history, becoming not much more than a footnote in the larger story of the assassination. The evidence that has survived regarding the relationship between the two Marylanders ultimately invites far more questions than it answers. As Martin's associate, the Confederate agent Beverley Tucker, remarked, perhaps with an implicit sense of relief, Booth's death "leaves behind his bloody tragedy a fearful mystery."[41]

It also left behind a wound in the American psyche and body politic that took a very long time to heal, as McKee Rankin discovered, years after he acquired Booth's wardrobe. In the fall of 1891, the Canadian actor mounted an ambitious play based on the life and death of Lincoln. The production, which was noted for its realism, focused very much on Booth's assassination plot, and ended, in fact, not with Lincoln's death, but rather that of Booth. Although the initial response to the play was largely positive, it was eventually shut down, partly as a result of the intervention of Lincoln's son, Robert Todd Lincoln, who felt that the tragedy of his father's death was still too sensitive for portrayal on the stage.[42] (Interestingly, after the First World War, one of Rankin's daughters, Doris, would appear, together with her husband, Lionel Barrymore, in *The Copperhead*, a popular play, and then movie, about the subversive activities of pro-Confederate conspirators during the Civil War.)[43]

Coincidentally, several months before Lincoln's assassination, John Wilkes Booth's brother, the actor Edwin Booth, had saved Robert Todd Lincoln's life after the young man had fallen off a crowded railway platform in Jersey City.[44] In 1890, in Detroit, as the twenty-fifth anniversary of Lincoln's death was being observed, the Quebec auctioneer Thomas Casey endeavoured to contact Edwin Booth to talk about the salvaging of John Wilkes Booth's wardrobe from the *Marie Victoria*. Booth ignored Casey's overtures, instructing his manager, Arthur Chase, to inform the auctioneer, in no uncertain terms, that "the great tragedian would tolerate no allusions or conversations about his brother from any source whatsoever."[45]

Clearly, for his family — and for those who had been involved with him in the shadowy world of the Confederate secret service — the less attention devoted to John Wilkes Booth and the details of the planning, financing, and execution of his act of retribution against the president, the better. As a result, the "fearful mystery" of his actions has persisted.

17

Aftermath

Once the Civil War ended, most of the combatants and other participants in the three Lake Erie expeditions and the related Buffalo raid adjusted to the Confederate defeat and the new post-war realities and drifted, like the majority of combatants in all wars, back into relative anonymity and obscurity. A few, however, went on to make their marks in history in other fields.

Lieutenant John Wilkinson, who had led the first Lake Erie expedition, ended his Confederate war service in Liverpool, where, as the commander of the CSS *Chameleon*, he arrived on April 9, 1865, the day of Lee's surrender to Grant. After turning over his ship, and the government funds then in his possession, to the CSN officer James Bulloch, the senior Confederate agent in Europe, Wilkinson made his way to Halifax, Nova Scotia, where a small colony of former Confederate naval officers and their families was being established. Here, in the seaport that had warmly welcomed so many Confederates during the war, Wilkinson joined the noted Confederate naval commando leader John Taylor Wood and a fellow participant in the first Lake Erie expedition, the CSN engineer Charles Schroeder, in the founding of a merchant house — Wilkinson, Wood and Company. Specializing in Southern produce, the company also eventually represented several American and British firms, including the Liverpool-based merchant house co-owned by James Bulloch.[1]

In March 1866, when the Maritime provinces were threatened by a possible invasion by the Fenian Brotherhood, which had acquired a former Confederate schooner and was assembling a hostile force (composed mostly of Union veterans) in various Maine communities, Wilkinson, Wood, Schroeder, and other Confederate exiles in Halifax sent a petition to the lieutenant-governor of Nova Scotia, Sir Fenwick Williams, in which they offered to assist "in the defense of the province; in the present emergency." As it turned out, the Fenian scare soon abated and Nova Scotia did not find it necessary to call upon the services of the Southern naval volunteers, some of whom would have likely relished a final clash with their detested Yankee enemies.[2]

In the early 1870s, Wilkinson returned home to Virginia. Later, he relocated to Annapolis, Maryland, where he established a preparatory school for candidates for the U.S. Naval Academy. He died in Maryland in 1891. His book *The Narrative of a Blockade-Runner*, which includes an account of the first Lake Erie expedition, was published in 1877 and is regarded as one of the classic naval memoirs of the Civil War. It was reissued in Time-Life's Collector's Library of the Civil War in 1984.[3]

John Banister Tabb, who had served as his cousin John Wilkinson's clerk during the first Lake Erie expedition, spent most of the last year of the war as a prisoner at Point Lookout in Maryland, where he became close friends with a fellow prisoner, the poet and musician Sidney Lanier. After the war, Tabb became a teacher. In 1872, he converted from Episcopalianism to Catholicism. Later, he entered St. Mary's Seminary, Baltimore, graduating

Opposite Page: The Halifax-based merchant house Wilkinson, Wood and Company was operated after the war by three former Confederate naval officers: John Wilkinson, John Taylor Wood, and Charles Schroeder. [McAlpine's Halifax City Directory for 1869–70 *(David McAlpine, 1869)*]

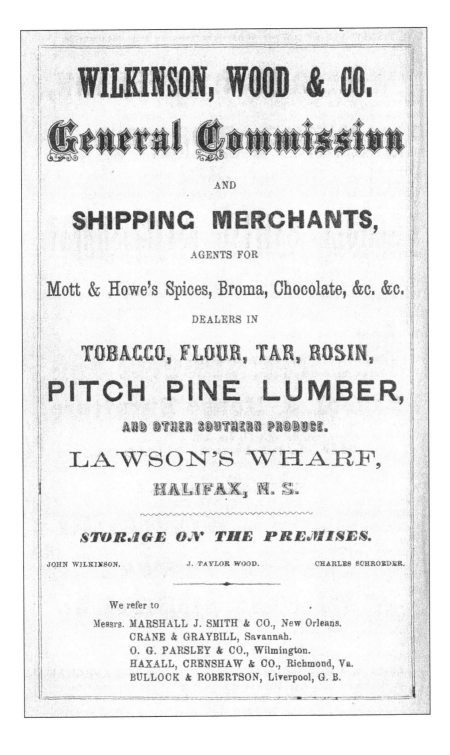

WILKINSON, WOOD & CO.

General Commission

AND

SHIPPING MERCHANTS,

AGENTS FOR

Mott & Howe's Spices, Broma, Chocolate, &c. &c.

DEALERS IN

TOBACCO, FLOUR, TAR, ROSIN,

PITCH PINE LUMBER,

AND OTHER SOUTHERN PRODUCE.

LAWSON'S WHARF,

HALIFAX, N. S.

STORAGE ON THE PREMISES.

JOHN WILKINSON.   J. TAYLOR WOOD.   CHARLES SCHROEDER.

We refer to

Messrs. MARSHALL J. SMITH & CO., New Orleans.
CRANE & GRAYBILL, Savannah.
O. G. PARSLEY & CO., Wilmington.
HAXALL, CRENSHAW & CO., Richmond, Va.
BULLOCK & ROBERTSON, Liverpool, G. B.

as a priest near the end of 1884. Long associated with St. Charles College in Maryland, Father Tabb emerged as one of America's most prolific and popular poets of the late-Victorian period. In addition to contributing to *Harper's*, *The Atlantic*, and other major periodicals of the day, he published numerous volumes of verse. He also wrote some prose, including short memoirs touching on his experiences in the Confederate Navy. Interestingly, in a short autobiographical essay, Tabb later recounted that one of his first encounters with Catholicism occurred during the first Lake Erie expedition, when, in his words, "in Montreal I had spent a little time with a Catholic family — the Martins, from Baltimore."[4]

Father Tabb died in 1909 and was buried in Richmond's Hollywood Cemetery, the resting place of many Confederate luminaries.[5] A few years before his death, in a short poem entitled "The United States to the Filipinos," the former Confederate commando offered a sharp rebuke to America's brutal suppression of another rebellion, the Philippine struggle for independence:

> We come to give you liberty
> To do whate'er *we* choose,
> Or clean extermination
> If you venture to refuse.[6]

George Proctor Kane, the Montreal-based Confederate exile and operative who had provided important logistical support to the first Lake Erie expedition in 1863 and who was alleged to have earlier been involved in the so-called Baltimore Plot (a conspiracy to kill Abraham Lincoln as the then president-elect made his way, in April 1861, to the inauguration), spent the last year or so of the war in Virginia, where he endeavoured to rally and organize Marylanders for the Confederate cause and also became active in the tobacco industry at Danville. In 1868, he returned to Baltimore, where he entered the fire-insurance business. A former marshal of police in the city, he was elected in 1871 as sheriff for a two-year term, after which he resumed his business career. In 1877, he won election as Baltimore's mayor, but died in office not long after, in June 1878.[7]

John Banister Tabb, also known as Father Tabb, became one of the most popular American poets of the late Victorian era. He was a celebrated master of the short lyric poem. [Jennie Masters Tabb, Father Tabb: His Life and Work *(Stratford Co., 1922)*]

Suspicions about Kane's involvement in Lincoln's assassination have persisted to this day, not only because of his prominent role in Baltimore secessionist activity, but also due to his subsequent activities in the Confederate secret service and the fact that he had earlier been involved in Baltimore theatrical circles and likely knew John Wilkes Booth.[8] In 1868, while still residing in Danville, Kane not only vehemently denied any connection to the so-called Baltimore Plot, but he even insisted that

Lincoln himself had come to realize that he was innocent. "I had the very best reason to know," Kane asserted, "that he was very soon undeceived, and that I could have enjoyed the most substantial evidence of his confidence and favor after he became the President, had I felt inclined to embrace it."[9]

Kane's inclinations, of course, had instead led him to secession and rebellion. In fact, for a time, one of his prize possessions, as the police marshal of Baltimore, was a 32-pound Union shell, the first fired at Fort Moultrie during the Battle of Fort Sumter. This souvenir, which had apparently been sent to him following the battle by Confederate general Pierre G.T. Beauregard, marked the beginning of a conflict that Kane eagerly embraced.[10]

Benjamin Wier, the Confederacy's chief agent in Halifax, who had assisted with financial and logistical arrangements for the first Lake Erie expedition, found himself confronting some difficult challenges in the immediate post-war period due to his close connections with the Confederate government. Although he was able to eventually re-establish some business ties with the northern states, he was prohibited from obtaining a visa that would permit him to visit the U.S. Partly as a result of such obstacles, Wier, who had supported the South's secession primarily out of self-interest, became an outspoken advocate of Canadian Confederation and a supporter of a projected railway line between Halifax and Quebec City. In 1867, his pro-Confederation activities were rewarded with an appointment to the new dominion's first senate. However, Wier's career as a senator was short-lived, as he died at Ottawa in April 1868.[11]

Wier's remains were returned to Halifax for burial in a family plot at Camp Hill Cemetery, where, just a few years before, he had arranged for the interment of Confederate Major J. Smith Stansbury, who had been in charge of Confederate ordnance procurement in Bermuda.

Today, Wier's elegant residence on Hollis Street, one of the few Rococo Italianate buildings ever built in Nova Scotia, is viewed as one of the jewels of architectural preservation in Halifax.[12]

Alexander "Sandy" Keith Jr., the nephew of the famous Halifax brewer, who had also provided some assistance to the Confederates during the first Lake

Erie expedition, left Halifax for the United States several months before the war's end. He subsequently moved to Europe, where, on December 16, 1875, he died from self-inflicted gunshot wounds at Bremerhaven, Germany. Five days before, eighty-one people had been killed or fatally injured and more than fifty wounded in a massive explosion that occurred during the loading of cargo owned by Keith (then using the alias William King Thomas) on board the steamship *Mosel*. Keith's shipment, it turned out, contained a powerful time bomb that was designed to explode once the vessel was at sea.[13]

During the Civil War, most Southerners who visited Halifax had come into contact with Keith, but not all were impressed by his overly solicitous manner. In fact, he was referred to facetiously by some Confederate visitors as the "Confederate Consul." John Wilkinson went further, characterizing Keith as "a coarse, ill-bred vulgarian," but not even this blunt, disparaging assessment captured the true nature of the man. As authorities investigated the Bremerhaven explosion, it became evident that Keith (who was also known as Thomassen) was not only an opportunist and swindler who had been eager to exploit the considerable financial opportunities presented by the American Civil War, but also, it turned out, a dangerous sociopath, very much seduced by the mayhem and carnage that had attended the conflict.[14]

In fact, after leaving Halifax, Keith increasingly succumbed to his darkest urges, eventually adopting the technology of war and applying it to insurance fraud by way of the destruction of transatlantic passenger ships, thereby aspiring to become not only a mass-murderer, but perhaps even a serial mass-murderer. Following his death in Bremerhaven, he became known in the European and American press as the Dynamite Fiend.

The full extent of Keith's crimes will probably never be known. John Wilkinson, like many other observers of maritime affairs in the post-war era of transatlantic travel, was convinced that Keith was likely responsible for the loss of the *City of Boston*, an Inman Line steamer that had left Halifax on January 28, 1870, for Liverpool and was never heard from again. More than 175 people died in that tragedy, including many prominent citizens of Halifax. Another Confederate who had probably come into contact with Keith in Halifax, George P. Kane, apparently insisted that the Dynamite Fiend was responsible for the death of Patrick Martin and the loss of the schooner *Marie Victoria* in 1864. Martin's former passenger, J.W.A. Wright, was likewise convinced of Keith's complicity in this disaster. Although it is now obvious that Keith was not involved, the nature of his crimes encouraged such speculation.[15]

The unparalleled depravity of Keith's crimes inspired the American journalist, former war correspondent, and sometime poet William A. Croffut to write a poem comparing the Halifax mass-murderer to two of history's most notorious fiends:

GUY FAWKES, WILKES BOOTH, THOMASSEN

Three miscreants in three distant countries born,
England, Virginia, Prussia, did adorn:
The first in appetite for blood surpassed,
The next in perfidy, in both the last.
To shape the third did Nature's self undo —
She broke the mould that formed the other two.[16]

The Halifax social elite, which had generally shown considerable sympathy for the Confederate cause, was determined to forget about the city's "Confederate Consul," expunging his crimes from the historical record and disassociating him from the highly respected Keith family and its business concerns. Surprisingly, these efforts were largely successful — until the year 2005, when the American academic Ann Larabee published a biography of Sandy Keith, *The Dynamite Fiend: The Chilling Story of Alexander Keith Jr., Nova Scotian Spy, Con-Artist and International Terrorist*. Her scholarly detective work finally reclaimed one of Canada's most vicious criminals from the historical black hole to which he been consigned for more than a century.

Bennett G. Burley, the young naval commando and bibliophile who had served as John Yates Beall's second-in-command during the second and third Lake Erie expeditions, left Canada after the Civil War, changed the spelling of his name to "Bennet Burleigh," and continued on his pursuit of adventure, spending several years travelling the world and campaigning as a soldier of fortune. In the 1870s, he embarked on a career as a journalist, first in Houston, Texas, and then, from about 1878, in England. In 1882, he was recruited as a war correspondent in Egypt by the London *Daily Telegraph*, then the largest-circulation daily newspaper in the United Kingdom, if not the world.

Bennet Burleigh, the renowned Victorian war correspondent, who, during the Civil War, had made his mark as an Acting Master in the Confederate States Navy, under the name Bennett Burley. [Bennet Burleigh, The Natal Campaign *(George Bell, 1900)*]

Over the course of the next thirty years or so, until his retirement in 1913, the year before his death, Burleigh covered more than twenty campaigns throughout the far-flung British Empire and beyond, including the Boer War and the Russo-Japanese War. Emerging as one of the leading war correspondents of the late-Victorian and the Edwardian eras, he was the author of six books incorporating his dispatches from various war fronts: *Desert Warfare: Being the Chronicle of the Eastern Soudan Campaign* (1884), *Two Campaigns: Madagascar and Ashantee* (1896), *Sirdar and Khyalifa, or the Re-Conquest of the Soudan, 1898* (1898), *Khartoum Campaign, 1898; or the Re-Conquest of the Soudan* (1899), *The Natal Campaign* (1900), and *Empire of the East; or Russia and Japan at War, 1904–5* (1905).

During the Boer War, Burleigh had occasion to escort Rudyard Kipling, on March 29, 1900, to the Battle of Karee Siding, where the two British writers were eventually spotted by Boer gunners. "Then they took to shelling us two poor wayfarers," Burleigh reported, "and I altered my tactics by moving zigzag to the east, and, though once or twice they got near, all was well, and by and by, we walked down the slope and so out of sight." According to Burleigh, Kipling appeared to have "enjoyed himself upon the veldt, otherwise he would not have taken to making and humming over new verses, like Robert Burns was wont to do." [17]

Despite his prolific journalistic output, Burleigh apparently never did write about his experiences as a Confederate naval commando. In fact, according to his obituary in *The Times*, he was reticent about this period of his life: "It has never been possible to get a very clear and consistent story of the young fire-eater's adventures during these stirring times." [18]

His grandson, Michael Burleigh, is a distinguished British historian who has written many highly regarded works, including a cultural history of terrorism.

Jacob Thompson, who had orchestrated the Northwest Conspiracy from his headquarters in Toronto, hastily fled from Canada in April 1865 for the safety of exile in Europe. Thompson remained abroad, first in Europe and then Canada, beyond the reach of Union authorities, until the spring of 1869, when he was confident that he could resume his life in the conquered South without fear of reprisal. Returning to his hometown of Oxford, Mississippi, on May 3, he was welcomed by a large crowd headed by Colonel L.Q.C. Lamar, previously one of the Confederacy's representatives in Europe. Here, in the community where Union troops had looted and burned his home just a few years before, Thompson urged his fellow citizens to accept the verdict of history: "In the late war the power of arms decided that we should remain one people, now and forever. The God of battles decided the case in favor of Union."[19]

Thompson, who had also encouraged his fellow Southerners to "build up the waste places and secure prosperity and plenty," certainly heeded his own advice. Moving to Memphis, he shrewdly managed his business affairs, acquiring undervalued plantation property and selling timber. As a result of his wise investments, Thompson amassed a sizable fortune, which permitted him to leave an exceedingly generous gift of $100,000 in Bell Telephone stock to the University of the South in Sewanhee, Tennessee, upon his death in 1885.[20]

Thompson was buried in a family plot in Memphis. Curiously, his death caused a furor in Washington, due to the fact that Thompson's friend L.Q.C. Lamar, who was then serving as secretary of the interior, ordered that the flags of departmental buildings fly at half-mast to mark the death of Thompson, a former secretary of the department. Other buildings in the capital were apparently draped in mourning. The outcry in the North over the honouring of a rebel who had once been suspected of involvement in the Lincoln assassination was such that strict restrictions on public displays of mourning by federal departments were passed by Congress. These restrictions had unintended consequences in 1901, when departments were prohibited from draping their buildings following the assassination of President McKinley.[21]

Although Thompson certainly remains one of the most prominent people associated with Oxford, Mississippi, he is not the town's most famous resident. That distinction falls to the great American writer William Faulkner, who won the Nobel Prize for Literature in 1950. In 1930, as he began to earn money from his writing, Faulkner bought what proved to be a lifelong restoration project, the "old Bailey place," a once-splendid, but then dilapidated house in Oxford that he renamed Rowan Oak. The home was located across the street from where Jacob Thompson's antebellum mansion had once stood. Interestingly, the gardens at Rowan Oak had been designed by Thompson's gardener (and later butler), the Nova Scotian Joseph MacDonald.[22] Faulkner, of course, was familiar with Jacob Thompson's career. In fact, it is probable that the character Jason Compson in his 1929 novel *The Sound and the Fury* is based, at least in part, on the former Confederate commissioner to Canada.[23] (Faulkner, of course, had a wartime Canadian connection, as well, having enlisted in the Royal Canadian Air Force during the First World War.)

John W. Headley, who had participated in both the ill-fated third Lake Erie expedition and the even more disastrous Buffalo raid, briefly joined President Jefferson Davis's entourage as it fled through South Carolina and Georgia at the war's end. Following the complete collapse of the Confederacy, as others endeavoured to escape into exile, Headley resolved to apply for a pardon that would extend to his activities as a raider, and made his way to Tennessee, where he married his sweetheart, Mary Overall, who had also worked in the Confederate underground.[24]

After spending two years in Kentucky, Headley moved to Indiana, where he was engaged for many years in the tobacco business. He eventually returned to Kentucky, co-founding the Louisville-based tobacco firm Givens, Headley & Company. A prominent businessman, he served as Kentucky's secretary of state from 1891 until the January 1, 1896.[25] However, the hot-headed rebel raider still lurked under the politician's smooth exterior; for during his time in office, Headley briefly came to national attention when, during an argument over the state printing contract, he pulled a knife in a judge's chambers in Georgetown, Kentucky, and lunged at an adversary.[26]

In 1906, Headley published an ambitious memoir-cum-history entitled *Confederate Operations in Canada and New York*. Issued by the pro-Confederate, New York–based publisher Walter Neale, the book is rightly regarded as a classic Civil War text, probably the most important single source relating to Jacob Thompson's labyrinthine Northwest Conspiracy. In the book, an unreconstructed Headley makes no apologies for his wartime activities, as evidenced by his rather defiant and unrepentant dedication: "To the memory of the defenseless non-combatant people of the South who suffered the untold horrors of merciless warfare — desolation, destitution, imprisonment or death; of the persecuted people of the North whose sense of justice and humanity revolted at a crusade for the cause of John Brown, and of Horace Greeley, Gerrit Smith and Cornelius Vanderbilt, this volume is reverently dedicated by the author."[27]

Not long after the publication of his memoir, Headley moved to Beverly Hills, California, where he died in 1930.[28] His book, like John Wilkinson's post-war memoir, was reissued in Time-Life's Collector's Library of the Civil War in 1984. The book remains in print today.

Charles C. Hemming, who as a teenager had likewise participated in the third Lake Erie expedition and the subsequent Buffalo raid, was serving in North Carolina at the end of the war. After being mustered out of his regiment, he returned to his home state of Florida. He then settled in Texas, where he worked briefly as a dockworker in Galveston before embarking on an extremely successful banking career, eventually becoming president of the Gainesville National Bank and then president of the State Banker's Association of Texas. He later became president of the El Paso National Bank and moved to Colorado Springs, where he died in 1916.[29]

In 1896, at a meeting of Confederate veterans in Ocala, Florida, Hemming announced his intention to construct an imposing sixty-two-foot monument to commemorate Florida's Confederate soldiers. Committing $20,000 to the project, Hemming insisted that it be constructed of materials that would "last for a million years," namely, Vermont granite and Austrian bronze.[30] Installed in St. James Park in Jacksonville, the city of Hemming's birth, the monument was unveiled on June 16, 1898. According to the *New York Times*, the dedication reflected America's newfound national unity:

> The circumstances of the dedication illustrated in an impressive manner the fact that sectional bitterness that grew out of the war of the rebellion is at an end.
>
> Soldiers from the North and the West marched with their Southern comrades of the Federal Army in the parade preceding the dedication.
>
> A notable figure on the reviewing stand was the grandson of Gen. Grant, wearing the uniform of a United States officer.[31]

The year following the unveiling of the Jacksonville Confederate Monument, St. James Park was renamed Hemming Park (now Hemming

Plaza), in Hemming's honour. On August 27, 1960, the park was the site of a vicious race riot, when a white mob, including several Ku Klux Klan members, attacked a group of black civil-rights protesters. Forty years later, this event, known as Ax Handle Saturday, was commemorated with an official city marker, so now both the Confederate rebellion and the black struggle for freedom are commemorated in the same park.[32]

In 1984, Hemming's granddaughter, Lucy W. Sturgis, arranged for his Civil War memoirs to be published in *American Heritage* magazine. The text, which appeared under the title "A Confederate Odyssey," is certainly an entertaining read; however, Hemming's account of his wartime adventures appears to be liberally embellished in places and must be approached with a degree of skepticism.[33]

George Taylor Denison III, the young lawyer and militia officer who had provided crucial support to the Confederate operatives in Canada during the Civil War, soon discovered that he would pay a price for his wartime activities. Not only was he forced to spend a considerable amount of money in a frustrating and ultimately fruitless pursuit of his claims relating to the steamer *Georgian*, but he was also stymied in his efforts to pursue a regular army career, despite the fact that he commanded a militia regiment, the Governor General's Body Guard, during the Fenian raids of 1866 and published a scholarly military study, *Modern Cavalry: It's Organization, Armament, and Employment in War*, in 1868.[34]

Ever wary of American expansionism and continental hegemony, in 1868 Denison was an enthusiastic co-founder of the patriotic movement Canada First, which sought to encourage the development of a distinct Canadian identity, preferably within the context of an imperial federation with Britain. In 1869, the group urged a decisive military response to the Red River Rebellion, a major regional challenge to federal authority. The following year, the Canada Firsters founded the North-West Emigration Aid Society to encourage British immigration to the Canadian West.

In 1872, Denison ran unsuccessfully in the Ontario provincial election as a Liberal candidate. However, he was rewarded for his efforts with a short-term appointment as Ontario's emigration commissioner in London. Returning to Canada in 1874, he was somewhat at loose ends, until he learned that Grand Duke Nicholas, the inspector-general of Russian cavalry, was sponsoring a competition that offered three substantial cash prizes for the best histories of cavalry submitted by the deadline of January 1, 1877. Denison threw himself into this project with gusto and determination, spending about a year reviewing more than seven hundred military texts before he even began writing. He later recalled his demanding schedule: "I averaged eight hours work a day for over two years, and during two months in St. Petersburg, at the end, it was nearer twelve and fifteen hours."[35]

Throughout the process, Denison was determined to be very discreet about his participation in the competition:

> I was very anxious to keep it private that I was writing at all. I felt that the odds were against me, and I knew that no matter how gallant a struggle I made against what seemed insurmountable difficulties, I would be laughed at and ridiculed if I failed to secure at least one of the prizes, for I knew it looked absurd for a militia officer, a lawyer, one who had never attended a military school of any kind, one removed from the centres of military thought and away from the great military libraries, to attempt to compete in a competition open to all the trained officers of the regular armies of the world.[36]

Denison's apprehensions about his prospects as a military scholar proved to be unfounded. His submission, "A History of Cavalry from the Earliest Times with Lessons for the Future," which includes a chapter on the role of cavalry in the American Civil War, not only won the competition, earning him the first prize of five thousand rubles, but was subsequently published in English, German, and Russian editions, and is today still regarded as one of the definitive treatises on the subject.

Not long after his return to Canada in 1877, Denison had the good fortune to be appointed as the police magistrate for Toronto, a position that he held until 1921 and one that enabled him to have a good part of his day free for other pursuits, due to his remarkable dispatch as a judge. Disposing of more than twenty thousand cases a year, Denison explained that he was running "a court of justice — not a court of law." His decisive performance on the bench in police court even became something of a local attraction.[37]

Active in Loyalist circles, he was also a staunch imperialist, co-founding the Canadian branch of the Imperial Federation League and then the British Empire League. He also served with the Governor General's Body Guard during the Northwest Rebellion and was an avid supporter of Canadian participation in the Boer War. As well, he was extremely active as a writer, publishing numerous articles and several pamphlets and books, including *Soldiering in Canada: Recollections and Experiences* (1900), The *Struggle for Imperial Unity: Recollections and Experiences* (1909), and *Recollections of a Police Magistrate* (1920).

Although Denison is sometimes described as an anti-American, it might be more accurate to refer to him as anti-Yankee, as he remained a steadfast admirer of the "Lost Cause" and corresponded in the post-war period with Jubal Early, Bennett H. Young, John Mosby, and other Confederate notables. In 1916, Denison travelled to Birmingham, Alabama, for the Twenty-Sixth Annual Reunion of the Confederate Veterans' Association. According to Bennett H. Young, the leader of the St. Albans Raid, the assembled Confederates were grateful for the opportunity to acknowledge Denison's support: "The visit of Col. George T. Denison, of Toronto, the friend of Jefferson Davis, Robert E. Lee, and the glad helper of all who found refuge in his country, as he came to look, as he said, upon the survivors of the greatest volunteer army that was ever aligned under any flag, was a delightful occurrence, and those who constituted the Reunion were glad to do him honor and to express their appreciation of his generous kindness to the exiles, who, by the fortunes of war, came his way."[38]

In 1917, Confederate veterans expressed their admiration and gratitude once again when they learned that Denison's son, George T. Denison IV, had been killed in action in France. The United Confederate Veterans Association camp in Savannah, Georgia, wrote to Denison, offering their condolences and the assurance that young Denison had not died in vain: "Had he lived a thousand years there could not have been a nobler end." Bennett H. Young, writing from Louisville, Kentucky, echoed these sentiments and assured Denison: "Your friends in the South mourn with you in this hour of bereavement."[39]

Denison, probably the Confederacy's most devoted supporter in Canada, died at his home, Heydon Villa, in Toronto, in 1925.

William Armstrong, the Irish-born engineer, artist, and pioneer photographer who had helped George T. Denison prepare Jacob Thompson's secret dispatches for delivery to Richmond by courier, worked as a railway engineer and artist after the war, embarking on a tour of the remote Lakehead region at the head of Lake Superior in the late 1860s. In 1870, he continued his western travels, accompanying the military expedition under Colonel Garnet Wolseley to the Canadian West as the new Dominion of Canada responded to the Red River Rebellion. Armstrong not only recorded the expedition in watercolour paintings, but also supplied sketches to the *Canadian Illustrated News.*

In subsequent years, Armstrong emerged as one of Canada's leading artists. He was particularly noted for his watercolour paintings of Great Lakes scenes and vessels. He also became an important art instructor, teaching at the University of Toronto and the Toronto Normal School. Although he retired in 1897, he continued to give private lessons at his home in Toronto until his death in 1914.[40]

Armstrong remains an important figure in the history of art in Victorian Canada; however, he might be best remembered for the splendid photographs that he, his nephew Daniel M. Beere, and their partner H.L. Hime, took in Toronto, circa 1856–57. The earliest known photographic views of the city, they include an extraordinary thirteen-part panorama, which features prominently in the recent novel *Consolation* (2006) by the Baltimore-born Canadian writer Michael Redhill.[41]

Henry Starnes, who had been the Confederacy's main banker in Canada and who had been directly involved in Patrick Martin's blockade-running operations out of Montreal, rose to further prominence in both the political and business fields in the immediate post-war era. From 1866 to 1868 he served (for the second time) as the mayor of Montreal. In 1867, he also became a member of Quebec's legislative council. Moreover, he continued to be a major figure in Canadian banking, assuming the presidency of the Metropolitan Bank in 1871.

Starnes, who had relished working in the shadows during the Civil War with Jacob Thompson, Patrick Martin, and other Confederate agents, also began to play a crucial role in the murky world of federal backroom politics, becoming an important bagman for the Quebec wing of Sir John A. Macdonald's governing Conservative Party. However, Starnes was not able to remain in the background. In 1873, he found himself embroiled in a major patronage scandal involving kickbacks from railway developers that had been funnelled to politicians through his bank. Known as the Pacific Scandal, the affair ultimately resulted in the resignation of the Macdonald government. Not long after, in 1876, Starnes suffered another setback when his Metropolitan Bank collapsed and was forced to close its doors.

Despite these reversals, Starnes remained a prominent member of Quebec society. In 1878, he was appointed Speaker of the province's legislative council. He later served as a railway commissioner and very briefly as a commissioner of agriculture and public works. He also resumed his role as Speaker of the legislative council for a second time, from April 1889 to March 1892. He died at Montreal in 1896.[42]

In 1970, Starnes's grandson, John Starnes, became the first civilian to head the Security Service of the Royal Canadian Mounted Police (RCMP). Among his responsibilities, of course, was to counteract and monitor the activities of foreign agents in Canada.[43] (Curiously, one of the most prominent commissioners of the RCMP, someone who was also very preoccupied with security and the activities of foreign agents, was Stuart Taylor Wood, the grandson of the Confederate naval commando leader John Taylor Wood.)

Afterword

There is a memorable scene set in Sandusky, Ohio, toward the end of Harriet
Beecher Stowe's *Uncle Tom's Cabin* (1852), the abolitionist bestseller that
contributed significantly to the sectional divide that culminated in the
American Civil War.[1] Two of the novel's main protagonists, the escaped slaves
George and Eliza Harris, together with their son Harry, have reached Sandusky,
the last station on their perilous trip north by way of the Underground
Railroad. In disguise, they manage to elude slave hunters and board a steamer
to Amherstburg in Canada West. As they cross Lake Erie, they remain on
deck, eagerly anticipating their approaching freedom, until "at last, clear and
full rose the blessed English shores; shores charmed by a mighty spell — with
one touch to dissolve every incantation of slavery, no matter in what language
pronounced, or by what national power confirmed."[2]

It is one of history's many ironies, perhaps, that a little over a decade
after the appearance of *Uncle Tom's Cabin*, thousands of Southerners

would find themselves imprisoned in a POW camp just offshore from the city of Sandusky, on Johnson's Island, where they would dream of their own "underground railroad" that could take them south through Ohio and Kentucky or north across Lake Erie to the freedom of the Canadian shores. Their strong desire for freedom was communicated to the Confederate authorities by a variety of means and would lead to three concerted attempts by naval commandos to storm the camp and seize the warship stationed there, the USS *Michigan*, with a view to both freeing the camp's prisoners and then conducting punishing raids against the North.

Although the three naval commando operations launched on the Great Lakes by the Confederacy during the 1863–64 period were ultimately unsuccessful, they did not fail for lack of will. Nor were they, as some commentators have implied, *opéras bouffes*. The Confederates committed serious resources to these operations, both in terms of finances and personnel (this is particularly true of the first Lake Erie expedition). Furthermore, all three operations were led by experienced Confederate naval officers who had demonstrated an appetite for fighting. If the *Michigan* had been seized or destroyed by any one of the commando parties that were dispatched against her, the blow against the Union in the Great Lakes region would likely have been considerable, as would the impact on Northern morale and confidence. (It takes very little counterfactual historical speculation to imagine the possibilities.)

The 1863 Lake Erie expedition, involving more than twenty naval officers, was probably the most promising, but even it was compromised virtually from the start by an extremely efficient and pervasive surveillance network maintained by the American and Canadian authorities. It was also undermined by the effective and timely use of disinformation. Clearly, well-placed informers and other agents allowed the Union to constantly remain one step ahead of their Confederate adversaries on the lakes. Both George P. Kane in Montreal and Jacob Thompson in Toronto, who were responsible for logistical support and security for their respective commando operations, seemed incapable of undertaking effective counter-intelligence measures. From a security point of view, their organizations were sieves, which meant that the Confederates were always at a serious disadvantage when it came to the critical war in the shadows.

The Confederate burial ground on Johnson's Island in 1898. Nearly 270 prisoners died during their captivity, two of whom were shot by guards. The United Daughters of the Confederacy purchased the cemetery in 1905, managing the property until 1932, when it was acquired by the American federal government. [Theresa Thorndale, Sketches and Stories of the Lake Erie Islands *(I.F. Mack & Brothers, 1898)]*

Furthermore, as the prospect of a Confederate defeat became more and more probable, British and Canadian authorities were increasingly determined to avoid provoking the North. In fact, from the Confederate perspective, British neutrality slowly evolved into tacit support for the Union.

Nor were American and Canadian surveillance and governmental cooperation the only obstacles to Confederate success. With each successive raid, Union defences and military preparedness on the Great Lakes were bolstered. (In fact, as the war ended, the Union was preparing to increase its naval presence on the lakes.)[3] Nonetheless, the allure of Murdaugh's original plan for a commando raid on the Great Lakes persisted, probably until the end of the Southern rebellion (otherwise, Jacob Thompson would have sold the *Georgian* outright, rather than continue in his efforts to disguise the vessel's Confederate ownership).

Although Confederate naval commandos on the Great Lakes did not win the glory that William Murdaugh and Robert D. Minor had hoped for in 1863, they did conduct themselves with daring against formidable odds. Far from home, in enemy waters, they attempted the impossible. Certainly there was no dishonour for them in their failures — only bitter disappointment (even the *Parsons* "mutineers" acted in an honourable fashion). Contemplating the collapse of the first Lake Erie expedition, a philosophical Minor pointed to the reality that ultimately faced all the Southern commandos on the North's inland seas: "The fortunes of war were against us."[4]

Ultimately, of course, the fortunes of war were against the entire Southern struggle for independence. In April 1865, the dream of a Confederate States of America ended, becoming a lost cause — and then, over time, something larger, the mythic "Lost Cause." (Ulysses S. Grant, who recognized the courage displayed time and time again by the Confederates, bluntly characterized their cause as "one of the worst for which a people ever fought.")[5] The Confederate failure at nationhood would have a profound impact on British North America, contributing enormously to the post-war struggle for a Confederation of the Canadian colonies.

Proponents of Confederation learned two main lessons from the American Civil War. First, they saw United States belligerence and continental aspirations as a very real threat to the continued existence of separate British North American colonies. Second, the ill-fated Southern rebellion illustrated the perils of too much local sovereignty in the form of "states' rights."[6]

The politician and poet Thomas D'Arcy McGee, one of the most passionate supporters of Canadian Confederation — and a man very sympathetic to the South — was horrified by the carnage of the American Civil War. In 1863, as tentative discussions about Confederation began, he urged any British North Americans who were at a loss to identify reasons for the Canadian colonies to join together to "look around to the valley of Virginia, look around to the mountains of Georgia, and you will find reasons as thick as blackberries."[7]

With the failure of the Southern Confederacy, British North American Confederation took on a new urgency. The Union, having amassed the largest army in the world, was not pleased with its northern neighbours. The Lake Erie raids and other provocations during the war had left a sour taste in America. Thus Confederation became, in part, a defensive measure to forestall American expansionism across the border that had been brazenly crisscrossed by the Confederate naval commandos and other Southern raiders. For Alexander Galt, a future Father of Confederation who had met with President Lincoln in Washington during the Trent Affair, a naval action that had nearly precipitated a war between Great Britain and the

United States, the choice following the war was a stark one: "It becomes a question of whether we prefer the good old flag we are under to that of the United States."[8]

In 1867, British North America made its choice. The Union Jack would fly over the new northern dominion. Curiously, as soon as its creation was proclaimed, Canada would confront its own separatist movement; in this case led by the Nova Scotian patriot Joseph Howe (whose son had been severely wounded fighting for the Union in the American Civil War). However, Howe's struggle against Confederation was not another Southern-style rebellion. In Canada, the separatists were known as anti-Confederates and would challenge the central government with ballots, rather than bullets. British North Americans living in the long shadow of America's bloody war and its difficult aftermath were determined to find a different path to nation-building.

Appendix

Rosters of the Confederate Naval Commando Operations on the Great Lakes, 1863–64

It is likely that more than 250 people were involved — in various capacities and to varying degrees — in the three Confederate naval commando operations on the Great Lakes during the 1863–64 period and the related Buffalo raid. The following rosters, which are largely compiled from primary sources, identify as many of these individuals as possible.[1] Because the commando expeditions launched from British North America formed part of the Confederacy's war in the shadows, the identities of many of the participants, including some key players, have been lost to history — probably irretrievably.

The First Lake Erie Expedition (October–November 1863)

Commanding Officer: Lieutenant John Wilkinson

Second-in-Command: Lieutenant Robert D. Minor

Main CSN Commando Force:

Lieutenants — James Otey Bradford, Joseph M. Gardner, George Washington Gift, Matthew Peterson Goodwyn, Albert Gallatin Hudgins, Benjamin Pollard Loyall, Patrick McCarrick, Francis Marion Roby

Acting Masters — William B. Ball (Colonel, 15th Virginia Cavalry), William W. Finney (Paymaster), H.W. Perrin, Henry Wilkinson

Engineers — Chief-Engineer J. Charles Schroeder, First Assistant-Engineer Henry X. Wright, Second-Assistant-Engineer John T. Tucker

Other Officers — Assistant-Paymaster Perry M. DeLeon, Assistant-Surgeon William Shepardson, Gunners Crawford H. Gormley and John Waters, Captain's Clerk John Banister Tabb

Civilian Member of the Main Commando Force: Leggett (released by Wilkinson in Halifax on suspicion of spying)[2]

Advance Party: unidentified "Scotchman" (a trusted operative of the commanding officer)[3]

Logistical Support (Halifax): Alexander "Sandy" Keith, Benjamin Wier

Logistical Support and Operations (Montreal): George P. Kane, James Simeon McCuaig, Patrick C. Martin, James B. Clay, Dr. Montrose A. Pallen

Logistical Support and Operations (Toronto/Windsor): Mr. Bishop and Captain Murray (both Confederate Army)

Secondary Raider Force (Volunteers in British North America): the only identified members of this group of about thirty-two Southern volunteers are a man named Thompson, who had previously escaped from Johnson's Island, and another man, a private named Connelly, who was given the assignment of crossing to Ogdensburg, New York, in order to purchase steamer tickets in advance for a portion of the Confederate party.[4]

Secondary Raider Force (Volunteers in the Johnson's Island POW Camp): the only identified members of this group of approximately fifty prisoners who volunteered to participate in the operation in the event of a successful attack on the camp are Major-General Isaac Ridgeway Trimble, Brigadier-General James Jay Archer, and Lieutenant-Colonel William H. Payne; however, Robert D. Minor's report on the expedition also mentions "the Berkleys" and "Randolphs."[5]

Secret Courier (Montreal-Ohio): Mrs. Patrick C. Martin

Reconnaissance Personnel (Ohio): unidentified British North American (former British Army officer)

The Second Lake Erie Expedition (July–September 1864)

Commanding Officers: Captain Charles H. Cole (Cavalry) and Acting Master John Yates Beall

Second-in-Command: Acting Master Bennett G. Burley

Main Commando Force (under Beall and Burley): H.B. Barkley, John Bristol, James Brotherton, William Byland, Joseph Y. Clark, W.C. Colt, R.B. Drake, M.H. Duncan, Robert G. Harris, N.S. Johnston, W.B. King, Tom S. Major, J.G. Odoer, Dr. J.S. Riley,[6] David H. Ross, R.F. Smith, F.H. Thomas; plus two unidentified men.

Secondary Raider Force (Volunteers in the Johnson's Island POW Camp): only one member of this group has been definitively identified: Captain (and Assistant Quartermaster) Archibald Smith McKennon (Sixteenth Arkansas Infantry); however, based on the number of prisoners who stepped forward during the first Lake Erie expedition and McKennon's brief account of the activities of the prisoner volunteers, it is likely that a group of at least forty to fifty men (including some of the 1863 volunteers) were willing to join the commandos should an attack on the camp prove successful.[7]

Volunteer Covert Operatives in Sandusky, Ohio (Under Cole): John M. Brown, J.B. Merrick, John B. Robinson, Louis Rosenthal, Dr. Ellwood Stanley, Abraham Strain, and John H. Williams (although all these individuals were named as participants by Cole and were accordingly arrested by Union authorities, Robinson was the only one whose participation in Cole's covert activities is beyond doubt; it is possible, if not probable, that Merrick and Rosenthal played some role; however, the involvement of the others is open to question).

Secret Couriers (Sandusky–Canada West): Lieutenant Bennett H. Young, John B. Robinson, Annie Brown (aka Emma Bison, Jennie Brown, Mrs. Annie Cole, Annie Davis, and Pinkey)

Logistical Support and Operations (Toronto and Windsor): Jacob Thompson, Colonel Steele

The Third Lake Erie Expedition (September–November 1864)

Chief Planner and Coordinator of Operations (Toronto and Windsor): Jacob Thompson

Main Commando Force:
Commanding Officer (CSN) — Acting Master John Yates Beall
Second-in-Command (CSN) — Acting Master Bennett G. Burley
Commandos (Cavalry and Army) — four members of this group have been identified: Colonel Robert M. Martin, Lieutenant John W. Headley, George S. Anderson, and Charles C. Hemming (also possibly engaged in reconnaissance).

Secondary Raider Force (Volunteers in the Johnson's Island POW Camp): none of the prisoner volunteers have been identified; however, based on the number who stepped forward during the 1863 Lake Erie expedition, it is probable that at least forty to fifty men (including some of those who had volunteered to participate in the previous expeditions) were prepared to join the commando force in the event of a successful attack on the camp.

Ordnance:
Guelph: Acting Master Bennett G. Burley, Adam Robertson
Toronto: William Lawrence "Larry" MacDonald
Windsor: unknown number of Confederate operatives manufacturing "Greek Fire"

Operation of the Steamer Georgian:
Proxy Owner and Chief Coordinator: John Bates
Subsequent Proxy Owner: George T. Denison (with probable assistance from Colonel George Dewson)
Captain (for Bates) — Milne (an experienced Great Lakes captain)[8]
First Crew — eight unknown individuals served on the *Georgian* during her brief cruise under Captain Milne[9]
Captain (for Denison) — Nettleton Balme Whitby
Second Crew — three men have been identified: William Lawrence "Larry" MacDonald (ship's carpenter), James Huton (fireman), and William Ridout (purser); in addition, Captain Whitby had been authorized to select a crew comprising one mate, two wheelsmen, and three deckhands.[10]

Prize Crews — an unknown number of unidentified volunteers in various Lake Erie communities were prepared to man three steamers that were to be captured by the *Georgian* and turned into Confederate raiders.

Secret Couriers (Toronto–Richmond) — two unidentified couriers were dispatched from Toronto by Jacob Thompson; William Armstrong and George Walker assisted in the preparation of Thompson's secret messages; Lieutenant Samuel Boyer Davis was sent to Toronto from Richmond and was then ordered by Thompson to return to Richmond, utilizing a passport supplied by Willoughby Cummings and carrying messages that had been hidden with assistance from George T. Denison and his wife, Caroline Denison.

The Buffalo Raid (December 1864)

Commanding Officers: Acting Master John Yates Beall and Colonel Robert
M. Martin

Commando Force: Lieutenant John W. Headley, Captain Robert Cobb
Kennedy, Lieutenant James T. Harrington, Lieutenant John T.
Ashbrook, Charles C. Hemming, George S. Anderson, W.P. Rutland,
and Forney Holt

Notes

Introduction

1. [Epigraph] Daniel Bedinger Lucas, *Memoir of John Yates Beall: His Life; Trial; Correspondence; Diary; and Private Manuscript Found Among His Papers, Including His Own Account of the Raid on Lake Erie* (Montreal: John Lovell, 1865), 96.
2. The two best works on the history of the Confederate States Navy are Raimondo Luraghi's *A History of the Confederate Navy* (Annapolis, MD: Naval Institute Press, 1996) and J. Thomas Scharf's *History of the Confederate Navy from Its Organization to the Surrender of Its Last Vessel* (New York: Rogers and Sherwood, 1887).
3. Luraghi, *A History of the Confederate Navy*, 67–69.
4. Mallory's career is examined in depth in Joseph T. Durkin's *Stephen R. Mallory: Confederate Navy Chief* (Chapel Hill, NC: University of

North Carolina Press, 1954).

5. For a useful overview of the Confederate States Navy's main commando operations, see Luraghi, *A History of the Confederate Navy*, 300–14. For more on the Confederacy's approach to the authorization of irregular naval operations, see United States War Department, *The War of the Rebellion: A Compilation of the Official Records of the Union and Confederate Armies in The War of the Rebellion* (Washington, DC: Government Printing Office, 1880–1901) [hereafter cited as *OR*], ser. 1, vol. 22, 1,001–03, Stephen Mallory to E.C. Cabell, September 10, 1863.

6. United States Department of the Navy, *Official Records of the Union and Confederate Navies in the War of the Rebellion* (Washington, DC: Government Printing Office, 1894–1927) [hereafter cited as *ORN*], ser. 2, vol. 2, 256–57, J. Taylor Wood to Catesby ap R. Jones, August 30, 1862. For more on Wood's career, see Royce Gordon Shingleton, *John Taylor Wood: Sea Ghost of the Confederacy* (Athens, GA: University of Georgia Press, 1979); John Bell, *Confederate Seadog: John Taylor Wood in War and Exile* (Jefferson, NC: McFarland & Company, 2002).

7. Aside from the ambitious Great Lakes operations that are the focus of this volume, the most significant Confederate naval commando operation with a Canadian connection was the seizure in December 1863 of the American steamer *Chesapeake* off Cape Cod, while she was en route from New York to Portland, Maine. Not only were several British North Americans actively involved in this operation, but the vessel was subsequently captured by the American Navy in British waters. For a useful summary of the incident, sometimes referred to as the "Second *Chesapeake* Affair," see Greg Marquis, *In Armageddon's Shadow: The Civil War and Canada's Maritime Provinces* (Montreal and Kingston: McGill-Queen's University Press, 1998), 134–210. It should also be noted that there is some evidence of several unrealized plans by Confederate sympathizers to attack U.S. vessels in British Columbia waters. See Robin W. Winks, *Canada and the United States: The Civil War Years* (Baltimore. MD: Johns Hopkins Press, 1960), 162–65.

8. *Ibid.* 55–56; Lester Burrell Shippee, *Canadian-American Relations 1849–1874* (New Haven, CT: Yale University Press, 1939), 130–33.

9. *ORN*, ser. 1, vol. 2, 825, Robert Minor to Franklin Buchanan, February 2, 1864. Minor's letter also appeared in the *Richmond*

Dispatch (December 15, 1895) and *The Southern Historical Society Papers*. See *Southern Historical Society Papers*, vol. XXIII (Richmond, VA: Southern Historical Society, 1895), 283–90. A handwritten copy of the text is found in Minor's papers at the Virginia Historical Society (hereafter VHS). See VHS, Minor Family Papers (Mss1 M6663), Robert Dabney Minor Papers, Section 18, bound commonplace book, 1850–66, Minor to Buchanan, February 2, 1864.

10. Scharf, *History of the Confederate Navy from Its Organization to the Surrender of Its Last Vessel*, 113–17.

11. Frederick J. Shepard, "The Johnson's Island Plot: An Historical Narrative of the Conspiracy of the Confederates, in 1864, to Capture the U.S. Steamship *Michigan* on Lake Erie, and Release the Prisoners of War in Sandusky Bay," in Frank H. Severance, ed., *Publications of the Buffalo Historical Society Volume IX* (Buffalo, NY: Buffalo Historical Society, 1906), 4. Shepard's lengthy article, comprising 51 pages, was based on first-rate primary research and offered the first scholarly examination of the Confederate expeditions against Johnson's Island. Regrettably, the problems that he pointed to in 1906, regarding the slipshod research that had characterized previous accounts of the expeditions, have persisted to this day.

Chapter 1: William Murdaugh's Plan

1. For a history of the James River Squadron, see John M. Coski, *Capital Navy: The Men, Ships and Operations of the James River Squadron* (Campbell, CA: Savas Publishing Company, 1996). For the basic service records of most of the Confederate States Navy personnel mentioned in this article, see Thomas Truxton Moebs, *Confederate States Navy Research Guide* (Williamsburg, VA: Moebs Publishing Co., 1991), 183–298.

2. See the *Beaufort*'s entry in the online *Dictionary of American Naval Fighting Ships* (*www.history.navy.mil/danfs/cfa1/beaufort.htm.*)

3. *ORN*, ser. 1, vol. 2, 828–29, William Murdaugh to Stephen Mallory, February 7, 1863.

4. *Ibid.*, 829; *ORN*, ser. 1, vol. 2, 823, Minor to Buchanan.

5. *ORN*, ser. 1, vol. 2, 829–30, Murdaugh to Mallory.

6. *ORN*, ser. 1, vol. 2, 823, Minor to Buchanan.

7. *Ibid.*; Bradley A. Rodger's *Guardian of the Great Lakes: The U.S. Paddle Frigate* Michigan (Ann Arbor, MI: University of Michigan Press, 1996) provides a scholarly account of the career of the USS *Michigan* (renamed USS *Wolverine* in 1905). Launched in 1843, she was not decommissioned until 1912. The prow of the vessel has been preserved and is now on display at the Erie Maritime Museum in Erie, Pennsylvania.

8. It is estimated that ten thousand Confederates passed through the military prison camp on Johnson's Island from April 1862 to September 1865. Of these, about three hundred died while in custody. Charles E. Frohman's *Rebels on Lake Erie: The Piracy, The Conspiracy, Prison Life* (Columbus, OH: Ohio Historical Society, 1965) remains the most thorough account of the camp's history. For information on current preservation activities and ongoing archaeological investigations relating to the camp, see *www.heidelberg.edu/johnsonsisland*.

Chapter 2: John Wilkinson's Expedition

1. *ORN*, ser. 1, vol. 2, 823, Minor to Buchanan; *OR*, ser. 2, vol. 6, 311, Y.H. Blackwell to James A. Seddon (with unsigned enclosure from James Jay Archer), September 21, 1863. The C.C. Egerton mentioned in Archer's letter was probably the Baltimore businessman and senior militia officer Charles C. Egerton, Jr. By the time that Archer's message arrived in Richmond, neither of the two naval officers recommended by him were available for the operation. Bier had resigned his naval commission in 1862 and transferred to the army, where he served as a staff officer (ordnance) with Lieutenant-General T.J. "Stonewall" Jackson. As for Parker, he was about to take charge of the Confederate Naval Academy, a pet project of Secretary Mallory.

2. Minor indicates that the naval officer John Wilkinson was specifically recommended in the letter that Seddon shared with him, which might suggest an author other than Archer. See *ORN*, ser. 1, vol. 2, 823, Minor to Buchanan. It is also possible that Seddon — and not the letter-writer — recommended Wilkinson, as the two were close

friends. See John Wilkinson, *The Narrative of a Blockade-Runner* (New York: Sheldon & Co., 1877), 174.

3. Lynda Laswell Crist, ed., *The Papers of Jefferson Davis; Volume 10, October 1863–August 1864* (Baton Rouge and London: Louisiana State University Press, 1999), 489. For more on Kane, who was often referred to as Marshal Kane, see the *Maryland Online Encyclopedia* (*www.mdoe.org/kanegeorge.html*).

4. Crist, ed., *The Papers of Jefferson Davis; Volume 9, January–September 1863* (Baton Rouge and London: Louisiana State University Press, 1997), 285–86.

5. *ORN*, ser. 1, vol. 2, 823, Minor to Buchanan.

6. *Ibid.*

7. *Ibid.*

8. Wilkinson, *The Narrative of a Blockade-Runner*, 169.

9. *ORN*, ser. 1, vol. 2, 823, Minor to Buchanan.

10. *Ibid.*, 824.

11. Wilkinson, *The Narrative of a Blockade-Runner*, 169.

12. *ORN*, ser. 1, vol. 2, 824, Minor to Buchanan.

13. Shepardson often wrote under the pseudonym "Bohemian." For more on his wartime journalistic career, see J. Cutler Andrews, *The South Reports the Civil War* (Princeton, NJ: Princeton University Press, 1970), 448–551.

14. *ORN*, ser. 1, vol. 2, 824, Minor to Buchanan.

15. *Ibid.* In his memoirs, Wilkinson gives the date of departure as October 10 (see Wilkinson, *The Narrative of a Blockade-Runner*, 169). It may be that the *Lee* left Wilmington on October 7 and Smithville on October 10; however, I have assumed that Minor's nearly contemporaneous account is more reliable in this regard than Wilkinson's memoir, written more than a decade after the events.

16. Wilkinson, *The Narrative of a Blockade-Runner*, 171.

17. *ORN*, ser. 1, vol. 2, 824, Minor to Buchanan; Wilkinson, *The Narrative of a Blockade-Runner*, 170.

18. *Ibid.*, 173.

19. *Ibid.*, 174; *ORN*, ser. 1, vol. 2, 824, Minor to Buchanan.

20. For more on the activities of Wier and the other leading Confederate sympathizers in Halifax during the American Civil War, see Marquis, *In Armageddon's Shadow*.

21. Wilkinson, *The Narrative of a Blockade-Runner*, 174–76; Stephen R. Wise, *Lifeline of the Confederacy: Blockade-Running During the Civil War* (Columbia, SC: University of South Carolina Press, 1988), 139, 318.

22. VHS, Robert Dabney Minor Papers, Section 18, commonplace book, 1850–66.

23. Wilkinson, *The Narrative of a Blockade-Runner*, 176, 187. For more on Judge Jackson's efforts to counteract Confederate operations in the Maritimes, see Marquis, *In Armageddon's Shadow*, 103–04.

24. Wilkinson, *The Narrative of a Blockade-Runner*, 176; *ORN*, ser. 1, vol. 2, 824, Minor to Buchanan. Neither Wilkinson nor Minor provide Leggett's name in full; however, it is worth noting that there was a Richmond engraver named William Leggett, who was a principal in the firm Leggett, Keatinge & Ball, which had a contract for the printing of Confederate currency. In March 1862, the Secretary of the Treasury, Christopher G. Memminger, forced the firm to release Leggett, who had been observed associating with a known Union spy. Apparently, William Leggett was not arrested, but he likely remained under a cloud of suspicion. See the following webpage on Confederate currency and bonds: *www.csaquotes.com/collectingcsa/ t33collection.html*.

25. Wilkinson, *The Narrative of a Blockade-Runner*, 173.

26. *Ibid.*, 180.

27. For more on Confederate operatives in British North America, see John W. Headley, *Confederate Operations in Canada and New York* (New York and Washington, DC: Neale Publishing Company, 1906); Winks, *Canada and the United States: The Civil War Years*; Oscar A. Kinchen, *Confederate Operations in Canada and the North* (North Quincy, MA: Christopher Publishing House, 1970).

28. Wilkinson, *The Narrative of a Blockade-Runner*, 181.

29. Marquis, *In Armageddon's Shadow*, 105–33.

30. *ORN*, ser. 1, vol. 2, 824, Minor to Buchanan. For Minor's use of *noms de guerre*, see the *New York Times*, November 19, 1863. Minor's annotated copy of this article confirms that he adopted the names "Brest" and "Kelly." See VHS, Robert Dabney Minor Papers, Section 18, commonplace book, 1850–66.

31. *Ibid.*

32. The first request to have the *Michigan* stationed at Sandusky Bay came in the late spring of 1862, not long after the establishment of the Johnson's Island POW camp. However, she apparently did not take up her new station until more than a year later. See *OR*, ser. 2, vol. 4, 42, William S. Pierson to William Hoffman, June 19, 1862; *Ibid.*, *OR*, ser. 2, vol. 6, 435, William S. Pierson to William Hoffman, October 28, 1863.

33. Wilkinson, *The Narrative of a Blockade-Runner*, 181–85.

34. VHS, Minor Family Papers (Mss1 M6663), Robert Dabney Minor Papers, Section 18, commonplace book, 1850–66.

35. Crist, ed., *The Papers of Jefferson Davis; Volume 10, October 1863–August 1864*, 86.

36. Clay and Pallen's role in the expedition is discussed in a lengthy report from Toronto that appeared in the *New York Times* on November 19, 1863. Signed by "Canada," the report, which was widely reprinted, is notable for its general accuracy regarding the Confederate commando operation and its key participants. For more on Pallen, see his obituary, *New York Times*, October 4, 1890. A succinct biography of Clay can be found at the Biographical Directory of the United States Congress website. Clay would die in Montreal on January 26. See the *New York Times*, January 28, 1864. One of the leading Canadian literary figures of the day, Rosanna Leprohon, marked his passing with an elegy that reflected the esteem in which Clay was held in British North America: "And other mourners leaves he, too,/Who had learned to love him well,/Though short the time since he had come,/Within our midst to dwell." See Rosanna Leprohon, *The Poetical Works of Mrs. Leprohon (Miss R.E. Mullins)* (Montreal: John Lovell & Son, 1881), 152–53.

37. *ORN*, ser. 1, vol. 2, 825, Minor to Buchanan.

38. Wilkinson, *The Narrative of a Blockade-Runner*, 182; *ORN*, ser. 1, vol. 2, 825, Minor to Buchanan.

39. Canada Parliament, *Sessional Papers of the Dominion of Canada; Volume VI; No. 75; Second Session of the First Parliament of the Dominion of Canada, Session 1869* (Ottawa, ON: Hunter, Rose, 1869) [hereafter cited as *1869 Sessional Papers No. 75*], 79. The Camp Chase military prison was located at Columbus, Ohio. The Camp Douglas prison was in Chicago.

40. *ORN*, ser. 1, vol. 2, 825, Minor to Buchanan.

41. Wilkinson, *The Narrative of a Blockade-Runner*, 184–85.

42. *Ibid.*, 185; *ORN*, ser. 1, vol. 2, 825, Minor to Buchanan; Crist, ed., *The Papers of Jefferson Davis; Volume 10, October 1863–August 1864*, 86. For a brief biography of McCuaig, see J.K. Johnson, ed., *The Canadian Directory of Parliament, 1867–1967* (Ottawa, ON: Public Archives of Canada, 1968), 391.

43. *ORN*, ser. 1, vol. 2, 825, Minor to Buchanan.

44. *Ibid.*, 825–26.

45. *Ibid.*, 826.

46. VHS, Robert Dabney Minor Papers, Section 11 (W–Y), John Wilkinson to Robert D. Minor, October 31, 1863. Interestingly, some names have been carefully excised from Minor's copy of this document, presumably to protect the identity of Confederate agents or British North American sympathizers.

47. Wilkinson, *The Narrative of a Blockade-Runner*, 185–86.

48. *Ibid.*; *ORN*, ser. 1, vol. 2, 826, Minor to Buchanan.

49. Wilkinson, *The Narrative of a Blockade-Runner*, 186.

50. *Ibid.*; *ORN*, ser. 1, vol. 2, 826, Minor to Buchanan; *OR*, ser. 3, vol. 3, 1,013–15; *1869 Sessional Papers No. 75*, 75–78. The behind-the-scenes story of the gathering and analyzing of intelligence relating to the first Lake Erie expedition is beyond the purview of this book. The best summary of this aspect of the expedition — and of the diplomatic response to the attempted raid and its aftermath — is found in Winks, *Canada and the United States*, 145–54.

51. Wilkinson, *The Narrative of a Blockade-Runner*, 186.

52. *Ibid.*, 187.

53. *ORN*, ser. 1, vol. 2, 826, Minor to Buchanan. Minor indicates here that the force comprised fifty-two men, whereas he had previously indicated that there were fifty-four. In this instance, he is probably referring to the number of men who were under his and Wilkinson's command.

54. *Ibid.*

55. Winks, *Canada and the United States*, 148. Unfortunately, Henry C. Klassen's recent biography of Holton, *Luther H. Holton: A Founding Canadian Entrepreneur* (Calgary: University of Calgary Press, 2001) sheds very little light on Holton's role during the Civil War. Although the Confederates were convinced that McCuaig had gotten cold feet, it

is possible that he had been asked to deliberately plant disinformation that would undermine the Confederate operation.

56. Crist, ed., *The Papers of Jefferson Davis; Volume 10, October 1863–August 1864*, 86.

57. Wilkinson, *The Narrative of a Blockade-Runner*, 186–87.

58. *Ibid.*, 188; *ORN*, ser. 1, vol. 2, 826, Minor to Buchanan.

59. Another party of returning Confederates, including George P. Kane and about sixteen other men, mostly former POWs, left Montreal for Halifax in late January or early February. It is possible that some of the former prisoners who had volunteered to serve in the commando force were among this group. See Halifax *Citizen* (February 4, 1864).

60. *ORN*, ser. 1, vol. 2, 827, Minor to Buchanan; Marquis, *In Armageddon's Shadow*, 134–75.

61. *ORN*, ser. 1, vol. 2, 827, Minor to Buchanan; Marquis, *In Armageddon's Shadow*, 158.

62. *Ibid.*, 826–27; Wilkinson, *The Narrative of a Blockade-Runner*, 188–93.

63. *ORN*, ser. 1, vol. 2, 826, Minor to Buchanan.

Chapter 3: The Propaganda War

1. *New York Times*, November 19, 1863.

2. United States Department of State, *Papers Relating to Foreign Affairs, Accompanying the Annual Message of the President to the Second Session Thirty-Eighth Congress, Part I (1864)* (Washington: Government Printing Office, 1865), 63–66, William H. Seward to Charles Francis Adams (with enclosure), January 4, 1864. [This source is often cited under a later series title, *Foreign Relations of the United States* (*FRUS* for short). Volumes from the 1861–68 period are also at times cited under the title *Diplomatic Correspondence*. Citations hereafter will be to *FRUS*.]

3. *Ibid.*, 46–48, Seward to Adams (with enclosure), December 20, 1863.

4. *Ibid.*, 73, Adams to Seward, January 8, 1864.

5. *Ibid.*, 82, Adams to Seward, January 14, 1864

6. *Ibid.*, 111, Adams to Lord Russell, January 19, 1864.
7. London *Herald*, January 29, 1864; *ORN*, ser. II, vol. 3, 1,059–60, J.P. Benjamin to John Slidell, March 11, 1864.
8. *FRUS, Part I (1864)*, 568, Adams to Russell, April 4, 1864.
9. *ORN*, ser. II, vol. 3, 1,060–63, Henry Hotze to J.P. Benjamin, March 12, 1864.
10. Winks, *Canada and the United States*, 152–53.
11. *FRUS, Part I (1864)*, 194–95, Benjamin Moran to Seward (with enclosure), February 20, 1864.
12. *ORN*, ser. II, vol. 3, 1,107–10, John Slidell to J.P. Benjamin, May 2, 1864.

Chapter 4: The Order of the Brotherhood of the Southern Cross

1. "A Plan to Escape," *Southern Historical Society Papers* (Richmond, VA: Southern Historical Society, 1891), XIX, 286–88.
2. *Ibid.*, 284–86.
3. *Ibid.*, 288.

Chapter 5: Privateers at Rondeau Harbour

1. *1869 Sessional Papers No. 75*, 105, L.C. Baker to E.M. Stanton, March 8, 1864.
2. *Ibid.*, William H. Seward to Lord Lyons, March 11, 1864.
3. *Ibid.*, 107, Lord Monck to Lord Lyons, March 18, 1864.
4. *OR*, ser. 1, vol. 32, part III, 219, Henry D. Terry to Carroll H. Potter, March 29, 1864.
5. *FRUS, Part II (1864)*, 585–86, Viscount Monck to Lord Lyons, March 31, 1864 (with confidential enclosure).
6. *OR*, ser. 1, vol. 32, part III, 219, Henry D. Terry to Carroll H. Potter, March 29, 1864.
7. *1869 Sessional Papers No. 75*, 108, Lord Monck to the Duke of Newcastle, March 31, 1864.
8. *OR*, ser. 1, vol. 32, part III, 218, S.P. Heintzelman to H.W. Halleck, April 1, 1864.

9. *Ibid.*
10. Kingston *Daily News* (October 1, 1864).

Chapter 6: Jacob Thompson's "Northwest Conspiracy"

1. *ORN*, ser. 2, vol. 3, 174, Jefferson Davis to Jacob Thompson, April 27, 1864.
2. For more on Thompson's activities in Canada, see Headley, *Confederate Operations in Canada and New York*; Winks, *Canada and the United States*; Kinchen, *Confederate Operations in Canada and the North*.
3. *OR*, ser. 1, vol. 43, pt. 2, 934, Jacob Thompson to Judah P. Benjamin, December 3, 1864.
4. *Ibid.*, 932.
5. *OR*, ser. 2, vol. 8, 708, A.A. Hosmer to W. Hoffman, July 18, 1865; Headley, *Confederate Operations in Canada and New York*, 310. Headley's book includes transcriptions of some archival documents that are not found in the *OR* or the *ORN*.
6. *OR*, ser. 1, vol. 43, pt. 2, 934, Thompson to Benjamin.
7. *Ibid.*; Headley, *Confederate Operations in Canada and New York*, 231–35; Frohman, *Rebels on Lake Erie*, 73, 78p. For more on Carter's career, see David W. Francis, "The United States Navy and the Johnson's Island Conspiracy: The Case of John C. Carter," *Northwest Ohio Quarterly* LII, 3 (Summer 1980), 229–43. Interestingly, Carter was born in Virginia and was descended from a distinguished Southern family. His strong connections to the South may have raised some doubts regarding his commitment to the Union and probably contributed to the decision to relieve him of his command of the *Michigan* in October 1864. See Francis, "The United States Navy and the Johnson's Island Conspiracy," 232.
8. The infamous leader of the Copperheads (also known as Peace Democrats), Clement Vallandigham, was exiled in Canada in 1863–64, during which time he ran for the governorship of Ohio. Vallandigham's banishment inspired Edward Everett Hale's famous patriotic short story "The Man Without a Country," which first appeared in the December 1863 issue of the *Atlantic Monthly*. While in Canada, Vallandigham

was welcomed by the political elite and was even introduced on the floor of Parliament by Thomas D'Arcy McGee. See Winks, *Canada and the United States*, 143. Interestingly, Vallandigham's exile prompted Henry J. Morgan, a young civil servant and the author of *Celebrated Canadians* (1862), to contact Vallandigham's brother, James, in an effort to compile biographical information on Vallandigham, lest the latter's exile from America become permanent. James L. Vallandigham's reply to Morgan is in the author's possession. For more on Vallandigham's time in Canada, see Frank L. Klement, "Vallandigham as an Exile in Canada," *Ohio History* 74, 3 (Summer 1965), 151–68, 208–10. For more on the Copperheads, see Jennifer L. Weber, *Copperheads: The Rise and Fall of Lincoln's Opponents in the North* (New York: Oxford University Press, 2006).

9. Headley, *Confederate Operations in Canada and New York*, 233.

10. *Ibid.*

11. Lucas, *Memoir of John Yates Beall*, 17–18.

12. *Ibid.*, 241–48, 252; Luraghi, *A History of the Confederate Navy*, 303–04, 312.

13. William Washington Baker, *Memoirs of Service with John Yates Beall* (Richmond, VA: The Richmond Press, 1910), 47–49. It has been suggested that Beall was actually the first person to propose a Lake Erie raid. See Lucas, *Memoir of John Yates Beall*, 19–20; Headley, *Confederate Operations in Canada and New York*, 242–43.

14. Baker, *Memoirs of Service with John Yates Beall*, 49.

15. Headley, *Confederate Operations in Canada and New York*, 233.

16. *OR*, ser. 1, vol. 43, pt. 2, 226, John A. Dix to E.M. Stanton, September 30, 1864.

17. Kelleys Island is also known as Kelley's Island.

18. *Ibid.*, 234–35, 252.

19. *OR*, ser. 1, vol. 43, pt. 2, 932, Thompson to Benjamin.

20. Headley, *Confederate Operations in Canada and New York*, 248.

21. Lucas, *Memoir of John Yates Beall*, 43–44.

22. Headley, *Confederate Operations in Canada and New York*, 251; *OR*, ser. 1, vol. 43, pt. 2, 239, affidavit of S.F. Atwood, September 25, 1864.

23. *Ibid.*, 229, Dix to Stanton.

24. Lucas, *Memoir of John Yates Beall*, 32.

25. *Ibid.*
26. Shepard, "The Johnson's Island Plot," 10.

Chapter 7: John Yates Beall Attacks

1. The Confederate's seizure of the *Philo Parsons* is now commemorated by an Ontario provincial heritage plaque at Amherstburg. See *www. ontarioplaques.com/Plaques_DEF/Plaque_Essex05.html.*
2. *Ibid.*, 242–43, affidavit of W.O. Ashley, September 25, 1864.
3. *Ibid.*, 243–44; 240, affidavit of De Witt C. Nichols, September 25, 1864; Headley, *Confederate Operations in Canada and New York*, 250.
4. *OR*, ser. 1, vol. 43, pt. 2, 240, affidavit of Nichols.
5. *Ibid.*, 235–37, 240, 243, affidavits of James Denison, Michael Campbell, Nichols, Ashley.
6. *Ibid.*, 236–37, 240–41, 243, affidavits of Denison, Campbell, Nichols, Ashley.
7. *Ibid.*, 236–39, 241, 243, affidavits of Denison, Campbell, Atwood, Nichols, Ashley.
8. *Ibid.*, 239, affidavit of Atwood.
9. *Ibid.*, 240.
10. *Ibid.*, 228, Dix to Stanton; 239, affidavit of Atwood. Interestingly, the *Island Queen* was the first vessel to transport prisoners from Sandusky to Johnson's Island, in April 1862. See Frohman, *Rebels on Lake Erie*, 8.
11. *OR*, ser. 1, vol. 43, pt. 2, 227, Dix to Stanton; 236, 239, 243, affidavits of Denison, Atwood, Ashley.
12. *Ibid.*, 244–45, affidavit of Henry Haines.
13. *Ibid.*, affidavits of Denison, Atwood, Nichols.
14. *New York Times* (August 11, 1895).
15. *OR*, ser. 1, vol. 43, pt. 2, 245, affidavit of Haines.
16. *Ibid.*
17. *Ibid.*, 244, affidavit of Ashley.
18. Lucas, *Memoir of John Yates Beall*, 296.
19. For more on the Brown family's connection with the Lake Erie Islands, see Theresa Thorndale, *Sketches and Stories of the Lake Erie Islands* (Sandusky, OH: I.F. Mack & Brother, 1898), 159–73. Thorndale was a

pseudonym of the journalist Lydia J. Ryall. Her book, a second edition of which was issued under her own name in 1913, includes a first-person account of the Confederate raid by George W. Orr, the *Island Queen*'s captain.

Chapter 8: John Brown Jr. Fights Back

1. Thorndale, *Sketches and Stories of the Lake Erie Islands*, 71; Frohman, *Rebels on Lake Erie*, 85.
2. Shepard, "The Johnson's Island Plot," 39, note 36.
3. Thorndale, *Sketches and Stories of the Lake Erie Islands*, 72–73.
4. *Ibid.*, 71–72, 159–61.
5. *Ibid.*, 72–74.
6. Frohman, *Rebels on Lake Erie*, 85.
7. Thorndale, *Sketches and Stories of the Lake Erie Islands*, 73–74.
8. *OR*, ser, 2, vol. 7, 903, Charles W. Hill to E.A. Hitchcock, October 1, 1864.
9. Thorndale, *Sketches and Stories of the Lake Erie Islands*, 74.
10. Frohman, *Rebels on Lake Erie*, 85.

Chapter 9: Rebel Mutineers

1. Thorndale, *Sketches and Stories of the Lake Erie Islands*, 78.
2. *OR*, ser. 1, vol. 43, pt. 2, 236–37, 241, 245, affidavits of Denison, Campbell, Nichols, Haines; Headley, *Confederate Operations in Canada and New York*, 250.
3. *OR*, ser. 1, vol. 43, pt. 2, 237, affidavit of Campbell.
4. Lucas, *Memoir of John Yates Beall*, 296.
5. Thorndale, *Sketches and Stories of the Lake Erie Islands*, 78.
6. Headley, *Confederate Operations in Canada and New York*, 250–51.
7. *OR*, ser. 1, vol. 43, pt. 2, 233, B.H. Hill to C.H. Potter, September 21, 1864. Although Hill does not identify his informant, it probably was Godfrey Joseph Hyams, who was active in Jacob Thompson's Canadian network of Southern operatives and later openly betrayed

the Confederates. See Headley, *Confederate Operations in Canada and New York*, 215, 281, 308, 381; *1869 Sessional Papers No. 75*, 112, James Cockburn to Denis Godley, June 1, 1865; Canada Parliament, *Journals of the House of Commons of the Dominion of Canada from November 6, 1867, to May 22, 1868, Both Days Inclusive; In the Thirty-First Year of the Reign of Our Sovereign, Lady Queen Victoria; Being the 1st session of the 1st Parliament of the Dominion of Canada; Session 1867–8* (Ottawa: Hunter, Rose, [1868]) [hereafter cited as *Journals of the House of Commons of the Dominion of Canada from November 6, 1867, to May 22, 1868*], Appendix No. 7, [1–3]. See also *OR*, ser. 1, vol. 3, 496, extract from D. Hunter's consular dispatch No. 21, April 7, 1865. Hyam's name in this latter document is misspelled as "Hyarns." It is interesting to note that John Wilson Murray, the most famous Canadian detective of the Victorian era, claims to have been a gunner on the USS *Michigan* during the Civil War and insists that he was ordered by Captain Carter to uncover and foil the Confederate plot to seize the gunboat. While his account of the incident, which was co-authored, if not entirely ghosted, by Victor Speers, is colourful and entertaining, it is so riddled with gross errors and improbabilities that it must be regarded as fiction. See John Wilson Murray, *Memoirs of a Great Detective: Incidents in the Life of John Wilson Murray* (London: William Heinemann, 1904), 10–19. For a scholarly critical assessment of the reliability of Murray's memoirs as a source, see Jim Phillips and Joel Fortune, "Murray, John Wilson," *Dictionary of Canadian Biography Online* (*www.biographi.ca/EN/ShowBio. asp?BioId=41073&query=*). See also Shepard, "The Johnson's Island Plot," 24–25 (note 25); Frohman, *Rebels on Lake Erie*, 99–100.

8. *OR*, ser. 1, vol. 43, pt. 2, 235, B.H. Hill to J.C. Carter, September 19, 1864.

9. *Ibid.*, J.C. Carter to B.H. Hill, September 19, 1864.

10. W.D. Ardagh, Robert A. Harrison, and Henry O'Brien, eds., *The Upper Canada Law Journal (New Series), Volume 1, From January to December 1865* (Toronto: W.C. Chewett & Co., 1865), 37, 47.

11. *Ibid.*, 237–38, affidavit of Campbell.

12. *Ibid.*, 236, 238, 241, 242, 245, affidavits of Denison, Campbell, Nichols, Haines.

13. *OR*, ser. 2, vol. 7, 850–51, Charles W. Hill to S.P. Heintzelman, September 20, 1864; *Ibid.*, 901, Charles W. Hill to E.A. Hitchcock, October 1, 1864.

14. Shepard, "The Johnson's Island Plot," 38–39; Frohman, *Rebels on Lake Erie*, 85–86.

15. Headley, *Confederate Operations in Canada and New York*, 251–52; Lucas, *Memoir of John Yates Beall*, 45.

16. *Ibid.*

Chapter 10: The Unlucky Cruise of the CSS Georgian

1. *OR*, ser. 2, Vol. 7, 864–65, Jacob Thompson and Clement C. Clay, Jr. to Jefferson Davis, September 22, 1864.

2. *Ibid.*, 864, Jacob Thompson and Clement C. Clay, Jr. to B.H. Hill, September 22, 1864.

3. Headley, *Confederate Operations in Canada and New York*, 231–32. For more on the St. Albans Raid, see *inter alia* Winks, *Canada and the United States*, 295–336; Kinchen, *Confederate Operations in Canada and the North*, 127–47; Oscar A. Kinchen, *Daredevils of the Confederate Army: The Story of the St. Albans Raiders* (North Quincy, MA: Christopher Publishing House, 1959); Dennis K. Wilson, *Justice Under Pressure: The St. Albans Raid and Its Aftermath* (Lanham, MD: University Press of America, 1992).

4. Headley, *Confederate Operations in Canada and New York*, 254.

5. In some respects this third Lake Erie plan resembled an earlier proposal, probably by James D. Bulloch, the Confederacy's chief agent in England, to purchase a steamer in the United Kingdom that could be converted into a warship and used to strike against the Union on the Great Lakes. One drawback to this plan was that the vessel would have to pass through the Welland Canal without her true ownership and purpose being detected by British, Canadian, and Union authorities — an increasingly unlikely scenario as the war progressed. See Wilkinson, *The Narrative of a Blockade-Runner*, 188.

6. Lucas, *Memoir of John Yates Beall*, 21–22; United Kingdom Parliament, *North America No. 1 (1865); Correspondence Respecting the Attack on*

St. Albans, Vermont and Naval Force on the North American Lakes; With Appendices (London: s.n., 1865), [hereafter cited as *North America No. 1 (1865)*], 37–39, 41; *OR*, ser 1, vol. 3, 495–96; Headley, *Confederate Operations in Canada and New York*, 244. Daniel Bedinger Lucas indicates that Burley and Robertson were related, but does not specify the nature of the relationship. See Lucas, *Memoir of John Yates Beall*, 44. Claire Hoy, among others, indicates that they were cousins. See Claire Hoy, *Canadians in the Civil War* (Toronto: McArthur & Company, 2004), 246.

7. *The Glasgow Herald* (December 11, 1939).

8. *North America No. 1 (1865)*, 39, J.J. Kingsmill to John A. Macdonald, November 19, 1864.

9. *OR*, ser 1, vol. 3, 496, Bennett Burley to Dr. S.B. [James T.] Bates, October 17, 1864. This letter was intercepted by the double agent Godfrey Hyams and supplied to Union authorities.

10. See the *Georgian*'s entry in the online *Dictionary of American Naval Fighting Ships* (*www.history.navy.mil/danfs/cfa4/georgian.htm*); *New York Times* (December 11, 1864).

11. *OR*, ser. 1, vol. 43, pt. 2, 934, Thompson to Benjamin; *1869 Sessional Papers No. 75*, 88–90; *New York Times* (December 11, 1864).

12. *Ibid.*, 89–91. Among the documents cited here is a report from "Fides," a Toronto-based undercover detective who was supplying information on Confederate activities to William G. Fargo, the mayor of Buffalo.

13. *North America No. 1 (1865)*, 37–39, 41–42, 53–55; Toronto *Globe* (April 17, 1865); *OR*, ser 1, vol. 3, 496, Burley to Bates; *1869 Sessional Papers No. 75*, 84–87. The Greek Fire of the Civil War era was an incendiary liquid that apparently consisted of a mixture of phosphorous and carbon bisulphide. The concoction was designed to burst into flames when exposed to the air, but was not an entirely reliable weapon. See Headley, *Confederate Operations in Canada and New York*, 272–73; Kinchen, *Confederate Operations in Canada and the North*, 60–61. For a fascinating account of the origin of such chemical warfare, see Adrienne Mayor, *Greek Fire, Poison Arrows, and Scorpion Bombs: Biological and Chemical Warfare in the Ancient World* (Woodstock and New York: Overlook Duckworth, 2003).

14. Toronto *Globe* (April 17, 1865).

15. Headley, *Confederate Operations in Canada and New York*, 254–55.

16. Charles C. Hemming, "A Confederate Odyssey," available online at the *American Heritage* website: *www.americanheritage.com/articles/ magazine/ah/1984/1/.*

17. *Ibid.*

18. *1869 Sessional Papers No. 75*, 90, 93–95; *ORN*, vol. 1, no. 3, F.A. Roe to Gideon Welles, December 6, 1864.

19. *North America No. 1 (1865)*, 39, Kingsmill to Macdonald. Now designated as a provincial heritage property, Ferndell is operated as a bed and breakfast. See *www.ferndell.ca.*

20. *North America No. 1 (1865)*, 39, Kingsmill to Macdonald.

21. *North America No. 1 (1865)*, 36–42.

22. Headley, *Confederate Operations in Canada and New York*, 255.

23. *Ibid.*

24. *1869 Sessional Papers No. 75*, 92–94.

25. For more on Denison's early career and his relationships with many leading Confederates, see Lieutenant-Colonel George T. Denison, *Soldiering in Canada: Recollections and Experiences* (Toronto: George N. Morang and Company, 1900), 29–82.

26. *1869 Sessional Papers No. 75*, 92, W.H. Seward to J.H. Burnley, February 19, 1865. (Dewson's name is misspelled two different ways in this transcription.) For more on the Canadian-born Dewson, see Winks, *Canada and the United States*, 297, 310, 313; William A. Tidwell, *April '65: Confederate Covert Actions in the American Civil War* (Kent, OH: Kent State University Press, 1995), 20–21. Dewson's obituary can be found in the *Southern Christian Advocate*, February 18, 1874. Dewson's father, Jeremiah Wilkes Dewson, had commanded the Simcoe Militia during the suppression of the 1837 Rebellion in Upper Canada. The extent of George Dewson's activities in Canada during the summer and fall of 1864 will probably never be known in full. During the period he was in Canada, Dewson's brother-in-law, Augustus O. MacDonell, was a prisoner at Johnson's Island. The author has in his possession a digital copy of a letter that Mary Denison, George Dewson's sister and George T. Denison's mother, wrote to MacDonell on February 14, 1865. In the letter, Mary Denison confirms that her brother arrived in Canada in July.

27. George T. Denison, *The Petition of George Taylor Denison, Jr., to the House of Assembly, Praying Redress in the Matter of the Seizure of the Steamer "Georgian," Together with Copies of the Petition and Affidavits, Filed in the County Court of the County of Simcoe* (Toronto: Leader and Patriot, 1865), 10–14.
28. *1869 Sessional Papers No. 75*, 93–94.
29. Denison, *Soldiering in Canada*, 59.

Chapter 11: The Buffalo Raid

1. Headley, *Confederate Operations in Canada and New York*, 301; *Southern Historical Society Papers*, XIX, 286–88.
2. Headley, *Confederate Operations in Canada and New York*, 301.
3. *Ibid.*
4. *Ibid.*, 301–02; Hemming, "A Confederate Odyssey."
5. Headley, *Confederate Operations in Canada and New York*, 302.
6. *Ibid.*
7. *Ibid.*, 302–04.
8. *Ibid.*, 304.
9. *Ibid.*; *OR*, ser. 1, vol. 43, pt. 2, 789–90, General Orders No. 97, December 11, 1864.
10. Headley, *Confederate Operations in Canada and New York*, 304.
11. *Ibid.*, 304–05.
12. *Ibid.*, 305–06.
13. *Trial of John Y. Beall: As a Spy and a Guerrillero, by Military Commission* (New York: D. Appleton and Company, 1865), 36; Headley, *Confederate Operations in Canada and New York*, 306.
14. *Ibid.*, 306–07; Hemming, "A Confederate Odyssey."
15. Headley, *Confederate Operations in Canada and New York*, 306; *Trial of John Y. Beall: As a Spy and a Guerrillero, by Military Commission*, 37–38.
16. *Ibid.*, 23.
17. *Ibid.*

Chapter 12: Charles Cole's Imprisonment

1. *OR*, ser. 2, vol. 7, 864–65.
2. *Ibid.*, vol. 8, 708–09, A.A. Hosmer to W. Hoffman, July 18, 1865.
3. *Ibid.*, vol. 7, 901–06, Charles W. Hill to E.A. Hitchcock, October 1, 1864.
4. Frohman, *Rebels on Lake Erie*, 96–97; Shepard, "The Johnson's Island Plot," 21; Cleveland *Leader* (June 16, 1865).
5. Frohman, *Rebels on Lake Erie*, 98.
6. *OR*, ser. 2, vol. 8, 708–09.
7. Frohman, *Rebels on Lake Erie*, 98–99; *OR*, ser. 2, vol. 8, 739, W. Hoffman to S.P. Lee, September 1, 1865.
8. Shepard, "The Johnson's Island Plot," 40.
9. *OR*, ser. 1, vol. 43, 230–31.

Chapter 13: Bennett G. Burley's Fate

1. *1869 Sessional Papers No. 75*, 82–83.
2. Charles S. Blue, "Famous Canadian Trials VIII: The Case of Bennett Burley, the Lake Erie 'Pirate,'" *The Canadian Magazine* XLV, 3 (July 1915), 192–93, 195.
3. Blue, "Famous Canadian Trials VIII: The Case of Bennett Burley, the Lake Erie 'Pirate,'" 192.
4. *OR*, ser. 2, vol. 8, 873, 878, 881.
5. Blue, "Famous Canadian Trials VIII: The Case of Bennett Burley, the Lake Erie 'Pirate,'" 193; W.D. Ardagh, Robert A Harrison, and Henry O'Brien, eds., *The Upper Canada Law Journal (New Series.), Vol. 1, From January to December, 1865* (Toronto: W.C. Chewett & Co., 1865), 36.
6. Shepard, "The Johnson's Island Plot," 45.
7. Denison, *Soldiering in Canada*, 60.
8. *Ibid.*
9. Ardagh, et al, *The Upper Canada Law Journal (New Series.), Vol. 1*, 37–38.
10. Blue, "Famous Canadian Trials VIII: The Case of Bennett Burley, the Lake Erie 'Pirate,'" 193.

11. *Ibid.*, 194; Ardagh, et al, *The Upper Canada Law Journal (New Series.)*, *Vol. 1*, 34–35.

12. Headley, *Confederate Operations in Canada and New York*, 322.

13. Ardagh, et al, *The Upper Canada Law Journal (New Series.)*, *Vol. 1*, 51.

14. *1869 Sessional Papers No. 75*, 83, Lord Monck to Edward Cardwell, February 5, 1865. According to the Toronto *Globe* (February 4, 1865), Burley was transported to the U.S. by a special train, arriving at Suspension Bridge on Friday, February 3.

15. Shepard, "The Johnson's Island Plot," 45.

16. *1869 Sessional Papers No. 75*, 83, J.H. Burnley to W.H. Seward, March 15, 1865.

17. *Ibid.*, 84, W.H. Seward to J.H. Burnley, March 20, 1865.

18. Zebulon R. Brockway, *Fifty Years of Prison Service: An Autobiography* (New York: Charities Publication Commission, 1912), 98.

19. Shepard, "The Johnson's Island Plot," 49.

20. Frohman, *Rebels on Lake Erie*, 118–19.

21. *Ibid.*, 119.

22. *Ibid.*, 120.

23. Shepard, "The Johnson's Island Plot," 50.

24. *Ibid.*, 50–51; Frohman, *Rebels on Lake Erie*, 120.

25. Shepard, "The Johnson's Island Plot," 51.

Chapter 14: John Yates Beall's Trial

1. *Trial of John Y. Beall: As a Spy and a Guerrillero, by Military Commission*, 45.

2. Headley, *Confederate Operations in Canada and New York*, 264–83. For a more detailed account, see Nat Brandt, *The Man Who Tried to Burn New York* (Syracuse: Syracuse University Press, 1986).

3. *Trial of John Y. Beall: As a Spy and a Guerrillero, by Military Commission*, 26, 46.

4. *Ibid.*, 26.

5. *Ibid.*, 27.

6. *Ibid.*, 47.

7. *Ibid.*, 18, 20–21.

8. Lucas, *Memoir of John Yates Beall*, 56.

9. *Ibid.*, 91.

10. *OR*, ser. 2, vol. 8, 83–84, Dix to Stanton, January 17, 1865.

11. *Ibid.*, 91, Dana to Dix, January 19, 1865.

12. Lucas, *Memoir of John Yates Beall*, 57, 92.

13. *Ibid.*, 93.

14. *Ibid.*, 60–62.

15. *Ibid.*, 93–94.

16. *Ibid.*, 94.

17. *OR*, ser. 2, vol. 8, 132–33, General Orders No. 4, Headquarters, Northern Department, January 26, 1865; Denison, *Soldiering in Canada*, 60–64.

18. *Ibid.*, 63–64.

19. Lucas, *Memoir of John Yates Beall*, 57–59.

20. *Ibid.*, 62–63.

21. *Ibid.*, 91–142.

22. *Ibid.*, 143, 151–54.

23. *Ibid.*, 154–56.

24. *Ibid.*, 156–61.

25. *Ibid.*, 161–62.

26. *Ibid.*, 162.

27. *Ibid.*, 172–73.

28. *Ibid.*, 175–76. Brady here refers to Colonel Benjamin Grierson, who led a major Union cavalry raid during Grant's Vicksburg Campaign in 1863.

29. *Ibid.*, 179–81.

30. *Ibid.*, 181–82.

31. *Ibid.*, 182–83.

32. *Ibid.*, 184–85.

33. *Ibid.*, 185.

34. *Ibid.*, 186–90.

35. *Ibid.*, 191–92.

36. *Ibid.*, 194.

37. *Ibid.*, 204. Lieber was the author of the army's *General Order No. 100*, known as the "Lieber Code." Following the war, he was responsible for the archival records of the Confederate government.

38. *Ibid.*, 207–08.

39. *Ibid.*, 211.

40. *Ibid.*, 212.

Chapter 15: Commandos on the Gallows

1. Headley, *Confederate Operations in Canada and New York*, 324–25.
2. *OR*, ser 2, vol. 8, 181.
3. *Ibid.*, 191–92, 216–17.
4. Lucas, *Memoir of John Yates Beall*, 213–14.
5. *Ibid.*, 68–69; Isaac Markens, *President Lincoln and the Case of John Y. Beall* (New York: Isaac Markens, 1911), 4–5.
6. Lucas, *Memoir of John Yates Beall*, 69–70.
7. *Ibid.*, 70.
8. Markens, *President Lincoln and the Case of John Y. Beall*, 4–5.
9. Lucas, *Memoir of John Yates Beall*, 71.
10. *Ibid.*, 71, 213–16.
11. Markens, *President Lincoln and the Case of John Y. Beall*, 7–8.
12. Lucas, *Memoir of John Yates Beall*, 72.
13. *Ibid.*
14. Markens, *President Lincoln and the Case of John Y. Beall*, 9.
15. Lucas, *Memoir of John Yates Beall*, 77.
16. *Ibid.*, 81–87.
17. *Ibid.*, 87–88.
18. Lieutenant-Colonel —, *John Y. Beall, the Pirate Spy* (New York: T.R. Dawley, 1865), 76.
19. *OR*, ser 2, vol. 8, 398–400, Davis to the House of Representatives (with enclosures), March 14, 1965.
20. *Ibid.*, 414–16, General Orders No. 24, Headquarters Department of the East, March 20, 1865.
21. *New York Times* (March 27, 1865). Apparently the ballad "Trust to Luck" was particularly popular with the condemned. See Alfred M. Williams, *The Poets and Poetry of Ireland* (Boston: James R. Osgood, 1881), 179–80.
22. Headley, *Confederate Operations in Canada and New York*, 331.
23. *New York Times* (March 21, 1865).
24. See Jay Winik, *April 1865: The Month that Saved America* (New York: HarperCollins, 2001) for an authoritative account of the war's end, which was less abrupt — and far less inevitable — than many historians have implied.

25. Kinchen, *Confederate Operations in Canada and the North*, 205–16, 238–39; Winks, *Canada and the United States*, 361–62. Winks states that Thompson travelled to Halifax by way of Portland, Maine, an extremely unlikely route, given the circumstances. Kinchen's arguments for an all-Canadian escape route are far more persuasive.

26. *1869 Sessional Papers No. 75*, 96–97; *Journals of the House of Commons of the Dominion of Canada from November 6, 1867, to May 22, 1868*, 291, 412; Appendix No. 7 [1–3].

27. Library and Archives Canada, R7617-0-4-E (formerly MG 29, E 29), George Taylor Denison III fonds, Diaries Series, Vol. 26, file "Diary 1864–1879," entries for April 10–13, 1865.

28. Markens, *President Lincoln and the Case of John Y. Beall*, 10–11. Immediately after the assassination, a rumour circulated that Beall was Booth's brother-in-law. See, for example, the Quebec *Morning Chronicle* (April 17, 1865). For more on the mythology of the Booth-Beall connection, see Mrs. B.G. Clifford, "Why John Wilkes Booth Shot Lincoln," *Southern Historical Society Papers*, vol. XXXII, 99–101. Also of interest is George Alfred Townsend's fictionalized account of the relationship in his popular novel *Katy of Catoctin, or, The Chain Breakers: A National Romance* (New York: Appleton, 1886).

Chapter 16: John Wilkes Booth's Connection

1. For more on the Kilpatrick-Dahlgren raid, see Duane P. Schultz, *The Dahlgren Affair: Terror and Conspiracy in the Civil War* (New York: W.W. Norton, 1998).

2. *New York Times* (May 22, 1867).

3. A Union detective was even dispatched to Quebec City to search for Booth. The detective's presence appears to have prompted a spate of unfounded Booth sightings. See Quebec *Morning Chronicle* (April 25, 1865).

4. Quebec *Morning Chronicle* (May 2, 1865).

5. Edward P. Doherty, "Captain Doherty's Narrative," *Century Magazine* 39, 3 (January 1890), 448–49.

6. Clayton Gray, *Conspiracy in Canada* (Montreal, QC: L'Atelier Press, 1957), 51–52; *Mackay's Montreal Directory for 1864–65* (Montreal: John Lovell, 1864), 369. Starnes's biography is available in the *Dictionary of Canadian Biography Online* (*www.biographi.ca*).

7. William A. Tidwell with James O. Hall and David Winfred Gaddy, *Come Retribution: The Confederate Secret Service and the Assassination of Abraham Lincoln* (Jackson and London: University Press of Mississippi, 1988), 265, 328.

8. *New York Times* (August 17, 1863).

9. Quebec *Morning Chronicle* (April 17, 1865). Horn's biography, which probably exaggerates her contact with Booth, is available in the *Dictionary of Canadian Biography Online* (*www.biographi.ca*).

10. Kinchen, *Confederate Operations in Canada and the North*, 232. For more on Sanders, see Tidwell, *Come Retribution*, 331–34.

11. *Mackay's Montreal Directory for 1863–64* (Montreal: John Lovell, 1863), 202.

12. J.W.A. Wright, "How the Blockade Was Run," *The Overland Monthly* VI (second series), 33 (September 1885), 247–51; *ORN*, ser. 2, vol. 2, 714, Stephen Mallory to James D. Bulloch, August 27, 1864. Carron is mentioned in Confederate records relating to blockade-running in Bermuda. See Frank E. Vandiver, *Confederate Blockade-Running Through Bermuda, 1861–1865: Letters and Cargo Manifests* (Austin: University of Texas Press, 1947), 136.

13. Wright, "How the Blockade Was Run," 250.

14. J.W.A. Wright, "Mysterious Fate of Blockade-Runners," *The Overland Monthly* VII (second series), 39 (March 1886), 298–302.

15. *The Trial of the Assassins and Conspirators at Washington, D.C., May and June 1865, for the Murder of President Abraham Lincoln* (Philadelphia: T.B. Peterson & Brothers, 1865), 157–58.

16. *New York Times* (November 15, 1891).

17. George Okill Stuart, ed., *Cases Selected from Those Heard and Determined in the Vice-Admiralty Court at Quebec* (London: Stevens & Sons, 1875), 109.

18. Ben Perley Poore, ed., *The Conspiracy Trial for the Murder of the President, and the Attempt to Overthrow the Government by the Assassination of Its Principal Officers*, Vol. 1 (Boston: J.E. Tilton, 1865), 39–42.

19. Stuart, ed., *Cases Selected from Those Heard and Determined in the Vice-Admiralty Court at Quebec*, 113. Saunders was apparently associated with H&A Saunders, a firm of watchmakers and jewellers. See *Mackay's Montreal Directory for 1865–66* (Montreal: John Lovell, 1865), 274.

20. *Ibid.*, 109.

21. Ben Perley Poore, ed., *The Conspiracy Trial for the Murder of the President, and the Attempt to Overthrow the Government by the Assassination of Its Principal Officers*, Vol. 2 (Boston: J.E. Tilton, 1865), 268–73.

22. Tidwell, *Come Retribution*, 333.

23. Poore, *The Conspiracy Trial for the Murder of the President*, Vol. 2, 87. In his testimony, Campbell indicated that Booth was likely introduced at the bank by either Davis or Patrick Martin. The former seems more likely, as Booth was depositing a bill of exchange from Davis, and Martin had presumably left Montreal by October 27, as the *Marie Victoria* had cleared the port on October 24.

24. *Ibid.*, 268–73.

25. Stuart, ed., *Cases Selected from Those Heard and Determined in the Vice-Admiralty Court at Quebec*, 109–11.

26. *Ibid.*, 111. Martin's wife, who had participated in the First Lake Erie expedition as a courier, later appears in the Montreal directory as a widow. See, for instance, *Mackay's Montreal Directory for 1867–68* (Montreal: John Lovell, 1867), 227.

27. *Ibid.*, 111–12.

28. *Ibid.*, 112.

29. *Ibid.*

30. Poore, *The Conspiracy Trial for the Murder of the President*, Vol. 2, 86.

31. Quebec *Morning Chronicle* (April 28, 1865).

32. *OR*, ser 1, vol. 49, pt. 2, 566–67, proclamation by President Johnson, May 2, 1865. The rewards for the apprehension of Thompson, Tucker, Sanders, and Cleary were revoked on November 24, 1865. See *OR*, ser 1, vol. 49, pt. 2, 1,116, E.D. Townsend, General Orders No. 164, November 24, 1865.

33. Jane Ellis Tucker, *Beverly Tucker: A Memoir by His Wife* (Richmond, VA: The Frank Baptist Printing Co., 1893), 56. For a useful overview of the response to, and aftermath of, Johnson's proclamation, see Thomas Reed Turner, *Beware the People Weeping: Public Opinion and*

the Assassination of Abraham Lincoln (Baton Rouge, LA: Louisiana State University Press, 1982), 125–37.

34. John Surratt was extradited to American in 1867 and was tried in a civilian court, rather than a military commission. He was subsequently released after a mistrial was declared. For more on John Surratt, see Andrew C.A. Jampoler, *The Last Lincoln Conspirator: John Surratt's Flight from the Gallows* (Annapolis, MD: Naval Institute Press, 2008).

35. Tidwell, *Come Retribution*, 343.

36. Quebec *Morning Chronicle* (July 17, 1865).

37. Quebec *Morning Chronicle* (July 19, 1865).

38. *New York Times* (November 15, 1891). Rankin later claimed to have sold his Booth costumes in 1867 to Barton Hill, a member of Edwin Booth's theatre company. He also suggested that the costumes had likely been destroyed very shortly thereafter in a fire at New York's Winter Garden Theatre. However, another account indicates that the wardrobe survived this fire, but that it was methodically destroyed at a later date by Edwin Booth. See David Beasley, *McKee Rankin and the Heyday of the American Theater* (Waterloo: Wilfrid Laurier University Press, 2002), 45–46, 53, 68, 452. Whatever the final fate of the majority of the Booth costumes owned by Rankin, at least one survived. In November 2008, a sleeveless leather jerkin once worn by Booth, together with a note on provenance signed by Rankin, sold at auction at Gettysburg. The item and note comprised lot 61209 in Heritage Auction Gallery's Historical Americana Auction # 6014 (the Dr. John K. Lattimer Collection of Lincolniana). The online auction catalogue can be viewed at Google Books (lot 61209 is on page 145).

39. *New York Times* (April 18, 1890).

40. Stuart, ed., *Cases Selected from Those Heard and Determined in the Vice-Admiralty Court at Quebec*, 112–13.

41. Tucker, *Beverly Tucker*, 56.

42. David Beasley, *McKee Rankin and the Heyday of the American Theater* (Waterloo: Wilfrid Laurier University Press, 2002), 261–62.

43. *New York Times* (May 19, 1918). Also see Doris Rankin's Wikipedia entry.

44. John S. Goff, *Robert Todd Lincoln: A Man in His Own Right* (Norman, OK: University of Oklahoma Press, 1969), 70–71.

45. *New York Times* (April 18, 1890).

Chapter 17: Aftermath

1. Bell, *Confederate Seadog*, 56.

2. *Ibid.*, 55.

3. John Wilkinson, *The Narrative of a Blockade-Runner* (Alexandria, VA: Time-Life Books, 1984), unpaginated introductory insert.

4. John Banister Tabb, "Autobiography," in Francis E. Litz, ed., *Letters — Grave and Gay, and Other Prose of John Banister Tabb* (Washington, DC: Catholic University of America Press, 1950), 249.

5. For more on Tabb's life, see Jennie Masters Tabb, *Father Tabb: His Life and Work* (Boston: The Stratford Company, 1922).

6. Francis A. Litz, ed., *The Poetry of Father Tabb: John Banister Tabb* (New York: Dodd, Mead, and Co., 1927), 390.

7. *New York Times* (June 24, 1878). For a full discussion of the Baltimore Plot, see Michael J. Kline, *The Baltimore Plot: The First Conspiracy to Assassinate Abraham Lincoln* (Yardley, PA: Westholme Publishing, 2008).

8. J. Thomas Scharf, *History of Baltimore City and County from the Earliest Period to the Present Day* (Philadelphia: Louis H. Everts, 1881), 694–95. For more on the supposed connections between Booth and Kane, see note 15 for Chapter 17.

9. *New York Times* (June 25, 1868).

10. Benson J. Lossing, *Pictorial History of the Civil War in the United States of America, Volume 1* (Hartford, CT: T. Belknap, 1868), 322.

11. See Wier's biography in *Dictionary of Canadian Biography Online* (*www.biographi.ca*).

12. Marquis, *In Armageddon's Shadow*, xviii. For more on Weir's Hollis Street home, see *www.metcalf.ns.ca/BenjaminWierHouse.html*

13. Ann Larabee, *The Dynamite Fiend: The Chilling Story of Alexander Keith Jr., Nova Scotian Spy, Con-Artist and International Terrorist* (Halifax: Nimbus Publishing, 2005), 143–60.

14. Wilkinson, *The Narrative of a Blockade-Runner*, 177.

15. *Ibid.*, 180; *Daily Graphic* (March 22, 1876); Townsend, *Katy of Catoctin*, 431; J.W.A. Wright, "Mysterious Fate of Blockade-Runners," *The Overland Monthly* VII (second series), 39 (March 1896), 298–302. The *Daily Graphic* story is by the writer George Alfred Townsend and purports to be based on an interview with George P. Kane; however, many of the events that it chronicles are improbable, if not impossible. Townsend, who subsequently covered much of the same ground in his novel *Katy of Catoctin*, was clearly tempted to exaggerate the connections between Alexander Keith Jr., Patrick Martin, George P. Kane, John Yates Beall, and John Wilkes Booth. His speculations have given rise to two myths in particular. First of all, he reported that while Booth was in Montreal in October 1864, he asked Martin to write a letter of introduction to Kane. There is no other evidence that such a letter was ever requested or supplied. Since Kane had by that time been openly living in Virginia for more than half a year and probably knew various members of the Booth family, including John Wilkes, such a request seems very unlikely. Townsend is also the main source for the assertion that Patrick Martin was an early victim of Alexander Keith, who managed to somehow smuggle an explosive device on board the *Marie Victoria*. However, the subsequent salvage of the vessel, which was loaded with highly explosive material (in the form of coal oil), clearly demonstrated that she was a victim of weather and possibly poor seamanship — not the Dynamite Fiend. Townsend's writings on the subject have led several researchers astray. Ann Larabee, for instance, who is generally prudent in her use of sources, accepts Townsend's dubious account of Kane's allegations regarding Keith's connections with Martin. See Larabee, *The Dynamite Fiend*, 203–04. Likewise, Michael J. Kline ultimately accepts Townsend's evidence that Booth received a letter of introduction to Kane from Martin; however, to his credit, Kline is somewhat skeptical about the claim and points to several obvious contradictions. See Kline, *The Baltimore Plot*, 384–87.

16. W.A. Croffut, *The Prophecy and Other Poems* (New York: Lovell Brothers, 1894), 45.

17. *New York Times* (May 11, 1900).

18. Roger T. Stearn, "Bennet Burleigh: Victorian War Correspondent," *Soldiers of the Queen: The Journal of the Victorian Military Society* 65 (June 1991), 5–10; *The Times* (June 18, 1914); *New York Times* (June 18, 1914). For more on Burleigh's remarkable career, also see Lucas, *Memoir of John Yates Beall*, 20–22, 42–45; Headley, *Confederate Operations in Canada and New York*, 243–44, 462.

19. *New York Times* (May 10, 1869).

20. Joel Williamson, *William Faulkner and Southern History* (New York: Oxford University Press, 1993), 128.

21. *New York Times* (September 15, 1901).

22. Williamson, *William Faulkner and Southern History*, 128, 228.

23. Arthur F. Kinney, "Faulkner's Families," in Richard C. Moreland, ed., *A Companion to William Faulkner* (Malden, MA: Blackwell Publishing, 2007), 190.

24. John W. Headley, *Confederate Operations in Canada and New York* (Alexandria, VA: Time-Life Books, 1984), unpaginated introductory insert.

25. See Headley's biography at *apps.sos.ky.gov/secdesk/sosinfo/default.aspx?id=52*.

26. *New York Times* (November 23, 1895).

27. Headley, *Confederate Operations in Canada and New York*, [viii].

28. *Louisville Courier-Journal* (November 13, 1930).

29. Joseph E. Miller, "Charles Cornelius Hemming (1844–1916)," on the *Jacksonville Observer* website: *www.jaxobserver.com /headstones/2009/09/19/charles-cornelius-hemming-1844%E2%80%931916/*.

30. *Florida Times-Union* (February 23, 1896).

31. *New York Times* (June 17, 1898).

32. Marisa Carbone and John Finotti, *Insider's Guide to Jacksonville; Second Edition* (Guilford, CT: Globe Pequot Press, 2005), 142.

33. As noted above, the article is available online at the *American Heritage* website: *www.americanheritage.com/articles/magazine/ah/1984 /1/1984_1_69.shtml*.

34. For a useful summary of Denison's post-war efforts to receive compensation for the seizure of the *Georgian*, see Guy MacLean, "The *Georgian* Affair: An Incident of the American Civil War," *Canadian Historical Review* XLII, 2 (June 1961), 133–44.

35. Denison, *Soldiering in Canada*, 193.

36. *Ibid.*, 192–93. Denison was obliged to purchase many of the texts that he required for his research. Upon his death, some seven hundred volumes relating to military matters were donated to the Royal Canadian Military Institute. See *www.rcmi.org/library/about-library.html.*

37. *Toronto Star* (May 22, 1982). Also see the biography of Denison in *Dictionary of Canadian Biography Online* (*www.biographi.ca*).

38. Bennett H. Young and William E. Mickle, *General Orders No. 37, May 18, 1916* (Birmingham, AL: Headquarters, United Confederate Veterans, 1916), [3].

39. Library and Archives Canada, George Taylor Denison III fonds, MG 29 E 29, Vols. 13–14, Correspondence Series, File "1917–1917," pages 6,304–05, Bennet H. Young to Denison, May 21, 1917; pages 6,317–18, C. Lucian Jones, Charles H. Olmstead, and Francis D. Bloodworth to Denison, June 13, 1917.

40. See the entry on Armstrong in the *Canadian Encyclopedia* online (*www.thecanadianencyclopedia.com*). Also of interest is Thorold J. Tronrud's on-line article "William Armstrong, 1822–1914; Artist and Engineer," (*www.thunderbaymuseum.com/armstrong.htm*); J. Russell Harper, *Painting in Canada: A History* (Toronto: University of Toronto Press, 1966), 153–54.

41. The City of Toronto Archives website (*www.toronto.ca/archives/earliest_4_whowere.htm*) features a virtual exhibition of Armstrong's photographs.

42. See Starnes's biography in *Dictionary of Canadian Biography Online* (*www.biographi.ca*).

43. See John Starnes, *Closely Guarded: A Life in Canadian Security and Intelligence* (Toronto: University of Toronto Press, 1998).

Afterword

1. Stowe's book was partly inspired by the memoirs of Josiah Henson, who founded Dawn Settlement, a black community just outside Dresden, Ontario.

2. Harriet Beecher Stowe, *Three Novels: Uncle Tom's Cabin; The Minister's Wooing; Oldtown Folks* (New York: Library of America, 1982), 451.

3. *North America No. 1 (1865)*, 101–06.

4. *ORN*, ser. 1, vol. 2, 822, Minor to Buchanan.

5. Ulysses S. Grant, *Memoirs and Selected Letters* (New York: Library of America, 1990), 735.

6. For numerous references to the issue of states' rights during the Confederation debates, see Janet Asjzenstat, Paul Romney, Ian Gentles, and William Gairdner, eds., *Canada's Founding Debates* (Toronto: Stoddart, 1999).

7. Edward Whelan, comp., *The Union of the British Provinces; A Brief Account of the Several Conferences Held in the Maritime Provinces and in Canada, in September and October, 1864, on the Proposed Confederation of the Provinces, Together with a Report of the Speeches Delivered by the Delegates from the Provinces on Important Public Occasions* (Charlottetown, PEI: Haszard, 1865), 123.

8. Hoy, *Canadians in the Civil War*, 374.

Appendix:
Rosters of the Confederate Naval Commando Operations on the Great Lakes, 1863–1864

1. The principal sources for these rosters are *ORN*, ser. 1, vol. 2, 822–28, Minor to Buchanan; Wilkinson, *The Narrative of a Blockade-Runner*, 168–93; *OR*, ser. 1, vol. 43, pt. 2, 930–36, Thompson to Benjamin; Headley, *Confederate Operations in Canada and New York*, 231–55; *OR*, ser. 1, vol. 43, pt. 2, 225–47, Dix to Stanton (with appended affidavits); *OR*, ser. 2, vol. 7, 901–06, Hill to Hitchcock.

2. See note 24 for Chapter 2.

3. It is possible that Wilkinson's trusted Scotsman was recruited from among the members of the British crew that had originally manned the *Giraffe*, the British vessel that became CSS *Robert E. Lee*. See Wilkinson, *The Narrative of a Blockade-Runner*, 111–15. See also John Banister Tabb, "My First Experience in Blockade-Running," in Francis E. Litz, ed., *Letters — Grave and Gay, and Other Prose of John Banister Tabb* (Washington, DC: Catholic University of America Press, 1950), 216–24.

4. Wilkinson, *The Narrative of a Blockade-Runner*, 182–83, 187; *ORN*, ser. 1, vol. 2, 825, Minor to Buchanan. Wilkinson does offer some

clues regarding Thompson's identity, indicating that the escaped prisoner was a daredevil who had been involved with Colonel William Finney (another member of the first Lake Erie expedition) in the founding of the Pony Express. This might suggest that Thompson was a rider. In any event, there were several Pony Express riders by the name of Thompson, at least one of whom, Charles Peck "Cyclone" Thompson, was known to have served in the Confederate States Army. See *www.ponyexpress.org/pony%20riders.htm*; *www.xphomestation.com/frm-riders.html*.

5. *ORN*, ser. 1, vol. 2, 826, Minor to Buchanan.

6. In his disposition on the seizure of the *Philo Parsons*, the vessel's captain indicated that the Confederate surgeon (Riley) was "the oldest man of the party." See *OR*, ser. 1, vol. 43, pt. 2, 239, affidavit of Atwood. It is thus possible that this was the Texan doctor named John S. Riley who was in his late forties and early fifties when he served in the Southern army (Waul's Texas Legion) and was the uncle of the noted American poet James Whitcomb Riley. See *http://mikecochran.net/JonesCemetery.html*.

7. Shepard, "The Johnson's Island Plot," 10. Although most of the volunteers in the Johnson's Island POW camp cannot be identified, we do know, as discussed in Chapter 5, that following the failure of the first Lake Erie expedition, Captain L.W. Allen and other prisoners organized a detailed command structure and prepared a plan for a large-scale escape. The documents relating to these activities identify more than twenty officers who would provide leadership during an escape attempt. See "A Plan to Escape," 283–89.

8. There was a family of well-known Great Lakes engineers by the name of Milne active during this era. See the online version of J.B. Mansfield's *History of the Great Lakes* (Chicago: J.H. Beers & Co., 1899): *www.halinet.on.ca/GreatLakes/Documents/HGL2/default.asp?ID=s799*.

9. *New York Times* (December 11, 1864).

10. Denison, *The Petition of George Taylor Denison, Jr., to the House of Assembly, Praying Redress in the Matter of the Seizure of the Steamer "Georgian,"* 10–14.

Selected Bibliography

Primary Sources: Archival Records

Library and Archives Canada, R7617-0-4-E (formerly MG29, E29), George Taylor Denison III fonds.

Virginia Historical Society, Mss1 M6663c, Minor Family Papers, Robert Dabney Minor Papers, Sections 11, 12, 18, 28, 33.

Primary Sources: Printed Material

[Allen, Captain L.W.] "A Plan to Escape" in *Southern Historical Society Papers, Volume XIX*. Richmond, VA: Southern Historical Society, 1891: 283–89.

[Anonymous] Lieutenant-Colonel ———. *John Y. Beall, the Pirate Spy*. New York: T.R. Dawley, 1865.

Anonymous. *Trial of John Y. Beall: As a Spy and a Guerrillero, by Military Commission.* New York: D. Appleton and Company, 1865.

Anonymous. *The Trial of the Assassins and Conspirators at Washington, D.C., May and June 1865, for the Murder of President Abraham Lincoln.* Philadelphia: T.B. Peterson & Brothers, 1865.

Ardagh, W.D., Robert A. Harrison, and Henry O'Brien, eds., *The Upper Canada Law Journal (New Series), Volume 1.* Toronto: W.C. Chewett & Co, 1865.

Baker, William Washington. *Memoirs of Service with John Yates Beall.* Richmond, VA: The Richmond Press, 1910.

Canada Parliament. *Journals of the House of Commons of the Dominion of Canada from November 6, 1867, to May 22, 1868, Both Days Inclusive; In the Thirty-First Year of the Reign of Our Sovereign, Lady Queen Victoria; Being the 1st Session of the 1st Parliament of the Dominion of Canada; Session 1867–8.* Ottawa, ON: Hunter, Rose, [1868].

Canada Parliament. *Sessional Papers of the Dominion of Canada; Volume VI; No. 75; Second Session of the First Parliament of the Dominion of Canada, Session 1869.* Ottawa, ON: Hunter, Rose, 1869.

Crist, Lynda Laswell, ed. *The Papers of Jefferson Davis; Vol. 9, January–September 1863.* Baton Rouge and London: Louisiana State University Press, 1997.

Crist, Lynda Laswell, ed. *The Papers of Jefferson Davis; Vol. 10, October 1863–August 1864.* Baton Rouge and London: Louisiana State University Press, 1999.

Davis, Samuel B. *Escape of a Confederate Officer from Prison; What He Saw at Andersonville; How He Was Sentenced to Death and Saved by the Interposition of President Abraham Lincoln.* Norfolk, VA: Landmark Publishing Company, 1892.

Denison, George T. *The Petition of George Taylor Denison, Jr., to the Honorable the House of Assembly, Praying Redress in the Matter of the Seizure of the Steamer "Georgian," Together with Copies of the Petition and Affidavits, Filed in the County Court of the County of Simcoe.* Toronto: Leader and Patriot, 1865.

Denison, Lieutenant-Colonel George T. *Soldiering in Canada: Recollections and Experiences.* Toronto: George N. Morang and Company, 1900.

Headley, John W. *Confederate Operations in Canada and New York.* New York and Washington, DC: Neale Publishing Company, 1906.

Hemming, Charles C. "A Confederate Odyssey," *www.americanheritage. com/articles/magazine/ah/1984/1/.*

Hines, Captain Thomas H. [and John B. Castleman]. "The Northwestern Conspiracy," *Southern Bivouac* II (June 1886–May 1887), 437–45, 500–10, 567–74, 699–704.

Lucas, Daniel Bedinger. *Memoir of John Yates Beall: His Life; Trial; Correspondence; Diary; and Private Manuscript Found Among His Papers, Including His Own Account of the Raid on Lake Erie.* Montreal: John Lovell, 1865.

Murray, John Wilson (with Victor Speers). *Memoirs of a Great Detective: Incidents in the Life of John Wilson Murray.* London: William Heinemann, 1904.

Poore, Ben Perley, ed. *The Conspiracy Trial for the Murder of the President, and the Attempt to Overthrow the Government by the Assassination of Its Principal Officers*, 3 Vols. Boston: J.E. Tilton, 1865–66.

Stuart, George Okill , ed. *Cases Selected from Those Heard and Determined in the Vice-Admiralty Court at Quebec.* London: Stevens & Sons, 1875.

Tabb, John Banister. "My First Experience in Blockade-Running" and "Autobiography," in Francis E. Litz, ed., *Letters — Grave and Gay and Other Prose of John Banister Tabb.* Washington, DC: Catholic University of American Press, 1950: 216–24, 247–49.

United Kingdom Parliament. *North America No. 1 (1865); Correspondence Respecting the Attack on St. Albans, Vermont and Naval Force on the North American Lakes; With Appendices.* London: s.n., 1865.

United States Department of State, *Papers Relating to Foreign Affairs, Accompanying the Annual Message of the President to the Second Session Thirty-Eighth Congress, Part II [1864].* Washington: Government Printing Office, 1865.

United States Department of the Navy. *Official Records of the Union and Confederate Navies in the War of the Rebellion.* Washington, DC: Government Printing Office, 1894–1927.

United States War Department. *The War of the Rebellion: A Compilation of the Official Records of the Union and Confederate Armies in the War of the Rebellion.* Washington, DC: Government Printing Office, 1880–1901.

Wilkinson, John. *The Narrative of a Blockade-Runner.* New York: Sheldon & Co., 1877.

Wright, J.W.A. "How the Blockade Was Run," *The Overland Monthly* VI (second series), 33 (September 1885), 247–51.

Wright, J.W.A. "Mysterious Fate of Blockade-Runners," *The Overland Monthly* VII (second series), 39 (March 1886), 298–302.

Secondary Sources

Bell, John. *Confederate Seadog: John Taylor Wood in War and Exile.* Jefferson, NC: McFarland & Company, 2002.

Bell, John. "The Lake Erie Expeditions: Confederate Naval Commandos on the Great Lakes, 1863–1864," in Bernd Horn, ed., *Show No Fear: Daring Actions in Canadian Military History.* Toronto: Dundurn Press, 2008: 167–212.

Blue, Charles S. "Famous Canadian Trials VIII: The Case of Bennett Burley, the Lake Erie 'Pirate,'" *The Canadian Magazine XLV*, 3 (July 1915), 190–96.

Coski, John M. *Capital Navy: The Men, Ships and Operations of the James River Squadron.* Campbell, CA: Savas Publishing Company, 1996.

Cumming, Carman. *Devil's Game: The Civil War Intrigues of Charles A. Dunham.* Urbana and Chicago: University of Illinois Press, 2004.

Durkin, Joseph T. *Stephen R. Mallory: Confederate Navy Chief.* Chapel Hill, NC: University of North Carolina Press, 1954.

Francis, David W. "The United States Navy and the Johnson's Island Conspiracy: The Case of John C. Carter," *Northwest Ohio Quarterly* LII, 3 (Summer 1980), 229–43.

Frohman, Charles E. *Rebels on Lake Erie: The Piracy, the Conspiracy, Prison Life.* Columbus, OH: Ohio Historical Society, 1965.

Gray, Clayton. *Conspiracy in Canada.* Montreal: L'Atelier Press, 1957.

Horan, James D. *Confederate Agent: A Discovery in History.* New York: Crown Publishers, 1954.

Hoy, Claire. *Canadians in the Civil War.* Toronto: McArthur & Company, 2004.

Kinchen, Oscar A. *Confederate Operations in Canada and the North.* North Quincy, MA: Christopher Publishing House, 1970.

Kline, Michael J. *The Baltimore Plot: The First Conspiracy to Assassinate Abraham Lincoln.* Yardley, PA: Westholme Publishing, 2008.

Larabee, Anne. *The Dynamite Fiend: The Chilling Story of Alexander Keith Jr., Nova Scotian Spy, Con-Artist and International Terrorist.* Halifax: Nimbus Publishing, 2005.

Luraghi, Raimondo. *A History of the Confederate Navy.* Annapolis, MD: Naval Institute Press, 1996.

Markens, Isaac. *President Lincoln and the Case of John Y. Beall*. New York: Isaac Markens, 1911.

Marquis, Greg. *In Armageddon's Shadow: The Civil War and Canada's Maritime Provinces.* Montreal and Kingston: McGill-Queen's University Press, 1998.

Moebs, Thomas Truxton. *Confederate States Navy Research Guide.* Williamsburg, VA: Moebs Publishing Co., 1991.

Rodgers, Bradley A. *Guardian of the Great Lakes: The U.S. Paddle Frigate Michigan.* Ann Arbor, MI: University of Michigan Press, 1996.

Ryall, Lydia J. (as Theresa Thorndale). *Sketches and Stories of the Lake Erie Islands.* Sandusky, OH: I.F. Mack & Brother, 1898.

Ryan, Daniel J. *The Civil War Literature of Ohio: A Bibliography with Explanatory and Historical Notes.* Cleveland, OH: Burrows Brothers Company, 1911.

Scharf, J. Thomas. *History of the Confederate Navy from Its Organization to the Surrender of Its Last Vessel.* New York: Rogers and Sherwood, 1887.

Shepard, Frederick J. "The Johnson's Island Plot" in Frank H. Severance, ed., *Publications of the Buffalo Historical Society, Volume IX.* Buffalo, NY: Buffalo Historical Society, 1909: 1–51.

Shingleton, Royce Gordon. *John Taylor Wood: Sea Ghost of the Confederacy.* Athens, GA: University of Georgia Press, 1979.

Shippee, Lester Burrell. *Canadian-American Relations 1849–1874.* New Haven and Toronto: Yale University Press and Ryerson Press, 1939.

Stearn, Roger T. "Bennet Burleigh: Victorian War Correspondent," *Soldiers of the Queen: The Journal of the Victorian Military Society* 65 (June 1991), 5–10.

Tidwell, William A. *April '65: Confederate Covert Actions in the American Civil War.* Kent, OH: Kent State University Press, 1995.

Tidwell, William A., with James O. Hall and David Winfred Gaddy. *Come Retribution: The Confederate Secret Service and the Assassination of Lincoln.* Jackson and London: University Press of Mississippi, 1988.

Townsend, George Alfred. *Katy of Catoctin, or, the Chain Breakers: A National Romance*. New York: Appleton, 1886.

Townsend, George Alfred. "Thomassen," *Daily Graphic* (March 22, 1876), 171, 174.

Winks, Robin W. *Canada and the United States: The Civil War Years*. Baltimore, MD: Johns Hopkins Press, 1960.

Wise, Stephen R. *Lifeline of the Confederacy: Blockade-Running During the Civil War*. Columbia, SC: University of South Carolina Press, 1988.

Woodford, Frank B. *Father Abraham's Children: Michigan Episodes in the Civil War*. Detroit: Wayne State University Press, 1999.

Index

By the Same Author

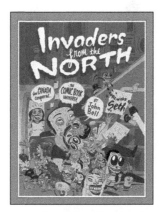

Invaders from the North
How Canada Conquered the Comic Book Universe
978-1550026597
$40.00

A profile of past and present comic geniuses, this book sheds light on unjustly neglected chapters in Canada's pop history and demonstrates how this nation has vaulted to the forefront of international comic art, successfully challenging the long-established boundaries between high and low culture. Generously illustrated, John Bell serves up a cheeky, brash cavalcade of flamboyant and outrageous personalities and characters that graphically attest to Canada's verve and invention in the world of visual storytelling.

Of Related Interest

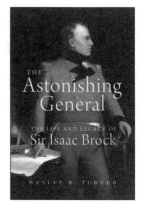

Four Years on the Great Lakes,
1813–1816
The Journal of Lieutenant David
Wingfield, Royal Navy
by Don Bamford and Paul Carroll
978-1554883936
$28.99

The Astonishing General
The Life and Legacy of Sir Isaac Brock
by Wesley B. Turner
978-1554887774
$35.00

This unique account of the history of Canada during the events of the War of 1812 and the stories of the people and places he was exposed to during this time is being made available in book form for the first time. This is the only account of the War of 1812 as seen through the eyes of a young seaman. Included is a Wingfield genealogical description that spans the modern world.

One of the most enduring legacies of the War of 1812 was the creation of heroes and heroines. The earliest of those heroic individuals was Isaac Brock. It's striking how a British general whose military role in that two-and-a-half-year war lasted less than five months became the best-known hero, and one revered far and wide.

Available at your favourite bookseller.

 **DUNDURN**
www.dundurn.com

What did you think of this book?
Visit www.dundurn.com for reviews, videos, updates, and more!